PRAISE FOR BERKSHIRE'S "THIS WORLD OF OURS" SERIES

This Is America: A Short History of the United States is the latest in Berkshire's "This World Of Ours" series, acclaimed by some of the world's leading scholars. *This Fleeting World: A Short History of Humanity,* the first in the series, was praised by Bill Gates, founder of Microsoft and author of *The Road Ahead.* The books tackle big subjects such as China, America, Islam, sports, environmental history, and Africa—even the universe—in about a hundred pages. Each book is designed to be read in one or two sittings.

This Is China

"It is hard to imagine that such a short book can cover such a vast span of time and space. *This Is China: The First 5,000 Years* will help teachers, students, and general readers alike, as they seek for a preliminary guide to the contexts and complexities of Chinese culture."

> Jonathan Spence, professor of history,
> Yale University; author of
> *The Search for Modern China*

This Fleeting World

"I first became an avid student of David Christian by watching his course on DVD, and so I am very happy to see his enlightening presentation of the world's history captured in *This Fleeting World.* I hope it will introduce a wider audience to this gifted scientist and teacher."

> Bill Gates, founder of Microsoft

This Is Islam

"*This Is Islam* provides interested general readers and students with a concise but remarkably comprehensive introduction to Islam. It is a clearly presented guide that provides both a broad overview and important specifics in a way that is easy for both experts and non-specialists to use."

> John Voll, professor of Islamic history,
> Georgetown University

Forthcoming titles in the series include *This Good Earth: A Short History of Human Impact on the Natural World, This Sporting World,* and *This Is Africa.*

S0-BZM-851

THIS IS AMERICA

A SHORT HISTORY OF THE UNITED STATES

THIS IS AMERICA

A SHORT HISTORY OF THE UNITED STATES

Duncan A. Campbell and David H. Levinson, Editors
Michael A. Rockland, Associate Editor

BERKSHIRE PUBLISHING GROUP
Great Barrington, Massachusetts

Digital editions and bulk orders: *This Is America* is available through most major ebook and database services; please check with them for pricing. Discounts on bulk orders are available; contact Berkshire Publishing (info@berkshirepublishing.com) for details.

Published by:
Berkshire Publishing Group LLC
122 Castle Street
Great Barrington, Massachusetts 01230, USA
www.berkshirepublishing.com

Berkshire Publishing specializes in international relations, cross-cultural communications, global business and economic information, and environmental sustainability.

This Is America is part of Berkshire's "This World of Ours" series. Other books in the series include *This Fleeting World, This Is China, This Is Islam, This Is Africa,* and *This Good Earth.*

Photo credits:
Front cover, top: collage of photos by Bill Siever. *Front cover, bottom*: collage of photos from the National Archives and Morguefile.com. Statue of Liberty from photo by Marjolijn Kaiser. *Back cover, background image*: Declaration of Independence, Library of Congress. *Back cover, left to right*: American flag; detail of photo by Bryan Niegel, National Archives. Statue of Liberty; photo by Marjolijn Kaiser. *Declaration of Independence*, painting by John Trumbull in US Capitol; Library of Congress. Golden Gate Bridge; photo by Marjolijn Kaiser. Other photo credits noted throughout the book.

Printed in the United States of America.

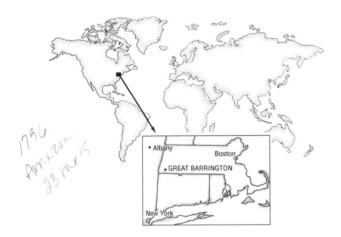

Library of Congress Cataloging-in-Publication Data
  This is America: a short history of the United States/edited by David H. Levinson and Duncan A. Campbell
    pages cm.—(This world of ours series)
  Includes bibliographical references and index.
  ISBN 978-1-61472-926-6 (hardcover: alk. paper)—ISBN 978-1-61472-571-8 (pbk.: alk. paper)—ISBN 978-1-61472-927-3 (ebook)
  1. United States–History.   I. Levinson, David, 1947–editor.   II. Campbell, Duncan A., 1968–editor.
  E178.T345 2013
  973—dc23   2013041821

CREDITS

Editors

Duncan A. Campbell, *National University*; David H. Levinson, *Berkshire Publishing Group*

Advisors

Mark Anderson, *University of Maine*; Thomas Bender, *New York University*; Gerald W. Fry, *University of Minnesota*; Hilary E. Kahn, *Indiana University*; Katherine Lester, *University of North Texas*; Lorna Lueker Zukas, *National University*; Joseph R. Oppong, *University of North Texas*; Michael Aaron Rockland, *Rutgers University*; Katherine L. Saffle, *University of Central Oklahoma*

Publishing Team

Karen Christensen, *Publisher*
Bill Siever, *Managing Editor*
Anna Myers, *Designer*
Kirsiah McNamara and Xiaoyun Helen Zhang, *Interns*
Amanda Prigge, *Indexer*
Aptara, Inc., *Page Composition*
Thomson-Shore, *Printer*

Contributors

"America's Name Problem" essay by Michael Aaron Rockland.

This Is America is informed and inspired, in part, by articles in the *Encyclopedia of Leadership*, the *Encyclopedia of Community*, *Global Perspectives on the United States*, the *Encyclopedia of World Environmental History*, the *Berkshire Encyclopedia of World History*, and the *Berkshire Encyclopedia of Sustainability*. Berkshire Publishing Group is grateful to the following authors for their contributions:

Michael Adas, *Rutgers University*; Laurien Alexandre, *Antioch University*; Laura Anderson, *University of Wisconsin–Stevens Point*; Curtis Andressen, *Flinders University* (Australia); Thomas Bender, *New York University;* Dharm P. S. Bhawuk, *University of Hawaii at Manoa*; Rebecca Bratspies, *City University of New York*; Joanna Burger, *Rutgers University*; Robert Buzzanco, *University of Houston*; John Broom, *Colorado Christian University*; Laura Calkins, *Texas Tech University*; James M. Carter, *Drew University*; Kisuk Cho, *Ewha University* (South Korea); Alfred Crosby, *University of Texas, Austin*; Irene Dameron Hager, *The Ohio State University*; Derek Davis, *University of Mary Hardin-Baylor*; Thomas Emerson, *University of Illinois, Urbana-Champaign*; Susan Flader, *University of Missouri, Columbia*; Richard Flanagan, *City University of New York*; J. Brooks Flippen, *Southeastern Oklahoma State University*; Charles Howard Ford, *Norfolk State University*; Janice E. Fowler, *Capella University*; Donald Franceschetti, *University of Memphis*; Delia Gillis, *University of Central Missouri*; John Martin Gillroy, *Lehigh University*; William Glass, *Warsaw University*; Stephen D. Glazier, *University of Nebraska, Lincoln*; Francisco E. González, *Johns Hopkins University*; Edward Harpham, *University of Texas, Dallas*; Maril Hazlett, *University of Kansas*; John von Heyking, *University of Lethbridge* (Canada); David Houghton, *King's College London*; Christopher Husbands, *London School of Economics and Political Science*; Denise R. Johnson, *Southern Illinois University, Carbondale*; Robert Johnstone, *Earlham College*; Arne Kislenko, *Ryerson University* (Canada); Larissa Larsen, *University of Michigan*; Tomasz M. Lebiecki, *Opole University* (Poland); Keith Leitich, *Pierce College Puyallup*; James G. Lewis, *Forest History Society*; Edwin Locke, *University of Maryland*; Ralph Luker, *Independent scholar, Atlanta, Georgia*; John Lyons, *Joliet Junior College*; Julian Madison, *Southern Connecticut State University*; Robert E. Manning, *University of Vermont*; Michael McClymond, *Saint Louis University*; Brendon O'Connor, *University of Sydney*; Daniel Pacella, *Ryerson University*; Chris Pennington, *University of Toronto*; Dorothy Pratt, *University of South Carolina*; Craig Roell, *Georgia Southern University*; Ingrid Shafer, *University of Science and Arts of Oklahoma* and the *University of Oklahoma*; David Sicilia, *University of Maryland, College Park*; David A. Smith, *Baylor University*; Michael Smith, *Arizona State University*; Robert Singh, *University of London, Birkbeck College*; Itai Sneh, *City University of New York*; Kristen Starr, *Auburn University*; Peter N. Stearns, *George Mason University*; Lee Trepanier, *Saginaw Valley State University*; Peter Ubertaccio, *Stonehill College*; Frank J. Williams, *Supreme Court of Rhode Island*; Alan Wood, *University of Washington, Bothell*; Noritaka Yagasaki, *Tokyo Gakugei University*

CONTENTS

PREFACE: AMERICA'S NAME PROBLEM

Whatʼs in a name? The United States is perhaps the most influential country in the world, yet it and its people have names which other nations and peoples do not accept. How can we be "America" and our people "the Americans," they ask, when all nations in the Western Hemisphere are in the Americas and their people Americans as well? Calling our country "America" and our people "Americans," without apology, is often construed by others as insensitive, if not downright arrogant.

But what then should we call our country and people? Most Spanish-speaking Latin Americans refer to our country as "Norteamerica" and our people as "Norteamericanos." But these words, in our culture, are not only awkward but inaccurate. Citizens of neighboring Canada and Mexico are also Northamericans, so we are not the only ones. Perhaps it is precisely because Canadians and Mexicans are Northamericans that they, of all the hemispheric peoples, feel most comfortable referring to our nation as "America" and our people as "Americans," a convenient way to distinguish us from them. But it does seem a bit unfair that, while they are just as much Northamericanos as we are, Latin Americans call them "Canadienses" and "Mejicanos." Like citizens of every other nation in the hemisphere, they have their own names. Donʼt we who live in the United States deserve a name too and, if so, what is it to be?

Some in Latin America try to get around the American-Northamerican problem by referring to us as "Estadounidenses." "Unitedstatesians" is the only way this can be translated into English. Not only is this word even more awkward than "Norteamericanos," it is equally inaccurate. There are other nations in the hemisphere with "United States" as part of their names: the United States of Brazil and the United States of Mexico. Is there any more justification in calling us "United Statesians" than Brazilians and Mexicans?

Some have suggested that we call ourselves "USonians." There are two difficulties with this. First, it might only be another way of saying "Unitedstatesians." Second, the architect Frank Lloyd Wright long ago appropriated this term with his Usonian house, and utilizing it would sow confusion—at least in architectural circles.

So, what to do? A Mexican friend has suggested we call ourselves "gringos." But surely a people need not embrace a word whose origins have come down to it from one of the least attractive events in its history, the Mexican-American War of 1846–1848, in which we grabbed California, Arizona, New Mexico, and part of Nevada, not to mention parts of several other states, largely to keep the South in the union by allowing it to extend slavery to the West.

Some Latin Americans refer to us as "Yanquis." While there is nothing offensive about this, it wouldn't work in our country. In the United States, "Yankees" is what Southerners call Northerners. But the word is reserved in the North for those who live in New England. And even within New England there are those who consider only residents of Maine to be true Yankees.

I really have no answer to the dilemma of what to call our country and its people that is not offensive to others in the Americas or unattractive or inaccurate to us. But let us not lose hope. Language is there for us to adapt and to create anew. For example, the word "Ms." is a late twentieth century invention that did a lot of good. At first it sounded strange, but by now it seems like it has always been part of the English language.

It is not impossible that we may solve the America/American dilemma someday. Until then, let us keep an open mind on the matter and, at least, be sensitive to present insensitivities. Nations and peoples need not always be prisoners of the past.

Michael Aaron Rockland

Rutgers University

CHAPTER ONE: PREHISTORY TO EARLY EUROPEAN SETTLEMENT

To understand the United States of America of today, it is crucial to understand the history of the physical terrain of the continent. The United States owes much of its development and power to the fact that it is protected from potential enemies by vast oceans on its east and west coasts, and it has enjoyed peaceful relations, with a few notable exceptions, with its two land neighbors to the north and south.

The United States is the fourth largest nation in the world, covering 3,717,813 square miles (9,826,675 square kilometers): slightly smaller than Canada, slightly larger than China, and less than half the size of Russia. The continental United States is bounded by the Atlantic Ocean to the east, the Gulf of Mexico and Mexico to the south, the Pacific Ocean to the west, and Canada to the north. The United States covers roughly forty percent of the North American continent; its population of 314 million (as of 2014) represents sixty percent of the continent's population. Moving from east to west, the land rises from the coastal plain of the East Coast to the relatively low Appalachian Mountains, to an enormous interior plain (the Great Plains), to the high Rocky Mountains, to the high deserts of the Great Basin (so-called because the region, centered on Nevada and Utah, is so dry that waters that flow into the basin never make it to the sea), and finally to more high mountains in the far west. The West Coast mountain ranges include the occasional large volcano, the most famous of which, Mount St. Helens, in Washington State, exploded violently in 1980, covering the lands surrounding it in ash.

The largest lakes are the Great Lakes in the north, shared with Canada. Major rivers (the Hudson, St. Lawrence, Ohio, Missouri, Mississippi, Colorado, and Columbia) have played key roles in the settlement, growth, and prosperity of the United States as sources of water and power, and as transportation routes. The climate ranges from tropical in the Hawaiian Islands, far out in the Pacific Ocean, to arctic in Alaska, with desert, semi-arid, continental, subtropical, and temperate regions found on the mainland. The Pacific Northwest is famous for its damp weather, which enables the growth of the tallest trees on Earth: the redwoods.

Compared to some nations, the United States has been relatively free of damaging natural disasters, although the East and Gulf coasts experience hurricanes, the Midwest and Plains experience flooding and tornadoes, the Southwest droughts, and the West earthquakes and large forest fires. The West Coast, as well as Hawaii and Alaska, is also in danger of tsunamis. All parts of the United States are susceptible to the effects of extreme weather—some more than others—although only 40 percent of Americans in a 2014 Pew survey said they felt climate change to be a major threat to the country. (By contrast, 85 percent of South Koreans and 54 percent of Canadians felt it was a major threat.)

The land hasn't always been in the familiar array of mountains, deserts, plains, and coastlines we know today. Two hundred million years ago, the continents of Earth were massed together in a gigantic supercontinent known as Pangaea. The opportunity for animals to migrate was virtually limitless. Then the continents split, drifting away from each other in an ongoing process spanning many millennia, and thereafter each continent's species evolved independently. North America and Asia reconnected several times in the far north as sea levels rose and fell, and therefore share many species, but there are many contrasts between the two. The Old World of Africa and Eurasia, for example, has such native species as nightingales and cobras, while the New World of the Americas has hummingbirds and rattlesnakes.

A gigantic ice sheet later covered nearly all of modern Canada, as well as the northern tier of what would eventually become the United States. Ten thousand years ago the most recent Ice Age ended, the continent-sized glaciers melted, and sea levels rose, dividing the Old and New Worlds once again. Before that a number of species had passed between the two, the most influential of which was the Old World anthropoid *Homo sapiens,* the scientific name for modern human beings. Thereafter the peoples of the Old World and the Americas evolved separately. The genetic differences that resulted were minor, but the cultural differences were major because the two peoples took different paths in exploiting their different environments.

The Indigenous Peoples of North America

There is considerable debate among anthropologists and archaeologists about when the first people arrived from Asia, and how, exactly, they got to the Americas. Many experts agree that the first humans arrived in the Americas at some point as early as 15,000 years ago—at least in part—by following migrating herds on open tundra and crossing the land bridge that had formed, due to a drop in sea level, between what is now the easternmost tip of Russia and Alaska. Other experts contend that the new arrivals came by boat: possibly in hide boats, since there likely was no wood available in the northern tundra. Still others contest that the first Americans arrived much later (or much earlier) than 15,000 years ago. Another theory, put forward by Norwegian anthropologist/explorer Thor Heyerdahl, was that the ancient Peruvians had the sailing technology necessary for long-distance ocean voyages, and that the islands of the Pacific could have been settled by people from the Americas, rather than the other way around; Heyerdahl's theory has been more or less discredited, although it continues to raise questions.

To be blunt, no one is quite sure how or when the first Americans got there. In any event, the new arrivals continued to cross in migratory waves throughout the Ice Age along alternative routes when the land bridge that had provided passage was again submerged by rising sea levels—this time, glacier-hopping across the 50 miles (80 kilometers) separating Siberia from North America on small craft and negotiating the narrow coastal paths left by ice sheets. These first settlers spread across the Americas in as little as a thousand years.

The Native Americans of North America were a varied and widely dispersed population when Christopher Columbus (1451–1506) arrived in what he thought was India (but was actually the Caribbean) in 1492. They inhabited all reaches of the continent and spoke as many as a thousand different languages, 250 of those in what would become the United States.

The total population of the original inhabitants is impossible to know with any degree of certainty; estimates range from one to eight million. With the great environmental diversity found across the continent, it is not surprising that the Native American nations were highly culturally diverse as well. Over those thousands of years of separation from the Old World they had developed different methods to exploit the environment for food, shelter, clothing, and other material objects; they developed different ways of organizing themselves politically; and they developed religions distinct from one another. Nations in the Northwest coast lived in large settlements of wood plank houses, lived mainly off of salmon and berry gathering, and enslaved people from other nations. Peoples in the Plains were nomadic hunter-gatherers whose primary source of food and raw material was the bison; they lived in the well-known portable tipi (also commonly spelled teepee). Peoples in the Northeast hunted and farmed and lived in semi-permanent villages of bark-covered longhouses. One of these nations, the Iroquois (actually a confederation of five nations) was in 1492 actively waging war on neighboring nations as it expanded its territory north and west. And peoples in the Southwest (later called the Pueblo nation) lived in large, settled communities of multi-story stone and mud houses while farming corn, beans, and squash. One of the

Indians? Native Americans?
American Indians? First Nations?

The term "Indians" was first applied by European explorers who thought they had arrived in India, and the name has stuck for centuries, for better or for worse, in much the same way that the term "America" has come to be applied to the United States, which is but a small part of the Americas. For years, schoolchildren played "cowboys and Indians," and a whole genre of movies (and television shows) known as Westerns came into being, invariably featuring Indians of one variety or another: stereotypically stoic and inscrutable, stereotypically sneaky, or stereotypically noble.

Eventually, two things happened: many people of European ancestry, seeking to be respectful or "politically correct," began to refer to native peoples as "Native Americans" or "American Indians," while many Native Americans began to refer to themselves more and more often simply as "Indians." In any case, in the same way that people who live in New York call themselves "New Yorkers" rather than "North Americans" or "Earthlings," most Native Americans refer to themselves as members of the particular nation to which they belong—for example, the Cherokee Nation, Mashantucket Pequot, Tohono O'odhom, or Lakota—rather than "Native Americans." Most (but not all) Canadian Aborigines are referred to as members of the First Nations.

Many of the names in use today for Native American tribes were bequeathed upon them by their enemies, or were mangled, Europeanized versions of the tribes' names for themselves. "Comanche," for instance, means "People who fight us all the time" in the language of the Hopi, one of their main rivals for land; the name "Sioux" is derived from an Ojibwa name (via French) for "snake" or "enemy." Many place names in the United States, including the names of several states—from Massachusetts and Connecticut in the Northeast to Illinois, Wisconsin, and Minnesota in the Midwest to Utah in the West—derive their names from Native American peoples.

best places to see evidence of this culture today is to visit the dramatic cliff dwellings of Mesa Verde National Park, located in southwestern Colorado.

These diverse nations did not live in isolation. Quite to the contrary, shortly after arriving in the New World they began trading with one another. Probably the first trade goods were high-quality chert (a variety of silica) and obsidian, used to make

Cahokia, the largest archeological site in North America, was located in the American Bottoms region of Illinois, across from modern-day St. Louis. By the thirteenth century the city was larger than London. Today it is possible to see the famous St. Louis Arch—the iconic "Gateway to the West"—from the top of the ancient mounds, which are now a UNESCO World Heritage site: one of twenty-four in North America. Source: Stephen D. Peet, *The Mound Builders: Their Works and Relics,* p. 158. Chicago: Office of the American Antiquarian, 1892.

projectile points, both of which were traded over moderate distances. Many millennia later, when populations were larger, and people were more settled and better able to exploit the environment, trade expanded to include marine shells, ceramics, and objects made of copper, galena (a variety of lead ore), obsidian, and other types of exotic stone. Some of the trade goods were used to make ornaments used in burials and other rituals, suggesting that social factors were more important than strictly economic factors as stimuli for trade.

The Columbian Exchange

Columbus's arrival in the Caribbean in 1492 began an interaction between the Old and New Worlds that continues to this day; an interaction that was to have enormous consequences, so much so that historians call the exchange of people, plants, animals, ideas, diseases, etc., the "Columbian Exchange." The Spanish Empire pioneered the cultural and commercial integration of the Americas, as well as connecting the commerce of the Americas with the rest of the world. Spain's creation of a territorial, rather than a merely commercial, empire like the Portuguese or the Dutch—in a populous continent rich in silver, gold, sugar, and other valuable resources—began to equalize and then reverse the world's economic balance in favor of Europe, until then a relatively poor promontory of Eurasia, and away from Asia. The process culminated centuries later with the rise of the United States and its later emergence as one of the world's foremost powers.

Agriculture was independently invented in both halves of the globe, roughly 5,000–6,000 years ago in the Americas, and roughly 10,000–11,000 years ago in various parts of Asia, although these dates are subject to much debate. The two systems were very different. The Native Americans domesticated few creatures in the Americas, because there were fewer large mammals to domesticate: the alpaca, the guinea pig, and several species of fowl. Various peoples throughout the Americas excelled as farmers, developing an astonishing array of today's most important food crops: maize (called "corn" in the United States), tomatoes, chili peppers, beans of several kinds, the white and sweet potatoes, manioc (cassava), squashes and pumpkins, peanuts, papayas, guavas, avocados, pineapples, and sunflower seeds, to name a few.

Old World peoples, who lived in a wider expanse of land and lived in a greater variety of ecosystems, domesticated more kinds of animals and plants. Horses, donkeys, cattle, pigs, sheep, goats, and chickens are all Old World in origin. The same is true of wheat, barley, rye, oats, rice, peas, turnips, sugarcane, onions, lettuce, olives, bananas, peaches, pears, and many other stock items of our diets today.

The Old World also had more infectious diseases to spread than the New World did. The greater number of people in more varied ecosystems was bound to have a greater variety of diseases, especially because they lived in close contact with their livestock. The intermixing of Old World humans across Eurasia and Africa, and their close association with their animals, produced many of the historically most significant diseases. An undoubtedly incomplete list includes smallpox, the bubonic plague, measles, influenza, malaria, yellow fever, and typhus. Even relatively harmless diseases such as chickenpox, which nearly all people in the Old World gained immunity to as children, could be deadly. Pre-Columbian Native Americans had tuberculosis and treponematosis and cultivated, unintentionally, new infections, but their indigenous diseases were few and mild compared with those native to the Old World. (One exception to the rule is syphilis, which is native to the Americas.)

The most profound early result of the contact with the Old World was the traumatic spread of these infections among the Native Americans. The European conquest of the Americas was not so much a matter of brutality, though there was undoubtedly plenty of that, as of imported diseases. Smallpox figures significantly in the Spanish conquests of Mexico and Peru, and again and again throughout the Americas. The Native American populations of both continents fell by as much as 95 percent (again, exact numbers are almost impossible to determine) before beginning a slow and incomplete recovery.

The arrival of Old World plants and animals increased immensely the capacity of America to support, in time, large human populations (unless, of course, those populations were being devastated by diseases). Horses, pigs, and cattle, for instance, within a century had propagated into the millions. Old World livestock revolutionized human life and whole ecosystems in the Americas. After the Columbian Exchange, meat became common in many regions.

The impact of the horse on Native American societies was particularly spectacular. Many Amerindians who had been strictly pedestrian became equestrian. From approximately 1750 to 1800, the native peoples of North America's Great Plains (Blackfoot, Sioux, Cheyenne, Comanche, Pawnee, and others) all took to the horse, which later partially contributed to the hunting of the bison—which at one time roamed the Plains in vast numbers—to near extinction, although this was overwhelmingly due to the later wholesale slaughter of the animals for sport by white pioneers. These sport hunters were best personified by "Buffalo Bill" Cody, born William Frederick Cody, who gained his nickname and his fame after killing some 4,000 bison in eighteen months to supply the United States Army with food and hides. Buffalo Bill's "Wild West Show" later toured extensively, including travel to Europe, doing much to establish the popular view of "cowboys and Indians."

New World crops had an enormous effect on the Old World. Most of those that became standard in Old World diets were brought back by the Spanish and Portuguese to the Iberian Peninsula, where they became widely cultivated by the sixteenth century; they spread out from there. Several American foods were more nourishing, more productive, and easier to cultivate and to harvest than traditional Old World crops. Maize became a standard crop in sub-Saharan Africa, in some regions the most important crop. It is impossible to imagine modern Italian cuisine, to pick one example of many, without many of these New World staples.

The white potato, from the high, cool Andes, became one of the most important food sources for the lower classes of northern Europe, which was another factor that was to have a profound influence on later history. In Ireland it became indispensable for the peasantry, and when, in the 1840s, an American fungus, *Phytophthora infestans*, arrived and destroyed the potato crop, a million people died of starvation and disease and a million and a half fled the country, the majority immigrating to the United States.

Among the most profitable Old World introductions was sugarcane, the source of a quasi-addictive substance: sugar. Sugarcane took a long time to reach the Americas: first known in New Guinea around 6,000 BCE, it made its way through

China's (First) Embrace of American Food

American fast food chains such as Pizza Hut and KFC have been enthusiastically embraced by modern China, but this is not the first time American food has become popular in China. No Old World people adopted alien plants such as potatoes, peanuts, and chili peppers faster than the Chinese of the Ming dynasty.

The eagerness with which the Chinese people accepted New World foods is related to population pressure. Between 1368 and 1644, the years of the Ming dynasty, the Chinese population doubled at the same time that farmers of the traditional staples—wheat in the cold, dry north and rice in the warm, wet south—were running into problems of diminishing returns. The Spanish and the Portuguese, both with empires in the Americas, carried the Amerindian crops to East Asia. The port of Manila (now the capital of the Philippines), newly Spanish and only a few days' sail from the coast of China, played a major role in the transfer of American crops to China. Sweet potatoes, a calorically rich food, arrived in China sometime in the last years of the sixteenth century. This crop did well in inferior soils, tolerated drought, resisted insect pests, and prospered with little care compared with existing staples such as paddy rice. By 1650 sweet potatoes were common in Guangdong and Fujian provinces (on China's coast, opposite Taiwan) and well on the way to becoming the staple of the poorer peasants wherever the climate would allow.

Maize arrived in China even before the mid-sixteenth century. It, too, was hardy and required little effort. It produced food faster than most crops and provided large amounts of calories. It soon became a common secondary crop from Shanxi in the northwest to Yunnan in the southwest and eventually a primary crop in several inland provinces. Peanuts, native to Paraguay and growing in China at least as early as 1538, have always been considered a novelty food in the West, but became a common item in Chinese meals.   —Alfred W. Crosby

China and India before Arab traders brought it to the Mediterranean; from there the Portuguese introduced it to the Canary Islands via Madeira, from whence Columbus brought it to the island of Hispaniola (now split between Haiti and the Dominican Republic) in 1493. The market for sugar in Europe seemed endlessly expansive for centuries, and therefore sugarcane became the single most important crop in the West Indies, Brazil, and other hot, wet regions in or contiguous to the American tropics.

Tobacco

In North America, the raising of another addictive crop—tobacco—would see vast numbers of people enslaved in the coming centuries. The issue of slavery—one of the more brutal chapters in the history of humanity—is discussed at more length in Chapters Two and Three. Tobacco (*Nicotiana tabacum*) is thought to have been first cultivated in the Peruvian Andes, where it was used for medicinal and ceremonial purposes. From there it spread throughout the continent. Evidence shows that the Aztecs smoked tobacco leaves stuffed in hollow reeds and that Central and North American natives smoked thick bundles of tobacco wrapped in palm leaves and maize husks.

Although tobacco was introduced from Mesoamerica to North America about 200 CE, Europeans did not come into contact with it until many centuries later. Christopher Columbus brought tobacco seeds and leaves with him back to Spain. By the early 1600s tobacco had spread throughout most of South America, Europe, the Caribbean, and the North American colonies.

Tobacco soon became an important commodity in Europe, but an even more important commodity for the American colonies. Virginia, Maryland, and North Carolina's eighteenth- and early nineteenth-century economies depended almost entirely on tobacco, which was harvested as a cash crop and sent to European and other North American colonial markets. Indeed, tobacco was the single greatest factor in the development of the southern colonies' economic, political, and social life.

The Englishman John Rolfe, who observed local Native Americans growing different strains of tobacco, cultivated the first successful commercial crop of *Nicotiana tabacum* in Virginia in 1612. The Native American princess Pocahontas was the first "poster girl" for tobacco; her marriage to Rolfe ensured that native peoples would not attack the Jamestown colony or destroy the new cash crop. By the 1620s tobacco had become Virginia's major crop.

Virginia's fledgling tobacco industry created great demands for land and labor. Because tobacco quickly depleted the land by removing nitrogen and potash from

Nicotania tobacum (cultivated tobacco), from *Tobacco, Its History and Associations: Including an Account of the Plant and its Manufacture; with its Modes of Use in All Ages and Countries*, by Frederick William Fairholt (1814–1866).

the soil and depositing toxic minerals and elements farmers seldom planted more than three or four crops on the same plot of land before they abandoned it to corn or wheat. Thus colonial planters constantly cleared forest to make room for more tobacco lands and began to establish large plantations deeper in the interior.

For the next two centuries, tobacco cultivation, which was labor-intensive, fueled the demand for labor, particularly imported African slave labor. To start a crop, seeds were sown in beds in late spring. Plants had to be carefully weeded and cut. In early autumn, ripe plants were cut and hung on pegs in a ventilated tobacco house to cure for a month or more. The leaves were then cut from the plant, tied into bundles, and shipped to England and the other colonies. At first, planters relied on indentured servants imported from England for this labor. But after 1700 tobacco plantations employing several dozen imported African slaves or more were common, and, by the 1790s, more than 650,000 slaves worked on tobacco plantations. By the time of the Civil War in the mid-nineteenth century, the South's agricultural economy rested on the labor of more than four million African slaves, although by that time tobacco had generally been replaced by cotton as the crop picked by slave labor.

European Settlement and Early Colonization

European activity in the Americas in the sixteenth and seventeenth centuries centered on the efforts by the Spanish, Dutch, French, and English to exploit and colonize the region. By the middle of the 1600s, the English had defeated the Dutch, with competition between the other three nations continuing into the eighteenth century. Spanish influence was limited mainly to the Southwest (with the exception of Florida), giving the English, after they defeated the French, freedom to colonize and rule most of eastern North America. The Europeans had enormous influences on the environment, and much of North America was transformed into a place more familiar to Europeans, with cleared land, familiar livestock, and widespread agriculture where conditions allowed. It is a commonly held—and very much erroneous—belief that Native Americans had little to no lasting effect on their environment, or that they did nothing to improve the land. They certainly lived more lightly on the land than the Europeans did, however, often by moving from place to place, depending on the season, thus allowing the land time to heal in their absence. The environmental history of America is discussed in Chapter Seven.

The Spanish

The initial Spanish forays into the North American continent were exploratory expeditions. These operated mainly as raids, searching for more of the mineral wealth, such as gold and silver, that had been found in abundance in Mexico and Peru; they quickly moved on when not finding it. The meandering of the Spanish was more often the result of rumors spread by native leaders than deliberate routes planned by the explorers and conquistadors. The Spanish generated hostility by their incessant demands for food and gold; this resulted in the local natives presenting them with various levels of noncooperation or outright resistance. These early expeditions, especially the efforts of Hernando de Soto, beginning in Florida and wandering as far north perhaps as the Carolinas and then west to the Mississippi Valley, were unsuccessful in locating any vast new areas of riches.

Subsequent Spanish expeditions established settlements in Florida and the Southwest, especially in New Mexico, starting in 1598. These settlements were a combination of military outposts and missionary churches. The Spanish were generally able to overawe the natives with firearms, steel, and cavalry, to which the native tribes of the Southeast and Southwest had no effective answer. The relatively easy, although at times violent and bloody, conquest of the borderlands was tested in 1680 by a widespread and successful uprising of the Pueblo nation. It would be thirteen years before another expedition would re-conquer the province of New Mexico. By 1700 the Spanish had again occupied the Pueblo territory and re-established settlements, decimating the Pueblo population in the process. After 1700 the Spanish continued

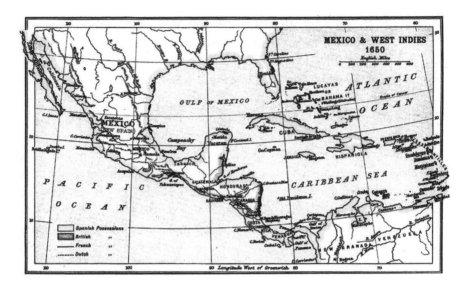

A 1911 map of New Spain (Mexico), Central America, and the West Indies in 1650. Spain would lose Mexico after the Mexican War of Independence (1810–1821); Mexico would, in turn, lose much of its northern territory to the United States in the course of the Mexican-American War (1846–1848). Source: Ernest Rhys, Ed., *A Literary and Historical Atlas of North & South America*. New York: E. P. Dutton & Co. Courtesy of the private collection of Roy Winkelman.

to expand the area under their direct control, settling parts of what would later become the states of Arizona (in 1700), Texas (in 1716), and California (in 1769). For a glimpse of Spanish colonial history today, the city of St. Augustine, Florida, is the oldest continuously settled city of European origin in the United States; it is known for its colonial Spanish architecture.

The Dutch

Toward the end of the sixteenth century, Dutch ships started to explore the waters beyond Europe. In 1602 the founding of the Dutch East India Company, which became the largest company in the world at the time, created an empire. The empire focused mostly on trade, however, and less on colonization. The Dutch established settlements in what is today New York City (originally called New Amsterdam) and along the Hudson River to the north of the city, prior to the settlement of the English Pilgrims and Puritans in New England to the east of New York's Hudson Valley.

The Amish: "Pennsylvania Dutch"

The Amish are members of a Christian subculture who trace their origins to the European Anabaptist movement. Extinct today in Europe, where they suffered terrible persecution, the Amish now live in Canada and twenty-five US states—most notably in Pennsylvania, where they are one of several groups (including the Mennonites) known inaccurately as the "Pennsylvania Dutch." (The term "Dutch" is thought to be a misnomer for "Deutsch," or German.)

Several public symbols of ethnic identity set the Amish and others apart as a distinctive community. Their homemade clothing proclaims them as members of a community that is separate from the mainstream American culture that surrounds them. The Amish speak a German dialect (Pennsilfaanisch Deitsch) and learn English as a second language in school. Their use of this dialect in everyday life gives them a sharp sense of separation from the outside "English" world, and a connection to their past.

Their use of horse and buggy for transportation is another public symbol of their rejection of modern ways. The Amish view some technology as a threat to the well-being of their communities, and so they screen new technologies to make sure that they will support, not disrupt, the Amish way of life. The car, for example, threatened to fragment their community, which is best sustained through face-to-face relationships. Thus Amish communities forbid owning and operating motor vehicles—a contrast with mainstream America, which is well known as a car culture.

The Dutch, while interested in settlement and agriculture, were also very interested in the fur trade, which resulted in a divided and inconsistent policy, on one hand displacing Native Americans in the Hudson River Valley, and on the other operating as suppliers and sometime allies to other Native Americans on the frontier. The British eventually displaced the Dutch as the overlords of the region, renaming New Amsterdam "New York" after their invasion of the town in 1664. The Dutch agreed to exchange Manhattan Island for the colony of Suriname, on the Caribbean coast of South America, in 1667.

Evidence of the early Dutch presence in New York State remains today in the many surnames and place names of Dutch origin, such as the Tappan Zee Bridge, Harlem, Brooklyn, and the Kill Van Kull River, as well as such literary figures as Rip Van Winkle, the Dutch protagonist of the story of the same name by Washington Irving who falls asleep for many years, awakening to profound changes that have taken place since the American Revolution; and Dietrich Knickerbocker, Irving's satirical pseudonym and source of the name of the New York Knicks basketball team. There is a noticeable difference in architectural styles between the Dutch-settled Hudson Valley and the neighboring states of New England. Martin Van Buren, the eighth president of the United States—the first president from New York and the first president born an American citizen—was of Dutch descent and remains the only president to have spoken English as a second language.

The English

English colonists established settlements at Jamestown, Virginia in 1607 and in Plymouth, Massachusetts, in 1620. Plymouth, like many of the colonies' earliest settlements, was built over the abandoned remains of a Native American (in this case Wampanoag) village. The village's inhabitants had been decimated by disease, most likely smallpox, shortly before the arrival of the colonists. It is likely that the English colonists—entirely unaccustomed to the harsh cold of a New England winter—would all have died of cold and starvation without the help of the remnants of the native peoples who came to their aid.

Many quintessential American traditions, such as the Thanksgiving holiday, date from the English settlement of New England. Thanksgiving is a blending of the Wampanoags' tradition of giving thanks for a successful harvest with traditional English harvest festivals, as well as less festive Puritan declarations of thanks to God for a bountiful harvest. Thanksgiving is today a favorite holiday for many Americans, as it a holiday that revolves around family and food and has so far escaped the commercialization of many other holidays. Roast turkey, stuffing, mashed potatoes, cranberry sauce, and pumpkin pie are the traditional elements, although there are variations.

On the political front, the English government tried to maintain a policy of mercantilism, buying only raw materials from the colonies and attempting to force them to buy their finished goods solely from the mother country, which led to an increase in smuggling. This arrangement was designed to maintain the flow of precious metals into Great Britain. Indeed, some evidence indicates that the eastern seaboard of North America—a captive market for British manufactured items—may have helped to give the British economy its push into full modernization.

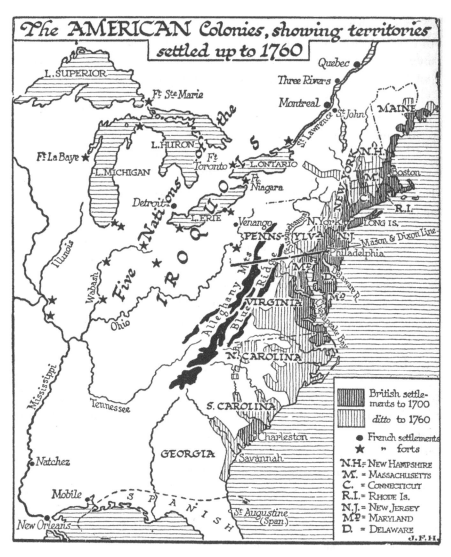

A 1921 map showing the expansion of the British colonies from 1700 to 1760; it also shows French settlements and forts, and indicates the Mason–Dixon Line (the symbolic dividing line between North and South) surveyed in 1763–1767. Source: H. G. Wells, *The Outline of History.* New York: Macmillan Co. Courtesy of the private collection of Roy Winkelman.

The English were almost exclusively interested in acquiring land for agricultural use, which entailed the displacement of the local native tribes and much resultant warfare. The English settlements relied on this militia force for both its defensive capability and its offensive capability against Native Americans and other threats to the security of the colony.

The most significant problem the English settlements faced was their dispersal on farms and in small villages along the frontier. As the frontier advanced inland, the Native Americans had a ready and vulnerable set of targets to strike with their traditional raid and ambush tactics. The English responded by fortifying houses in the villages, launching periodic punitive campaigns against the Native Americans, and conducting active militia patrols and ambushes along likely enemy approaches during times of trouble. The English faced repeated uprisings and minor wars with native tribes from 1622 in Virginia until 1675, in both King Philip's War in New England and Bacon's Rebellion in Virginia, as well as many other conflicts along their expanding frontiers. King Philip's War, named for the alias of Wampanoag chief Metacom, saw the highest number of deaths per capita of any subsequent American war, and represented the end of meaningful Native American resistance.

The French

The French in New France and the Mississippi River Basin had a much different colonial experience than the English. They were not quite as interested in large-scale settlement and agriculture or mining, although they had, of course, the desire of most colonizers to spread their language, culture, and Catholic religion far and wide. Instead, they were mainly interested in the fur trade, which required the cooperation of the Native Americans. The French therefore chose, with very few exceptions, to establish cordial relations with the native peoples. As a result, the warfare on the French-American frontiers that later developed saw both Europeans and Native Americans on both sides of the conflict.

France's colonial aspirations were ended with a war that started in North America known as the French and Indian War (1754–1763), fought largely over trading opportunities, before spreading to Europe and other parts of the world, where the conflict became known as the Seven Years' War (1756–1763). The British victory over the French in Quebec City stripped the French of their North American colonies. The French revenge against their British foes was to bankroll—and fight in, often to spectacular success—the American Revolution (1775–1781). The French monetary and military support for the American colonies' successful revolution, in turn, led

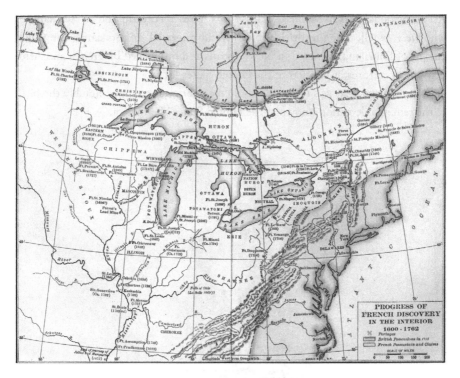

A 1906 map showing French territories between 1600 and the French and Indian War of the mid-eighteenth century. The French were generally on good terms with the Native Americans, with whom they traded furs and other commodities. Source: Albert Bushnell Hart, *The American Nation, Vol. 7.* New York: Harper and Brothers. Courtesy of the private collection of Roy Winkelman.

to bankruptcy of the French state and prepared the way for the French Revolution that began in 1789. The ideas of the English philosopher John Locke (1632–1704), discussed at more length in Chapter Three, were immensely influential on both the American and French revolutions.

French support of the Americans produced a close, although sometimes tense, relationship between the two nations, perhaps best symbolized by the Statue of Liberty in New York Harbor, given as a gift to the United States by France in 1886. While French control ended, some French people remained or moved south from Canada, creating enduring French ethnic enclaves in the six New England states (particularly Maine), Missouri, and Louisiana. The New France province of Acadia, which was absorbed into the present-day Canadian maritime provinces, explains the names of

Acadia National Park in Maine as well as the "Cajuns"—a corruption of "Acadians"—who were expelled by the British in 1755 and migrated to Louisiana. The Cajun cuisine of Louisiana, centered in New Orleans and influenced by French and Afro-Caribbean cultures, is popular in the United States today.

The century that was to follow would see enormous changes: notably the birth of the remarkable nation known as the United States of America.

The Statue of Liberty, given by France as a gift to the people of the United States in 1886, is an enduring symbol of American values. French political thinker and abolitionist Edouard de Laboulaye first had the idea for the colossal statue, which dominates New York Harbor, after the Union's victory in the Civil War in 1865. Photo by Marjolijn Kaiser.

CHAPTER TWO: FROM COLONY TO REPUBLIC

The eighteenth century began with North America under the control of the Spanish, French, and English empires. It ended with the United States of America an independent nation formed by the thirteen eastern colonies that had revolted against British rule in 1775. In the years in between slavery grew in importance, the British wrested control of eastern North America from the French, and the increasingly diverse population expanded by a factor of ten.

The Contest for North America

The eighteenth century opened with the English controlling the eastern seaboard from Georgia north to Maine; the Spanish controlling Florida and the Gulf Coast, the Southwest, and coastal California; and the French a vast territory that included eastern Canada and the American interior, including the immense Mississippi Valley. The French established forts, trading posts, and missions throughout their sparsely populated territory. The Dutch as a colonial force were long gone, although people of Dutch ancestry continued to live in the American colonies, and enclaves of Dutch-speaking communities lived on.

The Spanish focused their colonization efforts on exploiting the resources of their Caribbean and Central and South American colonies; they saw their territory in the north as a buffer zone protecting them from the French and English. They established missions and forts (called "presidios") across the region. The missions converted American Indians to Catholicism, and (with various degrees of success) they became agricultural enterprises. The Mission Trail in California, consisting of twenty-one missions that have survived, is the best-known showcase of the Spanish missions today. The missions brought European crops and animals, European farming methods, Spanish settlement plans, and Spanish architecture to the Southwest and California.

The British, meanwhile, established dozens of settlements in the 1600s and early 1700s, with the population increasing rapidly over the eighteenth century. England and Scotland joined together in 1707 to form Great Britain; the British Crown sought to expand its territory and power by driving out the French, and keeping the Spanish confined to the south.

The French and Indian War / Seven Years' War

The ongoing conflict between the French and British was settled by the French and Indian War, which began in 1754 with failed British attempts to drive the French from the interior of North America. For the first few years, the undermanned French held their own, with the help of their American Indian allies. In 1758, however, the tide of war shifted in favor of the British, in part because the British were able to convince some Native American tribes to remain neutral and others to actively give them aid. In 1759 the British took Quebec City, and France subsequently gave up its claims to territory in North America, leaving the British free to begin expanding further into the interior.

The Seven Years' War came to an end in 1763 with the Treaty of Paris. France lost its claims to Canada, and ceded Louisiana to Spain; Spain in return lost Florida to the British. The Treaty of Paris led to the supremacy of Britain throughout the region. The thirteen American colonies, meanwhile, were strengthened by the removal of their European rivals.

The war damaged relations between the colonists and Britain, however, and was an early cause of the American Revolution that was to come. The war left Britain deeply in debt; to increase its revenues, Britain began taxing the colonies heavily. This angered the colonists, who believed they remained British subjects entitled to equal treatment. "No taxation without representation"—meaning that it was unjust to tax people if they had no say in what the taxes would be used for—became the rallying cry of many of the increasingly restless colonists.

Colonial Society

Between 1700 and 1775 the population of the thirteen colonies increased from 300,000 to 2.5 million people. About ninety percent of the colonial population was rural, living on farms, plantations, and in small villages. The only true cities were the port cities such as New York, Boston, and Charleston. The port of Philadelphia (meaning "city of brotherly love" in Greek) was the largest, with 34,000 inhabitants. Philadelphia was the second-largest English-speaking city in the world at this time, after London.

Immigration and the slave trade produced an ethnically diverse population. Those born in England, or of English ancestry but born in America, remained the majority, but by 1775 twenty percent of the population was of African ancestry, seven percent Scots and Scots-Irish (i.e., people from Ulster, in northern Ireland), six percent German, and a total of about five percent were Swedish, Welsh, French, or Dutch. The colonial economy was based on farming, fishing, and trade; large-scale industry was limited to lumbering and tobacco. The American colonies' vast forests were a major boon for Britain (long stripped of a good part of its forests), which otherwise would be forced to depend on Scandinavia and Russia for its supplies. A single warship required hundreds of acres of trees to be cut down. In addition to the massive amounts of lumber needed for the ships, the tall white pines of New England, taller than any trees growing in Europe, were strictly reserved for use as masts for Britain's Royal Navy: an early source of vexation for the colonists. Those who did not farm were craftsmen and shopkeepers. Access to increased wealth was very easy compared to more class-bound European societies, primarily through the trade of farm products such as tobacco, fish on the coasts, and lumber. The poor were relatively few in number, compared with Europe, with widows and orphans making up a substantial percentage of the poor; there were no real social institutions at the time for the protection of the destitute.

As colonies of Britain, the colonial governments were controlled by the King. Eight colonies had governors appointed by the King, three had them appointed by proprietors, and two elected by the people (although only free, white men who owned property could vote). The colonies had two-chambered legislatures; the upper house appointed by the King or proprietor, and the lower one elected. The governments were controlled by the wealthy in the cities and larger towns, creating friction with farmers who felt that their needs were often ignored.

Religion and the Great Awakening

Religion was a central feature of colonial life, with the Anglican and Congregational churches the "established" religions, supported by taxes, in most of the colonies (with the exception of Maryland, which was Roman Catholic). The population was roughly 98 percent Protestant, with Catholics and Jews making up the remainder of the population. Catholics, Baptists, and members of smaller sects such as the Shakers were few in number and subject to discrimination. All over the American colonies, the church building was often the first and largest public structure in town, and served also as a public meeting house, with the village cemetery adjacent to it. The clergy was a highly respected profession and clergymen leaders in their communities.

Although Catholics had a small presence in the American colonies, much of French Canada became Catholic owing in large part to the zeal of the Franciscans and Jesuits, who established a bond with the Native Americans they encountered in their missionary travels. When France lost Canada to Britain in 1763, it was with the assurance that the rights of the Roman Catholics living there would be protected.

In 1634 a small group of English Catholics, failing to find the religious freedom they had hoped to find in Virginia, instead settled in Maryland. As Charles A. Goodrich wrote in his 1857 *A History of the United States*,

> Several circumstances contributed to the rapid growth and prosperity of Maryland. Her people were exempted from hostilities from the Indians, having satisfied them in the purchase of their land; the soil was fertile, and the seasons mild. But, more than all, their charter conferred on them more ample privileges than had been conferred in any other colony in America. It secured to emigrants equality in religious rights, and civil freedom; and it granted the privilege of passing laws, without any reservation on the part of the crown to revoke them. Even taxes could not be imposed upon the inhabitants without their consent.
>
> Source: Charles A. Goodrich (Ed.). (2011; originally published in 1858). *A History of the United States*. Charleston, SC: Nabu Press.

Much like Maryland, the colony of Rhode Island also was founded on the principal of the separation of church and state. Its founder, Roger Williams (c. 1604–1684), was forced to leave the Massachusetts Bay Colony in 1635 after speaking out against the habit of the authorities (hinted at by Goodrich) of taking the land of the Native Americans without payment; he further proclaimed that civil authorities had no rights over the consciences of men, which also did not much please the authorities. Another person exiled from the Massachusetts Bay Colony at this time was Anne Hutchinson (1591–1643), a mother of fifteen who held prayer meetings at her home attended by scores of women (and, later, men, including Governor Harry Vane,

> As I understand it, laws, commands, rules and edicts are for those who have not the light which makes plain the pathway.
>
> —ANNE HUTCHINSON, EARLY SETTLER OF RHODE ISLAND

one of her defenders). Hutchinson, too, fled to Rhode Island in 1637 after Vane was replaced by Governor John Winthrop, who did not share Vane's tolerance for her cause. Hutchinson was tried by a Massachusetts court and convicted of blasphemous and dangerous speech by the Puritan authorities and banished.

Religion is more a part of daily life in the United States today than it is in most of Europe. Part of the reason for this is that freedom to practice one's religion was one of America's major draws for various persecuted groups. This enthusiasm for religion has been a part of American history for some time. One such period was the "Great Awakening," a puritanical religious revival often described as "fire-and-brimstone" that took place in the North American colonies between 1730 and 1743.

The Great Awakening was the first of four such periods of religious zeal in America, each led by evangelical Protestant clergy and each leading to a more emotional, personal style of worship for followers. Many new churches were founded as a result of these revivals. The first Great Awakening was led by Jonathan Edwards, a Protestant preacher in Northampton, Massachusetts, and George Whitefield (sometimes spelled Whitfield), an Anglican clergyman from England who visited America several times. Both Edwards and Whitefield moved away from the traditional preaching style— heavy on theology and reason—and instead encouraged emotional worship and the personal experience of "grace," which was, essentially, the sense that one was on a mission from God.

An idea of the content of these preachers' sermons may be gleaned from the title of Edwards's most famous sermon, "Sinners in the Hands of an Angry God." Another sermon, preached by Gilbert Tennent, was titled "The Danger of an Unconverted Ministry."

Preachers such as these came to be known as the New Lights, and clergy who continued to follow the traditional approach were known as the Old Lights. The New Lights drew large audiences, which drew the ire of the Old Lights, whose services

SINNERS

In the Hands of an

Angry GOD.

A SERMON

Preached at *Enfield, July* 8th 1 7 4 1.

At a Time of great Awakenings ; and attended with remarkable Impreffions on many of the Hearers.

By *Jonathan Edwards,* A.M.

Paftor of the Church of CHRIST in *Northampton.*

Amos ix. 2, 3. *Though they dig into Hell, thence fhall mine Hand take them ; though they climb up to Heaven, thence will I bring them down. And though they hide themfelves in the Top of Carmel, I will fearch and take them out thence; and though they be hid from my Sight in the Bottom of the Sea, thence I will command the Serpent, and he fhall bite them.*

BOSTON : Printed and Sold by S. KNEELAND and T. GREEN. in Queen-Street over againft the Prifon. 1 7 4 1.

Protestant leaders such as Jonathan Edwards preached fiery sermons with titles such as "Sinners in the Hands of an Angry God" during the "Great Awakening" of religious feelings that occurred between 1730 and 1743. Source: "Sinners in the Hands of an Angry God. A Sermon Preached at Enfield, July 8th, 1741." Jonathan Edwards, Church of Christ, Northampton, Massachusetts.

subsequently had fewer attendees. The New Lights ultimately offered adherents a wider range of worship opportunities in the Congregational, Presbyterian, and Dutch Reformed churches.

The Great Awakening was the first of what were to be many mass movements in American history as the movement attracted people from across the thirteen colonies. It also made religion more democratic and open to the masses, and weakened the authority of the clergy. Several institutes of higher learning, including Princeton, Brown, Dartmouth, and Rutgers (originally Queen's College), were founded as a result of the religious fervor inspired by the Great Awakening.

The Great Awakening would also lead to an increase in contact between blacks and whites that would have a long-lasting effect on interracial relations in the colonies. While most preachers did not actively challenge slavery, they did preach to blacks and whites alike, and their ideas about a more egalitarian God would have a profound effect on the American people in the years that followed.

Slavery in the Colonial Period

The making of the "New World" by the Europeans was predicated upon the procurement of coerced labor: a system of indentured servitude at first, which in time led to outright slavery. Schemes for a quick and gushing fortune required much drudgery, which nearly all explorers and planters had come to the Americas to avoid. In an era when human inequality was taken for granted, indentured servitude came first. An indentured servant was an individual (usually British in the case of the American colonies) who agreed to work for a set period (usually seven years) without pay, in exchange for transportation to the New World. At the end of their period of service, masters traditionally, but not always, provided the newly freed servants with a patch of land or small sum of money to give them a start as newly freed individuals in the colonies. People entered indentured servitude both through choice and through coercion. In the seventeenth and eighteenth century, English courts sentenced convicted criminals to transportation to the colonies, where they were sold into indentured servitude. Daniel Defoe's eponymous heroine suffers this indignity in his novel *Moll Flanders* (1722). For a while indentured servitude appeared to meet the labor needs of the American colonies and, in fact, it is generally recognized that the first African Americans to arrive in Virginia did so as indentured servants. This situation, however, would soon change.

Slavery gradually replaced indentured servitude for a number of reasons. First, improving economic conditions and opportunities in England at the end of the seventeenth century greatly reduced the numbers of people willing to go to the New World as indentured servants. Second, indentured servants had to be freed at the end of their period of service and their condition was not passed on to their offspring; slaves were slaves for life and so were their children. Third, indentured servants frequently fled before their term of service had expired. As white Europeans, they could pass themselves off as free men (or women) once they got far enough away from their former masters. African Americans, by contrast, were identified as escaped slaves immediately.

Although attempts had been made initially to enslave the Native Americans, the Columbian exchange of diseases discussed in the first chapter decimated that source of labor. Accustomed to European diseases because of international trading contacts, enslaved Africans increasingly replaced sick and dying Native Americans, particularly in coastal, tropical, and disease-ridden areas prime for growing tobacco (an especially labor-intensive crop that gave Virginia and other southern colonies their *raison d'etre*), sugar, and other lucrative crops. Native American slaves, if they managed to escape both bondage and disease, could occasionally return to the protection of their own people. Slaves brought from Africa, on the other hand, had nowhere to go if they did manage to escape bondage.

The transatlantic slave trade, with its infamous Middle Passage from West Africa to the New World, ensnared roughly 11 million people between 1443 and 1870, although the exact number of people enslaved is impossible to determine. The majority of the enslaved went to the Caribbean and Brazil to labor on the sugar plantations. Estimates suggest that about 400,000 African men and women were brought to North America in the slave trade, less than 10 percent of the over four million brought to Brazil and even less than the number brought to the small island of Barbados. The slaves in America, however, tended to have more children (partly because the climate in which they lived was healthier), and so their number would grow in the following centuries. While children born of slaves in other parts of the world often were free, this was not the case in America: generations of slaves were born, lived their lives, and died enslaved.

Britain's first black indentured servants arrived in America in 1619, when a Dutch ship brought about twenty individuals to Jamestown, Virginia. There they sometimes developed friendships with white indentured servants who also had few (if any) rights.

Slavery grew slowly in North America in the 1600s, mainly due to the small numbers of people living there, many of whom were small-scale subsistence farmers. By the mid-1650s increased competition in the tobacco trade had cut profits, and newly freed servants were not getting the land or wealth they thought they would receive. Fearing a coalition of angry and frustrated poor whites and blacks, the Virginia and Maryland colonies took the lead in passing laws that mandated discrimination. Laws regarding marriage, punishment, personal property, and status of children born to slave mothers were all designed to give whites a common cause. Henceforth, nonwhites—particularly African Americans—were treated as the new enemy, and what became known as the "peculiar institution" of slavery enforced the ideas that blacks were inferior beings and that slavery was their natural and deserved status. ("Peculiar" here refers to being "peculiar" or "particular" to a place, not necessarily of being "weird," as the word is now more commonly used.)

Slavery grew more rapidly in the 1700s as the white population increased rapidly and large indigo, tobacco, and rice plantations were established, mainly in the South. In addition to the international slave trade, there was the internal slave trade, in which slaves were auctioned by their owners at slave markets. Many of the founding fathers of the United States, including Thomas Jefferson, Benjamin Franklin, Patrick Henry, James Madison, and George Washington, were slave owners.

Slave Masters and Their Children

The following is an extract from the Narrative of the Life of Frederick Douglass. *Douglass (1818–1895) was a former slave who escaped from bondage in Maryland. He went on to become an orator, writer, and social activist, doing much to spread the word of the evils of slavery. This passage from his autobiography (his first book) hints at the brutality of the system.*

Called thus suddenly away, [my mother] left me without the slightest intimation of who my father was. The whisper that my master was my father, may or may not be true; and, true or false, it is of but little consequence to my purpose whilst the fact remains, in all its glaring odiousness, that slaveholders have ordained, and by law established, that the children of slave women shall in all cases follow the condition of their mothers; and this is done too obviously to administer to their own lusts, and make a gratification of their wicked desires profitable as well as pleasurable; for by this cunning arrangement, the slaveholder, in cases not a few, sustains to his slaves the double relation of master and father.

I know of such cases; and it is worthy of remark that such slaves invariably suffer greater hardships, and have more to contend with, than others. They are, in the first place, a constant offence to their mistress. She is ever disposed to find fault with them; they can seldom do any thing to please her; she is never better pleased than when she sees them under the lash, especially when she suspects her husband of showing to his mulatto children favors which he withdraws from his black slaves. . . . For, unless he does this, he must not only whip them himself, but must stand by and see one white son tie up his brother, of but few shades darker complexion than himself, and ply the gory lash to his naked back; and if he lisp one word of disapproval, it is set down to his parental partiality, and only makes a bad matter worse, both for himself and the slave whom he would protect and defend.

Source: Frederick Douglas. *Narrative of the Life of Frederick Douglass*, pp. 2–3. (1995; originally published in 1845.) Mineola, NY: Dover Thrift Editions.

Only a minority of North American colonists had slaves; most were in the South, although there were slave owners in the northern colonies as well. One reason for this was that slavery was introduced for labor-intensive crops such as tobacco, mainly grown in the South. The smaller-scale household farms of New England—where the climate is cold and the soil rocky, thus limiting large-scale agriculture—did not require the large amounts of labor needed to run a massive tobacco plantation.

Slavery's increasing importance in the United States did not mean that all Southern blacks were slaves. Thousands of blacks were free, and several owned slaves. No matter their status as free men, however, they were constantly reminded that slavery was but a step away. Whites were angry and suspicious toward free blacks because the free blacks symbolized what could happen if the slaves were to rise up and revolt against their masters. Many slave rebellions were alleged to have been plotted by free blacks. As a result, they were viewed with suspicion as potential leaders of uprisings. Those who could read and write, be they slave or free, were viewed as dangerous potential rebellion leaders.

Although many colonists were indifferent to slavery, some people were opposed on moral grounds as well as for less noble political reasons. In 1687 the Spanish, to disrupt the English colonial economy, began offering English slaves freedom in Florida, requiring the slaves to convert to Catholicism and to give the Spanish crown four years of labor. In 1738 the first settlement of free blacks was established in North America, at Fort Mose, Florida. In 1688 the Pennsylvania Quakers passed the first anti-slavery resolution in North America. The slaves themselves resisted and launched revolts, with the Stono Revolt in South Carolina in 1739 causing the most concern among whites.

The United States Constitution written in the wake of the American Revolution did not end slavery—it did, in fact, protect it—but opposition continued to grow in the North and individual states began banning slavery or phasing it out over a period of years. It took the Civil War (discussed in Chapter Three) to ban slavery entirely, and then another one hundred years before African Americans received full legal rights. In the meantime, tens of millions of people led lives of humiliation, servitude, and misery under the Atlantic plantation system that endured for over four centuries.

Some historians believe that the institution of slavery led not only to the Civil War in the nineteenth century but to the American Revolution, discussed in the next section, as well. The 1772 court case *Somerset v Stewart*, in which a British judge ruled slavery to be illegal in England, was one such instance: colonists in the southern colonies thought the British courts would make slavery illegal in America, too, and were not pleased.

"Slave Driver"

> Ev'rytime I hear the crack of a whip,
> My blood runs cold.
> I remember on the slave ship,
> How they brutalize[d] our very souls.
> Today they say that we are free,
> Only to be chained in poverty.
> Good God, I think it's illiteracy;
> It's only a machine that makes money.
> Slave driver, the table is turn[ed].

—BOB MARLEY,
JAMAICAN REGGAE STAR

Independence and Revolution (1775–1783)

The American War of Independence, also called the American Revolutionary War or simply the American Revolution, did not occur in a vacuum; rather, it developed against the background of complex economic, political, religious, and social conditions (including a sizeable portion of the populace living in bondage) discussed in the previous pages.

Because the date 1776 is such a well-known year among Americans—it was the famous date of the signing of the Declaration of Independence—it is a commonly held belief, even among Americans, that the Revolutionary War started in 1776, and that it was short. This was not the case. The war actually took place between 1775 and 1781 (although it did not officially end until the signing of the Treaty of Paris in 1783) and pitted colonists of the thirteen British colonies against Great Britain. Until the twenty-first century war in Afghanistan (2001–present), it was the longest war in American history.

The Revolution was triggered, in part, by increased British efforts to control the colonies from 1763 onward, efforts largely designed to expand revenues for the British treasury, depleted by the Seven Years' War with France discussed earlier. New taxes and regulations on colonial economic activity infuriated many colonists, who were accustomed to their own semi-independent colonial legislatures and who had considerable commercial latitude. Patriotic societies formed, and leaders began to invoke Enlightenment ideas, such as those espoused by John Locke (discussed in the next chapter), about liberty and about popular control over government.

The patriotic Continental Congress assembled and began discussing the possibility of independence—not a small thing to contemplate—in 1774. Outright clashes between armed militia groups and British soldiers began in Massachusetts in 1775. George Washington (1732–1799), a military leader during the French and Indian War, was named commander in the summer of that year.

Numbers are difficult to estimate, but after the Revolution, John Adams estimated that perhaps a third of the American colonists had actively supported the struggle for independence from Britain. Another large minority—perhaps another third, many of them centered in and around New York City—preferred to remain loyal to the Crown. Many Loyalists (known as "Tories") fled north to Canada and were stripped of their former property. There are several places on the East Coast named "Tory Cave": places in which Tories attempted to hide, band together, or aid the British troops. Another large portion of the populace was either apolitical or waited to see

The Declaration of Independence

The Declaration of Independence, with its simple, direct language detailing the many reasons for Americans' grievances against Britain, generated a wave of revolutionary sentiment throughout Latin America and Western Europe in the late nineteenth century—most notably the French Revolution. It is perhaps the most revered document in American history.

July 4, 1776

When in the course of human events it becomes necessary for one people to dissolve the political bands which have connected them with another and to assume among the powers of the earth, the separate and equal station to which the Laws of Nature and of Nature's God entitle them, a decent respect to the opinions of mankind requires that they should declare the causes which impel them to the separation.

We hold these truths to be self-evident, that all men are created equal, that they are endowed by their Creator with certain unalienable Rights, that among these are Life, Liberty and the pursuit of Happiness. . . .

The history of the present King of Great Britain is a history of repeated injuries and usurpations, all having in direct object the establishment of an absolute Tyranny over these States. To prove this, let Facts be submitted to a candid world.

He has refused his Assent to Laws, the most wholesome and necessary for the public good.

He has forbidden his Governors to pass Laws of immediate and pressing importance, unless suspended in their operation till his Assent should be obtained; and when so suspended, he has utterly neglected to attend to them.

He has refused to pass other Laws for the accommodation of large districts of people, unless those people would relinquish the right of Representation in the Legislature, a right inestimable to them and formidable to tyrants only.

He has called together legislative bodies at places unusual, uncomfortable, and distant from the depository of their public Records, for the sole purpose of fatiguing them into compliance with his measures.

He has dissolved Representative Houses repeatedly, for opposing with manly firmness his invasions on the rights of the people. . . .

which way the wind blew: people who may have had family or business connections in England or who were afraid of losing their property (or their lives) if they came out on the wrong side of the war.

This widespread division of loyalties has led many to view the American Revolution as a civil war. Partisans included Virginia planters and New England political radicals, who agreed on Britain as a common enemy but disagreed about social change. A number of farmers, in what was still a largely agricultural society, participated in the struggle, as did some African Americans; the first colonist killed in the struggle was, in fact, an African American sailor, although most African Americans (as well as most Native Americans) supported the Crown.

The colonies officially declared independence from Britain on the Fourth of July, 1776, when the Continental Congress issued the Declaration of Independence, written mainly by Virginia aristocrat and gentleman farmer Thomas Jefferson (1743–1826), discussed below. The Declaration, and the ideals it represents, are discussed in the next chapter.

Declaring independence from one of the world's most powerful empires was one major step; gaining that independence was another. Fighting occurred in both the North and the South, with British troops, bolstered by German soldiers, known

Independence Hall in Philadelphia, site of the signing of both the Declaration of Independence and the Constitution. The building was known at the time as the Pennsylvania State House, and functioned as the colony's main courthouse. It is for this reason that the Declaration is, in part, an official list of crimes perpetrated by the accused, King George III of England. Photo by Bill Siever.

as Hessians, often holding the upper hand. Britain was hampered by cautious tactics but also by frequent overconfidence against the amateur colonial forces. Their bright red uniforms also made them easy targets for the colonists, although the colonists, too, fought in orderly, European-style ranks. (British soldiers were called, perhaps apocryphally, "lobsterbacks," as well as "bloody backs," in part due to the fact that flogging was a means of discipline in the British Army and in the Royal Navy.) The colonists had numbers and knowledge of the terrain on their side, although the actual number of combatants was small, with rarely more than fifteen thousand in the colonists' ranks at any given time. Many militiamen were part-time and ill-trained, and funding was a perpetual problem. France, and to a lesser degree Spain and the Netherlands, provided funds and weapons and direct military support after 1776; this support was crucial in the latter stages of the Revolution, and turned the tide in the Americans' favor.

By 1781 fighting concentrated in Virginia, where the British general Charles Cornwallis had to yield to a combined French-American force at the York River port of Yorktown. Although the war was essentially over, desultory fighting continued for two more years before a peace was signed in Paris to recognize the new United States, with territory running from Florida (ceded by Britain to Spain) to Canada, from the Atlantic to the Mississippi River. Britain feared even greater losses to its empire if war were to continue.

Profile of a Founding Father: George Washington (1732–1799)

Even with all the layers of legend that have accumulated around George Washington both during his lifetime and during the two hundred-plus years since his death, it would be difficult to overestimate his leadership and importance to the United States. Washington was the general responsible for winning independence on the Revolutionary War battlefield and the first president of the United States under the new Constitution. His achievements in the Revolutionary War earned him the title "father of his country" long before the job of president was designed. Later, when he was the first president, Washington's leadership ensured that the nation would survive its first tumultuous decade, and he set anti-monarchical precedents that were followed by all subsequent holders of the office.

Washington was born to a relatively prosperous Virginia planter named Augustine Washington and his second wife, Mary Ball. He received a small amount of formal schooling that consisted mainly of reading, writing, mathematics, and geometry. Later, like many young men, Washington joined the Virginia militia. In the 1750s he led several militia units in battles against the French in Ohio and Pennsylvania.

Although he was defeated at two major battles, he gained a reputation as a brave and solid—and perhaps very lucky—soldier.

After the French and Indian War ended in 1763, Washington married and lived the life of a wealthy Virginia planter. In 1774, however, with tensions increasing between the colonies and the British government, Washington's reputation and standing in the colony made him the natural choice to represent Virginia in the Continental Congress that was then meeting in Philadelphia. He was one of few prominent men who had seen battle firsthand; his career as a revolutionary leader had begun.

After fighting between the colonies and the British broke out in the towns of Lexington and Concord, Massachusetts, in April 1775, the Continental Congress selected Washington as commander of the Continental Army. He was an inspired choice for political reasons: placing a Virginian in command of a revolt that began in New England immediately made the Patriot cause appear less regional in nature.

In accepting command of the Continental Army, Washington the general became the unifying symbol for the entire colonial effort and was soon regarded as the personification of the Revolution itself. Washington kept the army together by his own strength of will and determination, through

> *By the rude bridge that arched the flood,*
> *Their flag to April's breeze unfurled,*
> *Here once the embattled farmers stood,*
> *And fired the shot heard round the world.*
>
> —RALPH WALDO EMERSON,
> "CONCORD HYMN"

miserable conditions, until achieving ultimate victory in Yorktown, Virginia, in 1781.

Although Washington is often viewed as a saintly figure in American history, he did have his flaws, and was at times exceedingly conflicted in his views: particularly on slavery. Like Thomas Jefferson—a fellow slave owner—his views on slavery evolved with time as he encountered black soldiers and freemen and travelled to parts of the new nation without slaves. He was also highly influenced by the French Marquis de Lafayette (1757–1834; full name Marie-Joseph Paul Yves Roch Gilbert du Motier de La Fayette, Marquis de La Fayette), an idealistic young aristocrat who came to America to fight what he saw as the tyranny of British rule, and who held adamantly anti-slavery views.

Washington added terms to his will that would free his over 300 slaves upon the death of his wife; he was the only slave-owning founding father to include such a clause in his will. People today may visit Mount Vernon, Washington's home of forty years, on the banks of the Potomac River to the south of Washington, DC.

Profile of a Founding Father:
Thomas Jefferson (1743–1826)

If George Washington was the heart and muscle of the new United States, Thomas Jefferson was the new nation's intellect. Second only to Washington in terms of his wide-ranging influences on early America, Thomas Jefferson, the main author of the Declaration of Independence, drew upon French and English Enlightenment political philosophy, and especially the work of the Englishman John Locke, to urge colonists to fight for a government based on popular consent—a government that could secure the right to life, liberty, and the pursuit of happiness. The Declaration and the American Revolution generated a wave of revolutionary sentiment throughout Latin America and Western Europe in the eighteenth and nineteenth centuries—most notably the French Revolution—and were even used to justify anti-colonial struggles in Asia and Africa in the twentieth century.

Jefferson became the third president of the United States in 1801 and secretly arranged the purchase of a vast swath of land known as the Louisiana Territory—an area larger than modern Mexico, and more than three times the size of France—from Napoleon Bonaparte in 1803. Jefferson doubled the size of the new nation and set the stage for the growth of the United States as the dominant power in the Americas.

Jefferson was born on 13 April 1743 in the colony of Virginia. His parents were wealthy tobacco planters and part of the colonial elite. Jefferson earned a living as both a lawyer and a farmer, living on his hilltop plantation, Monticello, in Virginia. In 1772 he married Martha Wayles Skelton, a widow, who died ten years later. Jefferson served as a member of the House of Burgesses, the lower house of Virginia's legislature, from 1769 to 1775 and became a leader of the developing opposition to British policies.

Jefferson went on to play a major role in the development of the United States. A deist, like many Enlightenment-era intellectuals, he managed to draft, after several attempts, the bill that established religious freedom and the separation of church and state in Virginia. (Deists saw God as, essentially, a celestial watchmaker, who created everything, wound it up, and then left it to run along mechanical lines; Ethan Allen, quoted at left, was another notable deist of the era.)

Jefferson served as Virginia governor from 1779 to 1781 and worked as United States minister to France from 1785 to 1789, where he was strongly impressed with the food and culture of that country but shocked by the

> While we are under the tyranny of Priests [. . .] it will ever be their interest, to invalidate the law of nature and reason, in order to establish systems incompatible therewith.
>
> —ETHAN ALLEN, FOUNDING FATHER OF VERMONT, from *Reason the Only Oracle of Man*

sad state of the impoverished French peasantry. Jefferson brought his slave, James Hemings, to France with him, to be trained in the art of French cuisine; Hemings would eventually gain his freedom from Jefferson once he'd bestowed the training he'd learned in France upon a successor. Historians are fairly certain that Jefferson later secretly fathered several children with James's sister, Sally Hemings.

Upon Jefferson's return home in 1789, President George Washington selected him to become the first secretary of state. Jefferson became a strong advocate for a weak central government and an economy based on agriculture. After Washington refused a third term as president in 1796, Jefferson stood for election against fellow founding father John Adams (1735–1826), an often cantankerous Boston lawyer and public figure with whom he disagreed on many topics. Adams won and became the second president of the United States; Jefferson became the vice president.

In the 1800 presidential contest Jefferson tied with fellow Republican Aaron Burr in the Electoral College, but the House of Representatives settled the tie in favor of Jefferson; this time, Jefferson became president and Burr vice president of the United States. Jefferson took office in March 1801 and served as president for two terms. As president, Jefferson's major accomplishment was the acquisition of the Louisiana Territory from France in 1803, as well as sending the Lewis and Clark expedition to explore the new lands; these are both discussed in the "Territorial Expansion in the 19th Century" section in the next chapter. In his retirement he founded the University of Virginia, and corresponded with hundreds of scientists around the world.

Jefferson died on the Fourth of July, 1826, the fiftieth anniversary of the signing of the Declaration of Independence, only hours before the death of his sometime nemesis and later close friend, John Adams, leaving behind a lasting political tradition that still influences America and the rest of the world.

Long a revered figure in America, Jefferson's reputation has been challenged by recent scholarship, which calls attention to his owning slaves throughout his life while advocating for liberty for others, as well as convincing evidence that he fathered children with Sally Hemings who, as a slave, by definition could not consent to such a relationship.

Jefferson was a complicated person; defenders of his legacy point out that he thought that abolishing slavery, while an admirable goal, was not something that could realistically be accomplished in his lifetime. Today Monticello, overlooking Charlottesville, Virginia, is open to the public, where visitors may learn much about the fundamentally different, but often parallel, lives of slaves and slave owners, as well as about early American agricultural innovation.

Significance of the American Revolution

The significance of the American Revolution in world history rests on several bases. It was part of the ongoing colonial struggle among European powers; the French monarchy was drawn into the conflict by the opportunity to weaken Britain's position. The British government believed the War of American Independence was caused by too little control over its American colonies, and took measures to tighten the reins over its remaining overseas colonies. French expenditures in the war contributed to financial crises at home and helped lead to the need to call the Estates General to consider new taxes.

The example of colonial independence, the strong principles embodied in the Declaration of Independence and other writings by leaders such as Jefferson, and the institutions ultimately established by the Constitution inspired revolutionaries and nationalists elsewhere. The American example loomed large during the French Revolution that was to come. The political philosopher and activist Thomas Paine, an Englishman who emigrated to the American colonies, where he became a widely read advocate of the colonists' rights, summed up this aspect of American influence by claiming that the Revolution "contributed more to enlighten the world and diffuse a spirit of freedom and liberty among mankind, than any human event that ever preceded it."

The Revolution was not a major social upheaval, as revolutions go, although a new generation of leaders did wrest power from their elders. Despite revolutionary principles, and some ensuing emancipations in northern states, slavery was not systematically attacked. The social structure and relations between men and women were not significantly altered. The American Revolution was far less sweeping than its later French counterpart. It was also unusually politically successful, compared with later independence struggles elsewhere, without the long, disruptive aftermath that often occurs after revolutions. The fact that the early leaders of the United States had considerable political experience in colonial legislatures may help explain this success. The country was also fortunate in having a considerable number of forceful, principled, and highly intelligent leaders in those early decades.

The quick resumption of close economic ties with Britain after the war encouraged the American economy. Indeed, British statesman Winston Churchill would later call this close tie with the former "mother country" the "Special Relationship," although there was to be another war with Britain (the War of 1812) in the years to come. Rifts between North and South, however, briefly bridged during the American Revolution, would soon reappear in the fledgling nation.

Opportunities for westward expansion across the Allegheny and Appalachian mountains followed quickly after the Revolutionary War. The nation began to set its own course.

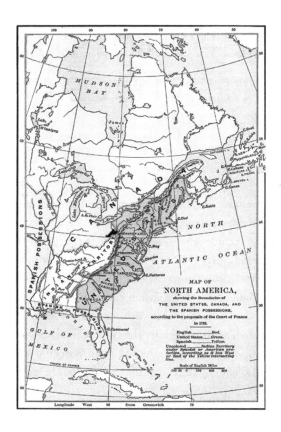

North America after the American Revolution. The Spanish controlled the lands to the west of the Mississippi River, as well as Florida and the Gulf Coast; the Indian Territories were east of the Mississippi, south of the Ohio River, and west of the Appalachian Mountains. Canada at this time dipped much further south than it does today.
Source: Justin Winsor, *Narrative and Critical History of North America Vol. VII* (1888). Boston: Houghton, Mifflin and Company. Courtesy of the private collection of Roy Winkelman.

CHAPTER THREE: AFTER THE REVOLUTION THROUGH THE NINETEENTH CENTURY

The period from victory in the American Revolution through the nineteenth century was one of tremendous growth for the United States. Its territory expanded to include what is now the entire contiguous United States, the number of states grew to forty-five, and the population grew by a factor of fifteen, from about five million in 1800 to seventy-six million in 1900. The economy shifted from agriculture to industry, and the nation continued to become more ethnically diverse while at the same time wrestling with the issue of slavery, which was ended only through a long and bloody civil war. The United States entered a period of relative isolation from world affairs, although the United States did assert its dominance in the Western Hemisphere. By the end of the century the United States had become a world power.

One event with far-reaching consequences for the nation (and the world) during this early period was the invention of the cotton gin in 1793 by Eli Whitney (1765–1825) in Connecticut. The machine allowed the easy and quick separation of cotton fibers and cotton seeds; this relatively simple machine altered agriculture in southern plantations and industry in the North. Cotton replaced tobacco as the South's major crop, and textile mills mushroomed across New England. The new machine also affected the social order, as worldwide demand for cotton increased the demand for slave labor in the South, involving the United States in the slave trade, and making slavery a key element of the southern and (to less of an extent) the northern economy. The increased use of slave labor correspondingly increased opposition to slavery, and sixty years later led indirectly to the Civil War and to the end of slavery.

Founding Principles of the United States

The founding of the United States of America after the war of independence from Britain was won was not a historical accident, but rather was the product of its leaders implementing certain philosophical ideas, most fundamentally the ideas of two philosophers: the Greek philosopher Aristotle (384–322 BCE) and the Englishman John Locke (1632–1704). The United States was founded at the peak of the intellectual period known as the Enlightenment, a period during which reason prevailed over religious dogma—a triumph that had its roots in ancient Greece but that took some two thousand years to reach fruition.

Aristotle, the foremost philosophical champion of reason in ancient Greece, held that people gain knowledge about the real world by using reason and logic to identify what they observe by means of their senses. Aristotle was also an advocate of the philosophy known as "egoism"; he held that one's proper goal in life is the achievement of one's own happiness. Reason and egoism form the base of the concept of individual rights, although the latter concept (which now has a rather negative connotation) was not formulated until much later.

John Locke was a leading philosopher in seventeenth-century England whose experiences in the English Civil War (1642–1651) and Glorious Revolution (1688) shaped his work in philosophy, political theory, education, and theology; his work played a major role in shaping eighteenth-century thought and in the founding of the United States. Locke's *Second Treatise of Civil Government*, published in 1689, was the first consistent, systematic presentation of the concept of individual rights.

Locke argued that individuals possessed "natural" rights, including the rights to life, liberty, and property. (By the right to property, Locke meant the right to earn it and to keep what was earned.) Locke held that these rights stemmed from man's nature and were prior to—and, importantly, superior to—governments and their laws. Thus individuals did not exist to serve governments; rather, governments were formed and existed in order to serve the individual by protecting his rights. Locke argued that people should be free from coercion and interference by others, including the state. This was one of the more revolutionary political ideas in human history—a complete reversal of the traditional conception of the relationship between the individual and the state.

Locke's ideas were grounded in a respect for the individual and the power of reason to order human affairs. He was sensitive to the role that experience plays in the education of youth and the development of one's moral character. He viewed a church as a voluntary association of people who come to worship together in matters of faith. He argued for tolerance among Protestant sects who were potentially willing to tolerate the religious opinions of the other sects. His goal was to convince Protestant groups that they had an interest in tolerating one another. Significantly, this toleration did not extend to Roman Catholics, who, Locke believed, were committed to the secular authority of the Pope.

The Constitution and the Bill of Rights

Following in the footsteps of the Declaration of Independence (1776), the founding principles of the United States after the war was won are set forth in the Constitution (1787), which provides the foundations for the United States government, and the Bill of Rights (1791), the name for the first ten amendments to the Constitution, written by Virginian James Madison (1751–1836) to address rights that were not specifically included in the original document.

The Constitution, written in Philadelphia in the summer of 1787 by delegates from twelve states (Rhode Island did not send a delegate), was meant to replace the previous Articles of Confederation with a more solid form of government. After much debate over the relative powers of the individual states and the central government, the new document created a federal system with a national government divided into three separated powers, each with a system of "checks and balances" on each others' powers:

- *Legislative branch*: The House of Representatives and the Senate, which together form the United States Congress, are responsible for creating laws. Laws can be vetoed (i.e., rejected) by the President (executive branch) or challenged by the judicial branch as unconstitutional. The United States Congress is divided into the Senate and the House of Representatives. The Constitution's Connecticut Compromise reached an agreement between large and small states: two senators represent each state in the Senate, regardless of population size, meaning that in a sparsely populated state such as Wyoming (which did not exist as a state at the time), the two senators each represent fewer than 300,000 people; the two California senators, meanwhile, currently represent around 19 million people each. In the House of Representatives, on the other hand, members are elected by population. California has 53 representatives as of 2014, while Wyoming has only one.

- *Judicial branch*: The federal court system, headed by the Supreme Court, administers justice. The nine members of the Supreme Court are nominated by the President (executive branch) but must be confirmed by the Senate (legislative branch). The Constitution states that the justices "shall hold their Offices during good Behaviour," meaning that they hold office as long as they choose—often a very long time—and can only be removed by impeachment. (Only one Justice, Samuel Chase, has ever been impeached, in 1805, although he was acquitted by the Senate.) The Supreme Court generally only reviews cases of national significance; some of the most well-known cases include *Dred Scott v. Sandford* (1857), which declared that African Americans (such as Scott, a slave) were not American citizens and thus did not have the right to sue in federal court, whether they were free or slaves; *Brown v. Board of Education* (1954), in which state laws establishing separate schools for black and white students were declared unconstitutional (discussed in Chapter Five); and *Roe v. Wade* (1973), on abortion rights (also discussed in Chapter Five).

- *Executive branch*: The President, as the head of the executive branch, is charged with carrying out the nation's laws. The President is also Commander-in-Chief of the nation's armed forces, but must have approval from the legislative branch for actions such as declaring war or signing treaties with other nations. The Constitution established a chain of succession in the event of the President's death: the Vice President, followed by the Speaker of House, then the president *pro tempore* of the Senate. (The Vice President is also automatically the president of the Senate, so the phrase *pro tempore* is used to denote a "temporary" officeholder.)

The nation's founders struggled over how best to find and keep good leadership. The system of institutional checks and balances created by the Constitution were meant to cultivate good leaders and to restrain bad ones, with each branch checking the powers of the other. As James Madison wrote in *Federalist Paper #51*, "ambition must be made to counteract ambition." (*The Federalist*, written by James Madison, John Jay, and Alexander Hamilton in 1787 and 1788, was a series of 85 essays written to promote the ratification of the Constitution; the articles later came to be known as *The Federalist Papers*.)

The basic idea of checks and balances informed other liberal democracies, including those of Great Britain and several other European states. John Jay of New York (1745–1829), writing in *Federalist Paper #64*, argued that leaders have to be trusted. The founders designed the Constitution, Jay noted, so that individuals of wisdom and keen judgment, with no interest other than the well-being of those they represented, would seek political office. If the system worked according to plan, the government would consist of the most able, the most virtuous, and the most trustworthy individuals. Toward the end of his analysis, however, Jay made an abrupt shift: if citizens were worried about the discretion granted to leaders, they should be reassured by another provision in the Constitution giving them the power to impeach a president who abuses his power.

In addition to the three-way separation of powers, the other notable features of the American political system are a federal system, dividing authority between the federal, state, and local levels of government, with the three-way division between executive, legislature, and judiciary replicated at each of the lower levels; and the Electoral College, in which the President is chosen by slates of electors rather than through direct popular vote.

CHECKS AND BALANCES IN THE US GOVERNMENT

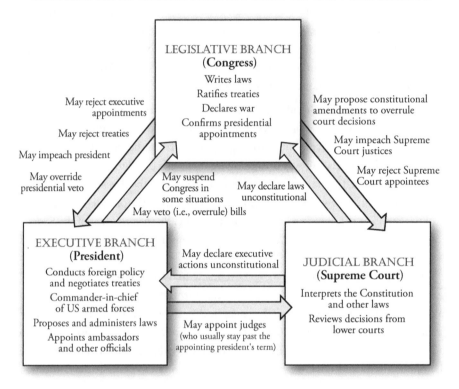

LEGISLATIVE BRANCH
(Congress)
Writes laws
Ratifies treaties
Declares war
Confirms presidential
appointments

May reject executive
appointments

May reject treaties

May impeach president

May override
presidential veto

May propose constitutional
amendments to overrule
court decisions

May impeach Supreme
Court justices

May reject Supreme
Court appointees

May suspend
Congress in
some situations

May declare laws
unconstitutional

May veto (i.e., overrule) bills

EXECUTIVE BRANCH
(President)
Conducts foreign policy
and negotiates treaties
Commander-in-chief
of US armed forces
Proposes and administers laws
Appoints ambassadors
and other officials

May declare executive
actions unconstitutional

JUDICIAL BRANCH
(Supreme Court)
Interprets the Constitution
and other laws
Reviews decisions from
lower courts

May appoint judges
(who usually stay past the
appointing president's term)

The product of compromise—see for example, the "three-fifths" compromise discussed below—the United States Constitution is considered one of the world's premiere showcases of democracy in action. It also makes the United States the oldest constitutional republic in the world.

James Madison created the Bill of Rights to address protections for individual liberties that were not specifically spelled out in the original Constitution. The powers of (and limits on) government enumerated by constitutional amendments were to be exercised for the purpose of protecting citizens' freedom of action, rather than destroying that freedom. For example, the First Amendment to the Constitution states that "Congress shall make no law respecting an establishment of religion, or prohibiting the free exercise thereof." By enacting that amendment, the founding fathers ensured that there would be no established church, such as the Church of England, in the United States. This did not mean that there were to be no powerful church interests—only that citizens would not be forced to pay taxes

(*continued on page 47*)

The Constitution of the United States (1787)

The United States Constitution, written in Philadelphia in 1787, set out the founding principles of the United States. The document, based in large part on James Madison's "Virginia Plan," provided the foundations for the United States government. The members of the Constitutional Convention included lawyers, merchants, educators, ministers, soldiers, doctors, and businessmen. The Connecticut Compromise, which addressed the concerns of large states such as Virginia and New York that their large populations would be underrepresented, and of small states such as Rhode Island and Delaware that their small populations would have no say in the new government, made for a Senate in which each state had two members, no matter their population, and a House of Representatives, in which states were represented based on their population.

We the People of the United States, in Order to form a more perfect Union, establish Justice, insure domestic Tranquility, provide for the common defence, promote the general Welfare, and secure the Blessings of Liberty to ourselves and our Posterity, do ordain and establish this Constitution for the United States of America.

Article. I.

Section. 1.
All legislative Powers herein granted shall be vested in a Congress of the United States, which shall consist of a Senate and House of Representatives.

Section. 2.
The House of Representatives shall be composed of Members chosen every second Year by the People of the several States, and the Electors in each State shall have the Qualifications requisite for Electors of the most numerous Branch of the State Legislature.

No Person shall be a Representative who shall not have attained to the Age of twenty five Years, and been seven Years a Citizen of the United States, and who shall not, when elected, be an Inhabitant of that State in which he shall be chosen. . . .

Source: National Archives.

The Bill of Rights (1791)

The following is a transcription of the first ten amendments to the Constitution, known as the Bill of Rights, created by James Madison. The Bill of Rights was ratified on 15 December 1791.

Amendment I. Congress shall make no law respecting an establishment of religion, or prohibiting the free exercise thereof; or abridging the freedom of speech, or of the press; or the right of the people peaceably to assemble, and to petition the Government for a redress of grievances.

Amendment II. A well regulated Militia, being necessary to the security of a free State, the right of the people to keep and bear Arms, shall not be infringed.

Amendment III. No Soldier shall, in time of peace be quartered in any house, without the consent of the Owner, nor in time of war, but in a manner to be prescribed by law.

Amendment IV. The right of the people to be secure in their persons, houses, papers, and effects, against unreasonable searches and seizures, shall not be violated, and no Warrants shall issue, but upon probable cause, supported by Oath or affirmation, and particularly describing the place to be searched, and the persons or things to be seized.

Amendment V. No person shall be held to answer for a capital, or otherwise infamous crime, unless on a presentment or indictment of a Grand Jury, except in cases arising in the land or naval forces, or in the Militia, when in actual service in time of War or public danger; nor shall any person be subject for the same offence to be twice put in jeopardy of life or limb; nor shall be compelled in any criminal case to be a witness against himself, nor be deprived of life, liberty, or property, without due process of law; nor shall private property be taken for public use, without just compensation.

Amendment VI. In all criminal prosecutions, the accused shall enjoy the right to a speedy and public trial, by an impartial jury of the State and district wherein the crime shall have been committed, which district shall have been previously ascertained by law, and to be informed of the nature and cause of the accusation; to be confronted with the witnesses against him; to have compulsory process for obtaining witnesses in his favor, and to have the Assistance of Counsel for his defence.

Amendment VII. In Suits at common law, where the value in controversy shall exceed twenty dollars, the right of trial by jury shall be preserved, and no fact tried by a jury, shall be otherwise re-examined in any Court of the United States, than according to the rules of the common law.

Amendment VIII. Excessive bail shall not be required, nor excessive fines imposed, nor cruel and unusual punishments inflicted.

Amendment IX. The enumeration in the Constitution, of certain rights, shall not be construed to deny or disparage others retained by the people.

Amendment X. The powers not delegated to the United States by the Constitution, nor prohibited by it to the States, are reserved to the States respectively, or to the people.

Source: National Archives.

(*continued from page 44*)

for any one church. Issues involving this separation of church and state crop up frequently throughout American history: starting in the 1960s, for instance, many Americans started to question the common practice of having prayers and bible studies in public schools.

The Second Amendment, which says that "A well regulated militia, being necessary to the security of a free state, the right of the people to keep and bear arms, shall not be infringed," is another source of contention, as discussed in the section on gun control laws in Chapter Six.

Interpreting the Constitution

While the Constitution and the Bill of Rights are clear on many topics, the documents cannot possibly cover every eventuality, nor could the framers of the documents foresee such inventions as radio and automobiles, let alone Twitter. As such, debates have raged over the years between several camps over how the Constitution should best be interpreted. Originalists believe the best method of interpreting the meaning of the law without unduly diluting its power is to try to interpret what the original framers had in mind when they wrote a specific passage, keeping in mind that they lived in a different world than the one in which we live today. Modernists, on the other hand, believe that the Constitution is a "living" document: one that evolves to suit modern circumstances (and inventions such as Twitter). Originalists and modernists are often found on opposite sides of the political spectrum.

Equality in the New Nation

When a principle as radical as that of individual rights is formally adopted by a country, the traditions and premises of past centuries are not suddenly overthrown. There will inevitably be opposition, and thus delay, in applying the new principles consistently.

Two not particularly positive traditions that the United States inherited from the past were slavery (by this time outlawed in England) and gender inequality, both of which lived on in the new nation. Many historians argue that the Revolution was in fact a setback for racial equality in America: white equality in the new nation depended upon racial inequality. On the positive side, the United States also inherited representative government, the concept of a bill of rights, and a solid rule of law.

There was an element of political compromise involved in the nascent United States' acceptance of slavery. Thomas Jefferson's original draft of the Declaration of Independence included a strongly worded repudiation of the slave trade (although not necessarily of the institution of slavery itself). This section was taken out, however, for fear that the southern states would not join the fight for independence against the British if that repudiation were retained.

Jefferson himself was a slave owner, albeit one who hoped that someday the "peculiar institution" would come to an end. He did not think that this would happen in his lifetime, however, and, like many at the time, did not think that freed blacks should stay in the country. Some abolition groups, notably the American Colonization Society (ACS; discussed later in this chapter), advocated the removal of freed blacks to the west coast of Africa; Liberia was settled partly as a result of efforts by the ACS and other groups. Other abolitionists, such as newspaper editor William Lloyd Garrison (1805–1879), a one-time member of the ACS in his youth, rejected such plans through his newspaper, *The Liberator*, and other outlets, and instead advocated for the immediate emancipation of all slaves. This belief marked him as a radical, even in the North. Garrison helped to organize the New England Anti-Slavery Society in 1832, followed by the American Anti-Slavery Society in 1833.

After the United States became independent, the nation was faced with a dilemma (although not one that many people were willing to discuss openly): slavery was obviously incompatible with the concept of individual rights. There were rationalizations to the effect that slaves were not fully human, but these rationalizations could last only so long. Either the country's core principles had to be repudiated, or slavery had to be abolished. It took almost ninety years to do it, but slavery was finally eradicated after a bitter and bloody civil war. It took many more decades before black people were treated as equal to white people before the law.

Full equality for women before the law (including the right to vote and the same property rights that men had) was exceedingly rare in Western history at the time the United States became independent. It took Americans almost 150 years to establish women's equality before the law: the Nineteenth Amendment, ratified in 1920. Also ignored by the founding principles were the Native Americans who, rather than being treated equally,

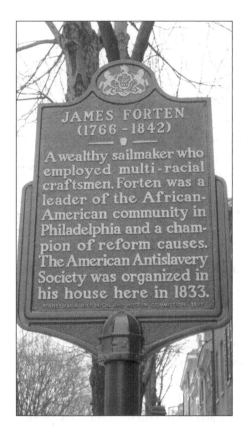

James Forten was a free-born African American who used his wealth from a prosperous sail-making business near the Philadelphia waterfront to advocate for the right of women and African Americans to vote. African Americans would gain that right in 1870, although they would not gain full rights until the enactment of the Voting Rights Act of 1965. Women did not gain the right to vote until 1920. Photo by Bill Siever.

were instead driven from their lands and subjected to forced assimilation.

Equality has been a core value of the United States since the first European settlers arrived. Many of the colonists who migrated from Europe during the 1600s and 1700s came to escape inequitable treatment because of race, religion, or creed. Many of the people who provided the basis for American culture were, in a sense, seeking equality. (Many others, such as the colonists who settled Jamestown, Virginia, in 1607—the first English settlement in America—came mainly for financial gain, with the backing of the Virginia Company of London.) Indeed, the American value of equality is clearly stated in the Declaration of Independence, which boldly begins, "We hold these truths to be self-evident, that all men are created equal. . . ."

Citizens of the United States enjoy an equality of individual opportunity. Rather than ascribing equal status to people throughout life, the essence of American equality is that all people begin life—at least in theory—with the same opportunities and the same potential. Someone born into poverty or born with a debilitating disease or a drug addiction could, no doubt, argue this point; but laws have been put in place over the years to ensure that no person may be discriminated against because of any of these disadvantages. What each person does with these opportunities and challenges—whatever they are—is a matter of his or her own ambition and work ethic. The Constitution clearly emphasizes many of these ideas, although, notably, it did not include the word "equal" until the Fourteenth Amendment was added after the Civil War. (This amendment, a magnet for many lawsuits over the years, is a somewhat complicated amendment that, among other things, prevents individual states from usurping the rights of United States citizens.)

Concern with equal opportunities for all people is strongly linked to the American belief in each person's inalienable right to self-direction and development. In this way the value of equality is bound inseparably with American individualism. Inequality is presumed to result not from different opportunities, which are contextual or situational characteristics. Rather, inequality is presumed to result from ambition and work ethic, which are individual characteristics.

Black Codes, and the "Three-Fifths" and Missouri Compromises

Politically, slavery and abolition were contentious issues that had already influenced the writing of the Declaration of Independence and the Constitution, as we have seen. In the drafting of the Constitution in 1787, a compromise was reached by the northern and southern delegates in which three-fifths of the total number of enumerated slaves in a state would count toward the state's official population, even though the slaves were not citizens. In other words, out of one hundred slaves, sixty would "count" toward the official population count that determined how many representatives the state would be assigned, even though those slaves could not vote. This compromise affected taxes and representation in the House of Representatives and inflated the southern states' populations, allowing them disproportionate power in Congress. Representatives of southern states supported slavery and fought abolition, while northerners were divided among several positions. One key concern for some northerners was keeping the fragile nation together, and toward that end they were willing to compromise on the slavery issue.

During this period, several states passed "Black Codes" that limited the activities that all blacks, free or enslaved, could engage in. The northern state of Illinois, for instance, passed its infamous Black Laws in 1819; in force until 1865, the laws required that all black residents carry a certificate of freedom, called "free papers." A person caught without the proper documentation could be arrested as a runaway slave. In the South, slave codes, enacted from the 1660s to the 1860s, had for centuries defined slaves as property. As such, slaves could not marry, sign contracts, or own property. Slave codes also had sections pertaining to free blacks, limiting their ability to travel and to seek employment.

Confronted with expansion and the incorporation of new territories and states in the West, Congress continued to struggle with the slavery issue, and in 1820 compromised again. The Missouri Compromise of 1820 probably forestalled the Civil War by prohibiting slavery in the northern portion of the Louisiana Territory (discussed below), purchased by Jefferson in 1803, permitting it in Missouri and Arkansas, and admitting Maine (previously a part of Massachusetts) as a free state. The compromise hardly settled the issue, as defenders of slavery continued to fear that the institution would be banned eventually, while opponents fretted over any action that enabled slavery to survive. In 1850 a second compromise was enacted, which again allowed some states and territories to be free and others to decide by popular vote if slavery were to be allowed. The most controversial provision of the compromise was the Fugitive Slave Act, which required slaves who escaped to the North to be captured and returned to their owners. The Act was, in part, a southern reaction to the Underground Railroad, a network of escape routes with safe houses and people willing to hide escaped slaves moving from the South to as far north as Canada. The Act, which outraged abolitionists, was routinely ignored in some northern states, such as Massachusetts, while it was zealously applied in others.

One of the most active and successful of the Underground Railroad "conductors" was Harriet Tubman (c. 1820–1913). Born a slave in Maryland, Tubman escaped from bondage, fled to the North, and risked her life repeatedly in several trips back to the South, during which she freed nearly seventy people.

Portrait of Harriet Tubman, Underground Railroad "conductor" who repeatedly risked her life to free slaves from the South. As was often the case with slaves (and escaped slaves such as Tubman), her exact date of birth is unknown. Source: National Archives.

Territorial Expansion in the 19th Century

The most dramatic physical change in the United States in the nineteenth century was the expansion of its territorial borders to encompass all the territory that is now the forty-eight contiguous states as well as Alaska. By 1900 the United States stretched from the Atlantic to the Pacific and consisted of forty-five states and three territories (Arizona, New Mexico, and Oklahoma) and the District of Alaska, all four of which would later become states. Over the course of the nineteenth century geographical expansion was intertwined with several other major transformations, including immigration from Europe, relocations from the East to the West, invention and innovation, industrialization, and ultimately with the emergence of America as a regional, then world, power.

Settlers had been moving west of the Allegheny and Appalachian mountains before independence, but the defeat of the British and the desire for expansion West (the British had forbidden such westward expansion across the mountains) led many more to move into the southern interior and the Midwest. But the major geographical expansions that created the opportunity for massive migration and settlement came through four major territorial acquisitions and several smaller ones from 1803 to 1868. The acquisitions were through purchase, warfare, treaties, and annexation.

The first and largest of these acquisitions was President Thomas Jefferson's Louisiana Purchase of 1803, in which he obtained an enormous tract of land from France for $15,000,000, or approximately five cents an acre. The purchase more than doubled the size of the United States, adding territory that would later encompass all or parts of fifteen states and two Canadian provinces. Even at the price, the purchase was controversial, as it was not at all clear that Jefferson had the constitutional authority to make it, but he did so on the grounds that it was in the national interest. History has undoubtedly proven him correct on the second point, although the jury is still out on the first point.

The Southwest started to come under the control of the United States in 1833 when white residents of Texas (then part of Mexico) who had migrated there from the southern United States revolted against Mexican rule. Whites were the majority and were displeased by Mexican restrictions on slavery and religious worship. Despite losing the Battle of the Alamo in the spring of 1836, the "Texians" prevailed and became an independent republic later that year. After much negotiation, Texas became the twenty-eighth state of the United States in 1845.

The Lewis and Clark Expedition

After acquiring the Louisiana Purchase, the land needed to be explored to fill the large blank spaces beyond the Rocky Mountains that were found on maps at the time. Thomas Jefferson chose his personal secretary, Meriwether Lewis, to explore the newly acquired land. In turn, Lewis asked William Clark, an experienced frontiersman, to aid in the expedition. Together, Lewis and Clark co-commanded a journey of exploration called the Corp of Discovery that would, over the course of the next two years, bring them through vast prairies, mountains, and deserts, and eventually to the Pacific Ocean.

Jefferson's original hope for the expedition was to find a system of waterways that would link the vast Mississippi/Missouri river system that flows to the Atlantic via the Gulf of Mexico with the Columbia River that flows to the Pacific. More riverside ports in the interior of the country, he believed, would be a boost to commerce. In the summer of 1804, Lewis and Clark embarked on their expedition to find out if such a waterway existed. Although the unified river system was not to be—the high crest of the Rocky Mountains intervened—the expedition was an unqualified success in nearly every other sense. (The completion of the Erie Canal linking New York's Hudson River with the Great Lakes in 1825 would bring this dream a little closer to reality.)

Throughout the entire journey, Lewis and Clark kept records of everything they did and saw. They also traded and established diplomatic relations with many of the Native American tribes they encountered. They were joined by a Shoshone woman named Sacagawea (pronounced "Sah-cah gah-we-ah," with a hard g), who helped Lewis and Clark on numerous occasions—in one notable instance, rescuing irreplaceable scientific equipment and specimens after the near capsizing of a canoe—and worked with her husband, a French fur trapper, to translate between English, French, Shoshone, and Hidatsa. The only woman on the expedition, she travelled with her infant son, Jean Baptiste, strapped to her back; her presence with a baby evidently reassured many of the Native Americans they encountered that the Corp of Discovery was not a war party.

In September 1806, the party returned to report back to Jefferson, bringing with them hundreds of specimens, observations, detailed maps, and invaluable insights into the newly acquired American lands to the west.

Known as the Lone Star State, and celebrated for its sense of individualism, Texas today is the second-most populous state in the United States, second only to California in terms of population. The name of the modern amusement park chain "Six Flags"—the first of which was Six Flags Over Texas—refers to Texas's many national flags over the years:

1. *Texas under Spanish rule* (1519–1685 and 1690–1821)
2. *Texas under French rule* (1685–1690)
      (Texas back under Spanish rule, 1690–1821)
3. *Texas under Mexican rule* (1821–1836)
4. *Republic of Texas* (1836–1845)
5. *28th state of the United States* (1845–1861 and 1865–present)
6. *Member of the Confederacy* (1861–1865)
      (Texas again the 28th state of the United States, 1865–present)

Texas statehood led to the Mexican–American War (1846–1848). The war was a one-sided rout; the American forces were victorious in all ten major battles and took Mexico City in 1847. In the subsequent treaty Mexico ceded a vast part of its northern territory—covering all or part of the current states of Arizona, New Mexico, California, Utah, Colorado, Nevada, and Wyoming—to the United States. This represents approximately 15 percent of the total size of the modern United States.

The final large acquisition of the United States was known as "Seward's Folly," the mocking name critics gave to Secretary of State William Seward's purchase of Alaska from Russia in 1867. Despite the bargain price of just seven million dollars that Russia offered to the United States, Seward's contemporaries saw little economic or political value in the vast expanse of cold and sparsely inhabited frontier. Of course, like Jefferson's Louisiana Purchase, history has proved Seward's purchase to be a wise one. Alaska would become an important buffer for the United States during the Cold War, and has yielded a rich haul of minerals and oil, as well as being a vast wilderness area of incomparable natural beauty.

In addition to these large acquisitions, several smaller acquisitions between 1810 and 1853 nearly finalized the creation of the United States (the exception was Hawaii, which became a territory in 1898 and a state in 1959):

- Portion of the Gulf Coast from Spain (1810)
- Another portion of the Gulf Coast from Spain (1813)
- Red River Basin in the northern Plains from Britain (although the United States ceded territory from the Louisiana Treaty to Canada in exchange) (1818)
- Florida from Spain (1819)
- Disputed territory in northern Maine from Great Britain (1842)

- Parts of Oregon and Washington from Great Britain (1846)
- Gadsden Purchase: southern Arizona and New Mexico from Spain (1853)

One impediment to settlement of the new territories was the presence of native peoples, although historians debate the degree to which these peoples' presence was a barrier to the settlers' westward push; other factors, such as lack of survival skills and disease, also played large parts. Before the Revolution most Native American tribes in the thirteen colonies had either been driven out or killed off by disease and war.

The Trail of Tears

The very foundation of the United States is mired in ethnic conflicts because European settlers decimated the Native Americans and drove them away from their lands to reservations. When European settlers arrived in North America, it was populated by perhaps as many as eight million Native Americans (although exact numbers are impossible to determine); after contact their numbers dwindled to roughly half that. The Native American population today is about 5 million, around 1.2 percent of the total US population. Most of the Native Americans were victims of disease that white settlers brought, and many others were killed in wars with settlers.

The United States government formally adopted a policy of Indian removal in 1825, motivated by the desire to capture Native American lands that contained gold and other minerals. This policy led to the forced removal of the Cherokee, Chickasaws, Choctaws, Creeks, and Seminoles in 1833. The entire Cherokee tribe was forced to move from Georgia by the federal government under the leadership of presidents Andrew Jackson and Martin Van Buren, despite the Supreme Court ruling against moving Native Americans from their homeland. Of the sixteen thousand Cherokees who were forced to move from Georgia to the settlements in Oklahoma, about four thousand died along the 1,000-mile (1,600-kilometer) trek. The Cherokees walked for a year to move to Oklahoma, and the trail they followed is referred to as the "Trail of Tears" because of their hardship and loss of life. Later, at the Sand Creek Massacre in Colorado on 29 November 1864, more than two hundred Southern Cheyennes and Arapahos were killed despite the fact that their leader, Black Kettle, raised the flag of peace as well as the flag of the United States. Such events have led people to call the killing of Native Americans the "American Genocide."

The approach to dealing with tribes in territory waiting to be settled in the South and Midwest was much the same—displace them through military action (the Indian Wars), force them to relocate through legal action (often done in underhanded and/or illegal ways), or place them on reservations in places where whites did not want to live. Even tribes that had made considerable progress toward assimilation into white society, such as the Mahicans (also spelled Mohicans) in the Northeast and the Five Civilized Nations in the Southeast were forced to abandon their territory and move West. Not all of them were willing to leave, however, and in the late twentieth century, several nations in the East and Midwest began waging a lengthy legal battle with state governments and the federal government to regain land that was taken from them, or to receive compensation. And some, like the Mashantucket Pequot, in Connecticut, who were thought to have been extinct, have gained status as federally recognized tribes.

The federal and state governments were on the side of white settlers. In 1830 Congress passed the controversial Indian Removal Act, which led to the entire Cherokee people being forced to travel the "Trail of Tears" to Indian Territory between 1831 and 1839. (See the sidebar at left.) In 1851 Congress passed additional legislation that led to the creation of reservations. The reservations were meant to isolate the Native Americans, thereby reducing conflict with whites moving into their traditional territory.

In 1887 Congress passed the Dawes Act, which ended the practice of giving land to Native American tribes and instead gave land to individuals; its aim was to assimilate Native Americans by allowing them the possibility of individual land ownership. Many soon lost their land to whites, who took it by means both legal and illegal. All of these and other actions had the desired effect of opening the vast interior of the United States to white settlement. They also had the effect—desired by some and objected to by others—of substantially damaging native cultures and leaving them dependent on the federal government for support. The Pine Ridge Reservation, a Sioux reservation the size of Connecticut amid the prairies of South Dakota, is frequently cited as the most impoverished place in the United States, with diabetes, alcoholism, and unemployment all rampant.

The soldiers did go away and their towns were torn down; and in the Moon of Falling Leaves [November], they made a treaty with Red Cloud that said our country would be ours as long as grass should grow and water flow.

—BLACK ELK (HEȞÁKA SÁPA), SIOUX MEDICINE MAN

The Civil War (1861–1865)

The American Civil War, the bloodiest in United States history, took place against a backdrop of worldwide independence and secessionist events. The Polish war for independence took place in 1863, Italian unification the decade before. Whether or not the United States would turn out to be an indivisible nation or a loose confederation of states after the war owed much to the changing ideas of nationality and nationhood prevalent around the world in the mid-nineteenth century.

The Civil War was fought over three main issues: the preservation of the union, the idea of federal versus state power, and slavery. The Constitution was open to interpretation regarding the latter two issues. In the nineteenth century, Americans had varied viewed about these matters. Some, particularly Republicans in the North, favored a strong federal (i.e., centralized) system. Others, particularly Democrats in the South, favored more rights for the states, and especially the right to regulate slavery within their borders. How the question of state versus federal authority was decided would have implications for the survival of the union.

At the time the Civil War began in 1861 it was not yet clear if the United States was to be one, indivisible nation or a loose confederation of states. (It was common before the war to refer to the United States as plural entities—"the United States *are* . . ."—rather than "the United States *is* . . .," as one refers to the country today.) The Union victory in 1865 created one indivisible nation and gave new powers to the federal government. It did not fully resolve the conflict over state versus federal authority, but it did determine the ultimate authority of the federal government. In the twenty-first century this question of states rights remains a contentious issue, shaping the debate over various issues such as gay rights, immigration reform, gun ownership rights, health care, and abortion.

In 1861 the nation was divided about slavery; there were nineteen free states and three free territories, and fifteen slave states and three slave territories. The American people had a variety of opinions about slavery. Some were indifferent, as they did not own slaves and slavery had little direct impact on their lives. This was especially true in the North, where slavery had been phased out by the 1840s; there had always been far fewer slaves than in the South, where slave labor was of more economic importance.

Those who did take an interest in slavery had a wide range of opinions and political positions, sometimes expressed loudly and sometimes violently. At one extreme were those who defended slavery and resisted any government attempt to limit or end it. Central to this defense was the portrayal of African Americans as inferior and

Frederick Douglass and the Governor

The following passage by the former slave-turned-orator Frederick Douglass (first discussed on page 29) demonstrates how times were slowly beginning to change since his recollections of a childhood spent in bondage.

Riding from Boston to Albany, a few years ago, I found myself in a large car, well filled with passengers. The seat next to me was about the only vacant one. At every stopping place we took in new passengers, all of whom, on reaching the seat next to me, cast a disdainful glance upon it, and passed to another car, leaving me in the full enjoyment of a whole form. For a time, I did not know but that my riding there was prejudicial to the interest of the railroad company. A circumstance occurred, however, which gave me an elevated position at once. Among the passengers on this train was [Massachusetts] Gov. George N. Briggs. I was not acquainted with him, and had no idea that I was known to him. Known to him, however, I was, for upon observing me, the governor left his place, and making his way toward me, respectfully asked the privilege of a seat by my side; and upon introducing himself, we entered into a conversation very pleasant and instructive to me. The despised seat now became honored. His excellency had removed all the prejudice against sitting by the side of a negro; and upon his leaving it, as he did, on reaching Pittsfield, there were at least one dozen applicants for the place. The governor had, without changing my skin a single shade, made the place respectable which before was despicable.

Source: Douglass, Frederick. (1855.) *My Bondage and My Freedom. Part II—Life as a Freeman*, pp. 402–403. New York: Miller, Orton & Mulligan.

---

subhuman. Slavery's defenders were mainly the slave-owning class in the Deep South (Louisiana, Mississippi, Alabama, Georgia, and South Carolina), who drew support from others—such as bankers, merchants, and textile mill owners both in the South and in the North—who also benefitted from slave labor. Defenders of slavery also believed that slavery was a state issue, not a federal issue, and each state had the right to decide the issue without federal interference.

At the other extreme were the abolitionists, who rallied for the immediate end of slavery across the nation. Abolitionism as a movement had emerged in Britain and the American colonies before the American Revolution and drew early support in America from the Quakers in Pennsylvania. In post-colonial America, the ranks of abolitionists included such well-known speakers and writers as the aforementioned William Lloyd Garrison, Harriet Beecher Stowe, Frederick Douglass, and Sojourner Truth. Their argument against slavery was that it was immoral and had no place in a nation that extolled freedom, liberty, and equality. Abolitionists like Garrison were the exception to the rule, however: a large percentage of abolitionists argued for "compensated abolition" and the expulsion of African Americans from the United States.

In between these two perspectives were people who took several other views. One group—which supported the American Colonization Society—believed that the nation and people of African ancestry in America would both be best served by blacks returning to Africa. They were not terribly successful (although they enjoyed far more popularity than did Garrison's brand of abolitionism), as most black people preferred freedom in the United States, but they did manage to establish the colony of Liberia in West Africa. Another group was opposed to slavery but argued that to protect the southern economy and to maintain the Union, it should be phased out slowly (this had been the opinion held by earlier figures, such as Thomas Jefferson). A third group, including the Republican Party with Abraham Lincoln as their presidential candidate in 1860, preferred to leave slavery alone in states that already had slavery, but to prohibit it in new states that entered the Union. Lincoln, too, was in favor of colonization.

1860: The South Secedes from the Union

In November of 1860, Abraham Lincoln was elected sixteenth president of the United States, running on a Republican Party platform that called for the banning of slavery in new territories in the West. Perceiving this as an assault on states' rights and a threat to slavery, the southern states began seceding from the union and forming their own nation, called the Confederate States of America, or CSA. The Civil War was not the first time that the issue of secession had come up: the War of 1812 had been extremely unpopular with people in New England, which nearly seceded from the United States. South Carolina seceded first, in December 1860, followed by six more southern states before Lincoln took office in March of 1861. Four more southern states seceded and joined the Confederacy later in the year.

The Civil War officially began on 12 April 1861, when troops of the newly formed Confederacy in South Carolina fired on federal troops attempting to resupply Fort Sumter, in Charleston Harbor. Historians disagree over responsibility for that event: Lincoln for ordering the fort resupplied, or the South for firing the first shots.

The Union entered the war with enormous advantages: more men, more equipment, more ships, a better railroad network, and more money: in short, an industry-based economy. Its goal was to invade the South and quickly and painlessly force the CSA to rejoin the Union. During the war's first major land battle, the First Battle of Bull Run (known to the Confederacy as First Manassas, for the city nearest the fighting), spectators from nearby Washington, DC, picnicked on the sidelines, expecting a short and entertaining skirmish.

Like Bull Run, the war that was to come would turn out to be anything but quick and painless. New inventions, from telegraphs and railroads to repeating rifles and the Gatling gun (a precursor to the modern machine gun, but mounted on wheels like a cannon), ushered in the modern era of ever more destructive warfare. Despite the Union's initial advantages, the Confederacy more than held its own in campaigns and battles before the war shifted to the Union's favor after the Battle of Gettysburg in 1863. That three-day battle, with upwards of 50,000 killed, wounded, or missing, remains the single largest loss of American life in the nation's history.

While the Confederacy initially benefitted from superior generals and higher morale, as well as the war being waged on terrain that they knew, the Union's advantages in material and manpower eventually proved overwhelming for the South. The war effectively ended on 9 April, 1865, when General Robert E. Lee surrendered to General (and future President) Ulysses S. Grant at Appomattox Courthouse, Virginia.

The Role of Abraham Lincoln (1809–1865)

President Abraham Lincoln, a lawyer and politician noted early on for his integrity and graceful rhetoric, is credited with saving the Union and freeing the slaves; like other presidents, he was a complex figure who became somewhat of a mythological figure after his assassination.

Lincoln was born 12 February 1809 in a log cabin in rural Kentucky, a frontier state where the South, the Midwest, and the East meet. His family eventually settled in Illinois. He had little formal schooling, and was taught to read by his stepmother. By 1832 Lincoln had developed an interest in politics, and served in the state legislature and in the United States Congress. He began his political career as a Whig, a party that advocated for a stronger Congress, but when that party disintegrated over the issue of the expansion of slavery into the territories, he, like most northern Whigs, joined the Republican Party.

His reputation both as a lawyer and for his personal integrity made him an obvious choice to challenge the incumbent Democratic senator from Illinois, Stephen A. Douglas, in 1858. Their campaign centered on a series of debates over the extension of slavery into the territories that commanded the attention of the entire nation. Newspapers printed the Douglas-Lincoln debates verbatim. Huge crowds swelled the populations of the towns hosting the debates, as hordes of spectators arrived by train, boat, and by horseback, shouting questions and approval (and opprobrium) to the two debaters. Lincoln lost the race but won the Republican nomination for president two years later.

Lincoln barely won the presidential election, and only had the support of the northern states. Many in the South saw Lincoln's Republican Party as dangerous, as it was composed entirely of northern sectional interests. In response to what they saw as a lack of representation in government, Southern states to begin to secede from the union in December 1860. In spite of calls for him to intervene, Lincoln remained silent, thinking that it would be imprudent to act before his inauguration the following March. By then, however, eleven states had seceded and had adopted a new constitution creating a Confederacy.

Lincoln had widespread popular support early in the war. He had difficulties, however, finding a general who could win. Frustrated by generals who lacked offensive drive and tactical knowledge, Lincoln resorted to reading everything he could about military tactics; he eventually settled on Ulysses S. Grant.

As the war dragged on, Lincoln faced increasing criticism domestically and even within his own cabinet. He responded by suspending the writ of *habeas corpus* (the legal principle that someone who is arrested must be brought before a judge or into a court), arresting and jailing those deemed a threat, and closing Democratic newspapers that criticized the war effort.

Following the Union victory at the Battle of Antietam, in Maryland, in September 1862 (the bloodiest single-day battle in United States history, with over 22,000 killed, wounded, or missing), Lincoln issued the Emancipation Proclamation, declaring that slaves would be freed in states still in rebellion on 1 January 1863. Lincoln issued the proclamation in response to congressional pressure, fears (most likely unfounded) of European intervention on the side of the South, and to force the South to divert its military resources to shoring up defense of its slave system. While critics noted that no one was actually freed, the proclamation gave new purpose to the war, deterred foreign intervention, allowed black men to serve in the Union army, and gave hope to those enslaved.

Following the Battle of Gettysburg (19 November 1863), during the dedication ceremony for the cemetery for Union soldiers who fought in the costly battle, Lincoln delivered the short, elegant Gettysburg Address, in which he expressed the pressing need for Americans to remember the great sacrifice made by the soldiers:

> Four score and seven years ago our fathers brought forth, upon this continent, a new nation, conceived in liberty, and dedicated to the proposition that "all men are created equal."
>
> Now we are engaged in a great civil war, testing whether that nation, or any nation so conceived, and so dedicated, can long endure. We are met on a great battle field of that war. We have come to dedicate a portion of it, as a final resting place for those who died here, that the nation might live. This we may, in all propriety do. But, in a larger sense, we can not dedicate—we can not consecrate—we can not hallow, this ground—The brave men, living and dead, who struggled here, have hallowed it, far above our poor power to add or detract. The world will little note, nor long remember what we say here; while it can never forget what they did here.
>
> It is rather for us, the living, we here be dedicated to the great task remaining before us—that, from these honored dead we take increased devotion to that cause for which they here, gave the last full measure of devotion—that we here highly resolve these dead shall not have died in vain; that the nation, shall have a new birth of freedom, and that government of the people by the people for the people, shall not perish from the earth.

Lincoln's Gettysburg Address was especially noteworthy for its brevity. The only known photograph of the President delivering his address is a blurry image; his address was so short (less than two minutes) that the photographer had not had time to properly set up his equipment. Lincoln's words were repeated later to newspapers by those fortunate enough to be within earshot of the speaker.

As the war continued, Lincoln's supporters feared that he could not be reelected. The fall of Atlanta in September 1864 restored confidence to the Union and brought a second term for Lincoln. With that election success, Lincoln pressed for the Thirteenth Amendment to the Constitution, which would actually free the slaves. Lincoln also turned toward the reconstruction of the war-ravaged South. His proposed leniency toward the South faced substantial opposition in Congress.

Lincoln addresses the crowd at the dedication of the Gettysburg National Cemetery, 19 November 1863. There is only one known contemporary photograph of Lincoln delivering the address, of Lincoln preparing to sit down; because the address was over so quickly, the photographer had not had time to set up his equipment properly. Source: Sherwood Lithograph Co., circa 1905. National Archives.

Only days after the war ended, on 14 April, John Wilkes Booth, a famous stage actor who was angry over the Confederacy's loss, assassinated Lincoln while he and his wife Mary were watching the British farce *Our American Cousin* in Ford's Theatre in Washington, DC. The assassin shouted either *"Sic semper tyrannis"* (Latin for "Thus always to tyrants!") or "The South is avenged!"—witnesses at the scene disagreed on what he actually said, and if he said it before or after the shooting—and then fatally shot the President before jumping to the stage and escaping through a back door.

On the same night of Lincoln's assassination, a co-conspirator also unsuccessfully attempted to assassinate Secretary of State William Seward (of "Seward's Folly" fame, although his purchase of Alaska was two years away at the time); in an attempt to sever the government's constitutionally mandated chain of succession, there was also an aborted attempt on the life of Vice President Andrew Johnson. During the period of national mourning that followed Lincoln's death, those who only shortly before had been vehement political opponents turned their rhetoric to praise.

After the War: Reconstruction (1865–1877)

The Civil War remains the bloodiest war in American history. Estimates place the number of soldiers killed in combat or by disease, accidents, or starvation at between 620,000 and 850,000. For comparison, around 405,000 Americans servicemen and women died in World War II, when the United States had roughly ten times the population than it had during the Civil War: 132 million people counted in the 1940 census versus 31 million counted in the 1860 census. The southern political system, economy, and social structure were left in ruins. There were now some four million formerly enslaved African Americans who were now technically free, thanks to the Thirteenth Amendment, but who had no legal rights nor place in southern life.

Aware of the devastation in the South, Union leaders began formulating plans to reconcile the two sides, rebuild the South, and give African Americans there a place in society. This period, known as Reconstruction, lasted from 1865 until 1877 (some historians put the starting date around 1863, while the war was still being waged). The Thirteenth, Fourteenth, and Fifteenth amendments to the Constitution, enacted from 1865 to 1870, afforded African Americans their place in America by banning slavery, making them citizens, and giving them the right to vote, although it was not until 1965 that the federal government fully enforced voting rights.

Taking advantage of the Homestead Act of 1862 and similar acts—which gave applicants, white or black, ownership of western land for little to no money in return for improving the land—a few "freedmen" moved West. Those who could ride a horse, or were willing to learn how, worked for cattle barons and took part in cattle drives. The United States was still in the process of "taming" the West, and former slaves took advantage by joining the military. Some of these freedmen, at least for a time, were able to adjust quickly to their newfound freedom.

Most freedmen, however, faced numerous problems. Trusting white men was one such problem. Freedmen had just been released from slavery; memories were still fresh. Now that freedmen were legally able to learn to read and write, educational facilities for freedmen were in demand. Freedmen also needed health services, and thousands of southern blacks (and a few whites) were homeless, with little money and fewer prospects. Congress recognized these problems and in March 1865 created the Bureau of Refugees, Freedmen, and Abandoned Lands—the Freedmen's Bureau, as it was commonly known—to help both freedmen and white refugees transition from slavery to freedom. Conflicts over administering and continuing Reconstruction marred President Andrew Johnson's relationship with Congress, however, resulting in his impeachment by Congress. Johnson pursued a policy of conciliation for white southerners while ignoring the plight of African Americans. This angered the radicals of the Republican Party, who wanted the southerners to be treated more harshly and the freedmen more justly. Johnson survived removal from office by one vote in the Senate.

With former Union general Ulysses S. Grant's election to the presidency in 1868, Reconstruction would continue to help African Americans. Some African Americans were elected to political office. Two were elected to the Senate (Hiram Rhodes Revels and Blanche Kelso Bruce, both in Mississippi), one became governor (P. B. S. Pinchback, the first African American governor, of Mississippi), and one was elected lieutenant governor (Oscar James Dunn of Louisiana, the first African American to be elected to that office). Others were elected to state positions, including secretary of state, superintendent of education, and treasurer. On the surface all seemed well.

A loud undercurrent of trouble still flowed, however. In the South there was deep resentment of the occupying Union troops, and of whites who came from the North, derided as carpetbaggers, who often came to cash in on economic ventures; others came for more noble causes, such as helping to educate African Americans. Most of all, there remained a powerful resistance to African Americans occupying an equal place in society. Frustrated southerners resorted to violence. The Ku Klux Klan, founded in 1866 by Confederate general Nathan Bedford Forrest, burned crosses, and tortured and lynched African Americans and their white supporters. (Commonly known as the KKK, the secret society's name likely derives from the Greek word *kyklos*, for "circle," and the Scottish-Gaelic word "clan.") In 1871 Congress was compelled to pass an anti-Klan bill, which effectively banned the Ku Klux Klan. Many white people sympathized with the Klan, however, and violence was the Klan's *modus operandi* in its crusade to redeem the South against reformers and their sympathizers. Violence would continue to be used against blacks in the twentieth century, as witnessed by the 1963 bombing of the 16th Street Baptist Church in Birmingham, Alabama, in which four young black girls were killed.

After an initial rush to help African Americans during Reconstruction, Congress appeared to lose interest. Despite laws against their running for office, former Confederate leaders were elected to Congress and served, mainly because former president Johnson had granted pardons to virtually anyone who asked. The Republican Party's Radical Reconstruction leaders were retired or had moved on to other interests, while President Grant (in office 1869–1877) presided over one of the most corrupt administrations in American history. Reconstruction officially ended in March 1877, when the last federal troops were withdrawn from the South.

"Jim Crow"

Come listen all you galls and boys,
I'm going to sing a little song,
My name is Jim Crow.
Weel about and turn about and do jis so,
Eb'ry time I weel about I jump Jim Crow.

—FROM THE SONG "JIM CROW"
BY WHITE ACTOR THOMAS
DARTMOUTH "DADDY" RICE

The brief and uneven attempt at securing equal rights for African Americans was abandoned in favor of reunification of the white North and the white South. The southern states quickly passed laws, colloquially referred to as "Jim Crow" laws, that limited the rights of African Americans and created a system of segregation—separate and unequal—in which by every measure of quality of life and equality of opportunity African Americans as a group were disadvantaged. (The name Jim Crow refers to white actor Thomas Dartmouth "Daddy" Rice, a popular performer who wore blackface and, as the character Jim Crow, danced in a highly stereotypical manner.) In the North, the war did little to improve the lives of African Americans, as most remained second-class citizens denied employment and educational opportunities open to whites.

In a survey conducted by the Pew Research Center in 2011, 56 percent of Americans believed that the Civil War was still relevant to American politics and life. This should not be surprising, as the war changed America in several major ways, and reminders of the war in the form of war memorials, grave markers, and battlefields are a ubiquitous feature across the American landscape; Memorial Day, the unofficial start of summer, dates from the Civil War. The Civil War produced the first military draft, the federal income tax, and a liberal pension system for veterans, as well as long-lasting resentments between northerners and southerners (and their descendants) who could not easily forget the war, or forgive the other side. A state historical park in Florida dedicated to a Civil War battleground made national news in 2014 when descendants of Union soldiers (who lost the Battle of Olustee there) made a request for an obelisk to be erected in the same three-acre area that holds three memorials to the victorious Confederate war dead.

Because of their brave service, African Americans were allowed to serve in the military from the time of the Civil War on, although they fought in segregated units until 1948. Lincoln also greatly increased the president's wartime powers, some argued illegally, by suspending *habeas corpus*, detaining without trial those suspected of aiding the South, and using military tribunals rather than civilian courts. Subsequent presidents have followed his lead, including Franklin Delano Roosevelt in World War II, Lyndon Johnson in the Vietnam War, and George W. Bush and Barack Obama in the War on Terror: all, like Lincoln, acting in what the leaders considered the interest of national security.

The end of the Civil War and the end of slavery also opened a new movement in black-white relations: the Civil Rights Movement, discussed in Chapter 5. Freedom empowered African Americans in the South as well as in the North to take more control over their communities and their futures; the African American community took the opportunity by establishing churches, schools, colleges, and other institutions while continuing to advocate with the government for enforcement of its rights.

Immigration in the 19th Century

Before continuing with the chronological record of events in American history, it is important to stop and examine the people who were affected by, and participated in, these events. The United States owes much of its reputation as a "melting pot" to the waves of immigrants from foreign shores who made their way to America in huge numbers in the nineteenth century. The arrival of these immigrants, who have not always been welcomed—as long ago as 1751, founding father/polymath Benjamin Franklin complained "why should the Palatine Boors [i.e., German and Dutch immigrants] be suffered to swarm into our Settlements, and by herding together establish their Language and Manners to the Exclusion of ours?"—has produced greater ethnic and cultural diversity.

The United States has sustained a magnetic force throughout its history, although the source areas of immigrants have changed. Historically the United States needed a large labor force to exploit natural resources, to build cities, to develop urban industries, to construct railroads, to advance the farming frontier, and to harvest crops. One solution has been to fill worker vacancies by attracting workers from the world over: both manual laborers and white collar workers. Such immigrants have been admitted to the United States on the assumption that they eventually will become Americans and contribute to the development of the nation.

Since the establishment of colonies on the Atlantic seaboard through the late nineteenth century, northwestern Europe was the largest source area of immigrants to the United States, as seen by the number of immigrants in the period 1841–1860. Among the total of 4.3 million immigrants, according to US census figures, almost 94 percent of those came from northwestern Europe, including Ireland (over a third), Germany (another third), and the United Kingdom (a sixth). The Irish were driven out of their homeland by the potato famine and by British colonial rule. Non-Irish British migrants mostly came across for economic reasons: they had industrial skills that were worth more in America than they were in England; cheap land was also a powerful lure. The Germans left their homeland mainly because of economic and political uncertainty that followed the Napoleonic conquest of the German states.

Immigration patterns began to change in the period from 1861 to 1880. While the vast majority of the 5.1 million immigrants during this time period—nearly 85 percent—still came from Europe, the percentage from northwestern Europe was reduced substantially, to three-quarters. Southern and eastern Europe contributed a small but growing percentage of the immigrants. During the middle years of the century the first wave of Chinese immigrants arrived to work on the building of the railroads, to mine for gold, and to work on plantations in the South after the Civil War.

Starting in the 1850s, a political party known as the "Know Nothings," reacting to the large influx of European immigrants, began advocating against immigration, particularly immigration by Catholics. (Initially a secret party, the members would say they "knew nothing" if non-members questioned their activities.) The party had widespread support both in the North and the South—Ulysses S. Grant was a member for a time—but eventually split into factions over the issue of slavery.

Seventy percent of immigrants in the 1800s arrived in New York. Many stayed in the area but many others dispersed across the nation, mainly elsewhere in the Northeast or in the Midwest. Most settled in cities where employment was available in factories; artisans and craftsmen such as carpenters and stone masons also found work in the growing cities. The one exception were the Germans, about half of whom settled in cities and half on farms in the Midwest and in Texas. Today, in the Texas Hill Country near Austin, one finds the more common Spanish town names of Texas, such as Amarillo, Llano, and El Paso—meaning "Yellow," "Plain," and "The Pass," respectively—replaced with place names such as New Braunfels and Fredericksburg. The Irish settled mainly in the Northeast, particularly in Boston, and in Ohio and Illinois. Italians also settled in cities in the Northeast and also the upper Midwest; immigrants from northern Italy headed for California, where they quickly established themselves in fishing, agriculture, and wine-making. Italians faced more discrimination than other European immigrants and often established "Little Italys" in reaction to housing discrimination. More Italians—perhaps about thirty percent—also returned home than did members of other ethnic groups. The third large immigrant group, the Poles, settled in New York, Chicago, and elsewhere in the upper Midwest.

Although a sustained demand for labor and an ample supply of land and natural resources promoted immigration to the United States, the American government began to selectively admit immigrants on the basis of national origin. The Chinese Exclusion Act of 1882 was the first law to exclude immigrants by nationality. The Immigration Act of 1924 introduced the system of national quotas, which admitted immigrants by national origin on the basis of population composition as surveyed in

The Chinese Exclusion Act (1882)

One of the less celebrated items of American legislation, the Chinese Exclusion Act of 1882 was passed as a reaction to the large numbers of laborers coming to the United States from China, which was plagued by warfare, civil unrest, famines and other natural disasters, and incompetence and corruption at the Qing imperial court. The following is an excerpt.

An Act to execute certain treaty stipulations relating to Chinese.

Whereas in the opinion of the Government of the United States the coming of Chinese laborers to this country endangers the good order of certain localities within the territory thereof: Therefore,

Be it enacted by the Senate and House of Representatives of the United States of America in Congress assembled, That from and after the expiration of ninety days next after the passage of this act, and until the expiration of ten years next after the passage of this act, the coming of Chinese laborers to the United States be, and the same is hereby, suspended; and during such suspension it shall not be lawful for any Chinese laborer to come, or having so come after the expiration of said ninety days to remain within the United States.

SEC. 2. That the master of any vessel who shall knowingly bring within the United States on such vessel, and land or permit to be landed, any Chinese laborer, from any foreign port or place, shall be deemed guilty of a misdemeanor, and on conviction thereof shall be punished by a fine of not more than five hundred dollars for each and every such Chinese laborer so brought, and maybe also imprisoned for a term not exceeding one year. . . .

the 1890 census. The quota provided immigration visas to two percent of the total number of people of each nationality in the United States; it excluded immigrants from Asia entirely. The law was intended to restrict immigration from southern and eastern Europe, and from Japan. The door to the United States remained closed to southern and eastern Europeans and Japanese until the 1960s, when the Immigration Act was revised to abolish the national quotas system.

Industry, Invention, and Labor Movements

The mass migrations of large numbers of people to America was made possible by the Industrial Revolution: without the advances in manufacturing, agriculture, communications, transportation, and other technologies that came about from the revolution, the nation would not have had a big enough economy (and enough jobs) to encourage migrants to leave their home countries for a better life.

The Industrial Revolution changed every aspect of American society. It began in Britain in the middle of the eighteenth century and subsequently spread to continental Europe and the northeastern United States. In 1800 the United States was still mainly an agricultural nation of farms, ranches, and small-town shopkeepers and craftsmen. The little industry there was (lumbering and textiles) was confined mainly to the Northeast, where mills could be powered by the fast-moving water of rivers and streams. Farm work was powered by horse and human power. Industrial innovation that arrived from Britain and Europe, along with "home-grown" inventions created in the United States—such as the cotton gin discussed at the beginning of this chapter—transformed the nation from an agricultural one to one that combined more efficient and productive agriculture with a range of industries and modern systems of communication and transportation. Industrialization developed in conjunction with geographic expansion, increased immigration, and the rise of the United States as a regional, and then world, power.

Industrialization was also accompanied by urbanization through the movement of people from rural areas to cities and the settlement of immigrants in cities. In 1800 there were only six cities in the new nation with a population over 10,000; New York, which had by now overtaken Philadelphia, was the largest, with over 60,000 inhabitants. One hundred years later three cities had populations over one million (New York had 3.4 million, Chicago had 1.7 million, and Philadelphia had 1.4 million) and three other cities with populations over 50,000 (St. Louis, Boston, and Baltimore). Employment in factories in these and many other growing cities was a major lure for European immigrants, who saw factory work as the first step in achieving what would come to be known in the 1930s as the American Dream.

Industrialization and urbanization also transformed American society. New types of communities—ethnic enclaves such as Little Italys and Chinatowns—developed in cities to accommodate immigrants who faced discrimination in housing. And a new class of the wealthy and powerful—the owners of industry—began to replace the landed gentry as the leaders of the nation, especially in the rapidly industrializing North. The more unscrupulous of these industrialists were known as the "robber barons," but this was also an age of unprecedented philanthropy by extremely wealthy businessmen

Something to think about:

Public offices in the United States, even the presidency, are relatively low-paying positions compared to chief executive officers of major corporations. President Barack Obama's 2012 base salary, for instance, was $400,000, roughly one-hundredth of the $41 million 2012 salary of Starbucks CEO Howard Schultz. Some argue that making public service more lucrative would attract the wrong kinds of people to run for office, while others argue that keeping public officials' salaries low means that only the wealthy can afford to run for, and hold, office. What do you think?

such as Andrew Carnegie, discussed below. Many people thought the very fabric of civil life in America was endangered by the large amounts of political power held by the extremely wealthy.

The nineteenth century was a time of much innovation in America, with inventors following in the footsteps of Eli Whitney coming out from all quarters: Morse code (Alfred Vail and Samuel Morse, 1832), the revolver (Samuel Colt, 1836), vulcanized rubber (Charles Goodyear, 1839), the grain elevator (Joseph Dart, 1842), barbed wire (Lucien B. Smith, 1867), the refrigerator car (J. B. Sutherland, 1867), the telephone (Alexander Graham Bell, 1876), and photographic film (George Eastman, 1885), to name a few, all date from this period. Many of the inventors became household names. Two of the most well-known figures of the era are the inventor Thomas Edison and the industrialist Andrew Carnegie, both discussed below.

Thomas Edison (1847–1931)

Thomas Alva Edison was one of the greatest (and most tireless) inventors in modern history. Edison's name is so well-known to schoolchildren in the United States that many people grow up mistakenly thinking he was one of the country's founding fathers.

Edison had over a thousand inventions patented and made major contributions to the development of several of the modern world's most important industries—telegraphy, telephony, electric light and power, recorded sound (the phonograph), motion pictures, and chemical energy storage (batteries), to name a few—as well as less sweeping but still notable contributions to the fields of railroads, cement, automobiles, ore separation, and others. Edison, however, was as much an entrepreneur and innovator as he was an inventor.

Born on a Midwestern farm in Milan, Ohio, Edison began his professional career as a telegrapher, which gave him a decent income and mobility. He went into business as an inventor and began to attract modest corporate capital in Boston during a stint there in 1868–1869. To launch his career as an independent inventor, he garnered the support of major telegraph companies. Leading financiers such as J. Pierpont Morgan (1837–1913; the first North American to install electric lights in his home) and Henry Villard were strong supporters of Edison's electric light and power endeavors. His initial work focused on improving telegraph, fire alarm, and facsimile telegraph systems. Edison soon moved to New York City. In 1876 he opened what he called an "invention factory" in the northeastern New Jersey farm community of Menlo Park. This was a predecessor of the twentieth-century research and development laboratory, an institution devoted to controlling the pace and direction of technological development.

As an inventor, Edison worked much more pragmatically than theoretically—by present-day standards—but this was largely a consequence of the times in which he lived. Edison exploited theoretical understandings as best he could; but the ends he sought quite often outran the limits of theory, forcing him and his researchers into uncharted territory, where laborious trial-and-error protocols were the only practical solution. He also had a great talent for assembling teams of skilled inventors.

Edison's reputation began to soar in the 1870s, thanks in large measure to his successes with the phonograph. The device's power to capture and reproduce voices and music awed and enchanted the press and the public. Journalists reveled in his eccentricities: he was famous for hardly sleeping, for instance, and is said to have refused to hire potential employees if they added seasoning to soup before tasting it.

Although Edison was extraordinarily foresighted in identifying areas of opportunity, at times he proved to be stubbornly committed to what proved to be technological and entrepreneurial dead ends, as in his insistence that America should run direct current (DC) electrical systems, rather than the more efficient alternating current (AC) systems introduced by his rival George Westinghouse and others. In his twilight years Edison sustained his image through interviews and historical reenactments. Unlike many who attained his level of celebrity, however, Edison demonstrated few ambitions as a social philosopher.

Edison's legacy still stands as an example of a heroic inventor and, more broadly, a heroic American citizen. His lack of much formal education, his strong practical bent, his independent and quirky habits, his apparent willingness to take on virtually any technical challenge—all resonated deeply with a nation that was becoming more and more bureaucratic, scientific, and professionalized but feeling ambivalent about the transition to the modern world.

I have not failed. I've just found 10,000 ways that won't work.

—THOMAS EDISON

Andrew Carnegie (1835–1919)

A good part of the modern industrial world involves steel: locating and extracting the ore, smelting the raw ore into steel, and moving the finished product to where it is needed. Andrew Carnegie essentially created the modern steel industry, which in turn fostered global economic preeminence for the United States. Authoring a new ethic in corporate social responsibility, Carnegie also pioneered the philanthropic industry. He endures symbolically as both hero and villain in the controversial era that humorist Mark Twain (1835–1910) dubbed "the Gilded Age." A prime symbol of rags-to-riches folklore, he was an elite business entrepreneur who personified the unprecedented power of big business.

Paradoxes defined Carnegie's life. He was born in Dunfermline, Scotland, to parents who were unemployed because industrial technology had made their jobs redundant. Carnegie emigrated to the United States at age thirteen, where he found employment in 1848 at a textile mill in Pittsburgh, Pennsylvania, studying accounting in night school after his arduous twelve-hour workday. With characteristic quickness and hard work, he soon became a messenger boy in a telegraph office, moving up quickly through the ranks.

He made his first fortune by buying into a company that manufactured iron rail-road bridges, which were in high demand during the Civil War, and as heavier trains became more commonplace, as well as selling bonds on commission in New York and Europe to fund the construction of bridges and railroads. Carnegie became convinced that the future of railroads was in steel production; he and other investors founded the Edgar Thomson Works in 1873, thus beginning his age of steel (1873–1892).

Under Carnegie, American steel production jumped dramatically; his ability to supply unlimited, inexpensive steel for railroads, skyscrapers, and bridges was unrivaled. His efforts to make production more efficient cut his companies' costs by more than half—and Carnegie's wealth continued to increase exponentially.

In 1892 Carnegie merged his various steel companies into the Carnegie Steel Company, an industrial colossus whose profits ballooned from $6 million in 1896 to $21 million in 1899 to $40 million in 1900. His desire to retire, combined with the challenge of rival financier J. P. Morgan's energetic move into the steel industry, prompted Carnegie's famous handwritten offer to his rival—$480 million—which Morgan accepted, resulting in the formation of United States Steel in March 1901, and the last phase of Carnegie's remarkable career: full-time philanthropist (1901–1919).

Carnegie embraced Social Darwinism's doctrines of extreme individualism and devotion to survival of the fittest, which helped him justify his hard-nosed acquisition of wealth, his merciless industrial competition, and his heavy-handed treatment of his workers. As the author of *Triumphant Democracy* (1886), Carnegie trumpeted

> **I resolved to stop accumulating and begin the infinitely more serious and difficult task of wise distribution.**
>
> —ANDREW CARNEGIE

American democracy and capitalism, and was celebrated as a defender of the common laborer. Yet Carnegie's workers toiled grueling twelve-hour shifts seven days a week, their only holiday the Fourth of July. Carnegie's image as a friend of the worker was tainted further by his participation in the crushing of the 1892 Homestead strike by steelworkers in Pittsburgh.

Nevertheless, Carnegie preached—to the disdain of his wealthy peers—that the rich were morally obligated to practice bountiful and altruistic philanthropy, for "the man who dies thus rich dies disgraced." While the Vanderbilts, Rockefellers, Morgans, and others passed fortunes of unprecedented size from one generation to the next, the renegade Carnegie argued for an inheritance tax, and, even more radically, that the wealthy should not burden their children with great fortunes, as he believed money gained in this way did more harm than good. To this end, he gave vast sums of money to educational institutions and public libraries and supported medical research and world peace. By 1917, Carnegie had invested over $68 million (equivalent to over one billion in 2013 dollars) in 2,811 libraries worldwide, including nearly two thousand in the United States. By the time of his death in 1919, he had given away 90 percent of his fortune. The Carnegie Endowment for International Peace, with branches in Moscow, Beijing, Brussels, Beirut, and Washington, DC, had net assets of $238 million in 2012.

Labor Movements in the 19th Century

Carnegie had practical reasons for his philanthropic activities. He believed that unless the wealthy class returned a portion of its wealth to society for the good of everyone, the appeal of socialism would be too strong among the poor and the working class. Some of Carnegie's writings were devoted to showing the interrelationship of *laissez-faire* capitalism (opposing governmental interference in economic affairs), philanthropy, and Social Darwinism; these argued that capitalists must spend their fortunes for the public good to prevent serious social unrest, because such unrest could lead to the loss of fortunes. Wise philanthropy not only protected individual survival of the fittest, it also guaranteed the fittest society.

Carnegie's fears of social unrest were well founded, as unrest was plentiful; Americans who have lived through the Cold War may be surprised at the widespread popularity of socialism and communism in the early twentieth century. The incalculable social, political, and economic impact of slavery in the United States, combined with large-scale European immigration in the late nineteenth and early twentieth centuries, led to multiple fractures within the skilled and unskilled labor force, all of which led to unrest. Workers were divided, and often pitted against one another, on the basis of race, ethnicity, and gender.

The first labor unions in the United States appeared in the early nineteenth century, growing directly out of the established guilds: blacksmiths, carpenters, cabinetmakers, and cobblers. By the 1820s, various trade unions were calling for the reduction of the work day from twelve to ten hours. As the use of steam engines along the Atlantic sea-board and internal waterways gave rise to new factory systems, paralleling the development of factories in England, labor unions in the United States sought to join together in citywide federations. In 1866 these federations formed the nationwide National Labor Union (NLU), which succeeded in persuading Congress to pass an eight-hour workday for federal workers. But by the early 1870s the NLU had unraveled.

Labor agitation resurfaced with unprecedented force later in the decade. In 1877, a national railroad strike paralyzed the nation's transportation system when workers in Martinsburg, West Virginia began a strike that quickly spread to St. Louis, Chicago, Baltimore, and New York, eventually reaching the steel capital of Pittsburgh, where discontent over reduced wages had originated. In several places workers resorted to violence, destroying railway lines to protest low wages and ill treatment. The national strike, known as "The Great Railroad Strike of 1877," attracted widespread public sympathy and was only suppressed through the force of state militias.

Over the following decade, the Knights of Labor, a union formed by Philadelphia garment cutters in 1869, became labor's preeminent organization. Expanding nation-ally under the leadership of Terrence V. Powderly (1849–1924), the Knights organized skilled and unskilled workers, men and women, blacks and whites. By 1886, the organization boasted a diverse membership of 750,000, which included urban and rural workers, although the southern branch had increasingly become all-black as southern white laborers refused to participate in interracial locals. The all-black membership soon joined the ranks of other African American workers in the Cooperative Workers of America and the Colored Farmers Alliance, whose combined membership grew to over one million strong, forming the largest movement of black agrarian workers and sharecroppers in American history. In the coming years many within the organized rural black labor movement—Black Populism—joined white farmers and laborers to establish the People's Party, which advocated on behalf of labor and agrarian interests.

In the 1880s, as the Knights of Labor became a national force demanding an eight-hour workday, both its leaders and the rank and file were targeted for retribution.

On 4 May 1886, the Knights held a mass rally to protest police brutality: the day before, striking employees at the McCormick Harvester Company in Chicago had been severely beaten; one was killed during a clash with the police. Following the mass rally, eight anarchists were accused of throwing a bomb that killed seven policemen, while the police were accused of indiscriminately shooting into the crowd, beating up dozens of workers, and killing four in the process. The incident became known as the Haymarket Massacre, for which the Knights were unjustly blamed. A precipitous decline in the union's northern, mostly white membership followed soon thereafter.

The year 1886 also saw the formation of the American Federation of Labor (AFL), led by a cigar roller named Samuel Gompers (1850–1924). The AFL would soon assume the preeminent position that had been occupied by the Knights of Labor. The AFL concentrated on organizing craft unions of highly skilled workers. Opposed to any alliances with radical political parties, Gompers emphasized economic rather than broad ideological goals. Under his stewardship, the AFL ushered in the modern era of organized labor, maintaining emergency funds to help members during strikes, and employing paid organizers to sign up members in nonunion shops. But the exclusive posture of the AFL precipitated a serious rift within the American labor movement, its ranks swelling with immigrant and mostly unskilled workers. In the long run, the organization's decision to focus on the economic interests of the nation's most

"Shift Change at the Pullman Car Works," in *The Story of Pullman*, c. 1893.
Source: Newberry Library: Pullman Company Archives.

skilled workers—a decision fueled by racism and growing anti-immigrant sentiment—debilitated the potential for a unified labor union movement.

Other labor unions competed with the AFL for membership. In 1894 the American Railroad Union, under the leadership of Eugene V. Debs (1855–1926), a leading socialist, organized a strike at the Pullman manufacturing plant near Chicago and called for a boycott by the men who handled the company's sleeping cars for the nation's railroads. Within a week, over 125,000 railroad workers across the nation went on a sympathy strike. At the request of the Illinois governor, President Grover Cleveland (1837–1908; held office 1893–1897) intervened, moving in federal troops to break the strike. Under the threat of military intervention and a broad injunction, the sympathy strike was ended. The Pullman strikers were defeated, and many were blacklisted for their involvement.

> **Chicago is the product of modern capitalism, and, like other great commercial centers, is unfit for human habitation.**
>
> —SOCIALIST PRESIDENTIAL CANDIDATE EUGENE V. DEBS

Regional and International Relations

As we have seen, waves of European immigration, the issue of labor, and industrialization all directed American attention inward until the end of the nineteenth century. Most scholars characterize this period of American history as one of isolationism. As a large nation with a rapidly growing population and economy, however, it had no choice but to begin forging relations with other nations and making a place for itself in the world. At this point we must once again step back from the chronological march of history in order to examine the United States' relations with other nations, in particular its neighbors to the north and south.

Relations with the United Kingdom and Canada

The notion of a special relationship existing between the United States and the United Kingdom has been a common reference point for politicians on both sides of the Atlantic for more than half a century. Originating in the close collaboration of the two nations during World War II, the relationship has been sustained by political leaders in Washington and London ever since. Yet the history of Anglo-American relations is one rich with contradictions and often mutual hostility. Assisted by the French, the United States was born in a revolution against British rule. The most serious foreign assault on mainland United States, prior to the terrorist attacks of September 11, 2001, was perpetrated by the British in the War of 1812, including the burning of much of Washington, DC (which had only recently been established as the capital, in 1790)—including the White House.

The War of 1812 had multiple causes, including the Royal Navy's impressment of American sailors; the British blockade of Continental Europe, which excluded American trade; the frontier conflicts against the Native Americans (whom the British were accused of arming); and expansionist ambitions aimed at Canada, which was vulnerable while Britain was at war with Napoleon Bonaparte. Both sides declared victory: the British because they successfully defended Canada and burned Washington; the Americans because they had stood up to Britain and won the last major engagement of the conflict, the Battle of New Orleans in 1815. The War of 1812 was declared for a variety of reasons, one of which was the hope that Canada could be taken from the British, preoccupied with its war with France. It was extremely unpopular in the Northeast; the states of Connecticut, Massachusetts, and Rhode Island refused to send militias against the British. The war saw a failed American three-pronged invasion of Canada, as well as a British invasion of the United States that led to, for a time, occupation of Maine, and would later lead to Maine's separation from Massachusetts, which had refused to help.

The octagonal guard tower of Fort Edgecomb on the coast of Maine, built in 1808–1809. The fort was used to house British prisoners of war during the War of 1812, a war that was extremely unpopular with New Englanders, in particular, due to President Thomas Jefferson's trade embargo with Britain that severely hampered the New England economy. The state of Maine seceded from Massachusetts in 1820, in part because of its lack of protection from the invading British during the War of 1812. Photo by Amy Siever.

One of the many low points of the war was the invading Americans' burning down of a Canadian village in the middle of the winter, sending its 400 inhabitants out into a blizzard. Relations between the two nations remained ambiguous well into the twentieth century. The conflict ended in a draw in 1815 and earned "Yankees" a withering reputation north of the border as a crass and warlike people. The two-hundredth anniversary of the war in 2012 was marked by widespread uncertainty about what, exactly, the war had been fought over.

The British continued to exert a profound influence on America, despite occasional hostilities. British industrialization was copied by the United States, as were various technological breakthroughs such as the steam engine and the spinning jenny, used in textile mills. The tariff policies the United States introduced during the nineteenth century were particularly aimed at protecting American manufacturers from more advanced British industry. Disputes over patents and copyrights plagued the relationship. Other sources of friction included disputes over the US-Canadian boundary, settled by a series of treaties, as well as imperial rivalry in Latin America and Asia.

As a former British colony, the United States shared a common language and often found itself—or believed itself to be—subject to cultural imperialism. Ralph Waldo Emerson (1803–1882) and many other early writers sought to create an American literary style distinct from Britain's. Sometimes, however, this process was reversed: Harriet Beecher Stowe's *Uncle Tom's Cabin* was a sensation in Britain, selling many more copies there than in the United States. (There is no evidence for the common belief that President Abraham Lincoln had referred to Stowe as the "little lady who started this great war.") Politicians and authors on both sides of the Atlantic typically satirized or disparaged each other's nations. But not all literary or political exchanges were hostile. Both the abolitionism movement and the temperance movement against the use of alcohol, which would lead to the constitutional ban on the sales and transport of alcohol in 1920 known as Prohibition, were transatlantic in membership, and both nations would later develop common peace and anti-imperial movements.

While the United States chose to split from Great Britain, Canada chose to stay, its population augmented by loyalists to the Crown who had fled in the wake of the Revolution. Although US-Canadian relations today are quite cordial—the long border between the two nations has long been known as the longest undefended border in the world—history has taught Canadians to be suspicious of the United States. English-speaking Canada was founded by those American colonists who opposed independence for various reasons and supported the Crown in the Revolutionary War, while French-speaking Canadians feared that their language and culture would be overwhelmed in an English-speaking America. American armies invaded Quebec in 1775 and again during the War of 1812, both unsuccessfully. While history is full of "what ifs," it is interesting to think that but for a string of bad luck and bad military decisions, large portions of Quebec and Ontario very well could have become part of the United States.

Despite the often acrimonious boundary disputes in which saber rattling was followed by treaty making, tensions gradually eased and trade flourished in the ensuing decades, despite occasional flair-ups such as those caused by British-American tensions during the Civil War and other conflicts.

As threats of war receded, trade increasingly became important. In the late nineteenth century both nations erected tariff walls to protect domestic industries. A sense that some Canadian leaders were considering political unification with the United States, and a border dispute over Alaska in 1903, revealed continuing anti-American sentiments in Canada in the early 1900s. Serving as allies in the two world wars turned the suspicion and animosity into friendship and collaboration, a pattern that continues despite disagreement over some issues such as the Vietnam War (Canada did not participate in that war, and became a haven for so-called draft dodgers) and the Second Iraq War (2003–2011).

Canadian humor is quite popular with many Americans. Comedy troupes such as the Kids in the Hall, SCTV, Bob and Doug McKenzie, and the Red Green Show are immensely popular south of the border, as are a large number of Canadian comedians and actors, a small sampling of which includes Will Arnett, Dan Aykroyd, John Candy, Jim Carrey, Michael J. Fox, Phil Hartman, Eugene Levy, Norm MacDonald, Howie Mandel, Lorne Michaels, Mike Myers, Leslie Nielsen, Catherine O'Hara, Seth Rogan, William Shatner, and Martin Short. British comedians, such as Benny Hill, Ricky Gervais, Rowan Atkinson, and the members of Monty Python, are also extremely popular in the United States.

Relations with Latin America and Mexico

In 1823 President James Monroe (1758–1831; held office 1817–1825), in his annual speech to Congress, congratulated the newly independent nations of South America and warned that the Western Hemisphere was no longer open to European colonial endeavors. His "Monroe Doctrine," as it came to be known, would become the basis for American foreign policy for the next two centuries. For the remainder of the nineteenth century the United States and Latin America dealt with their own internal issues. The United States was largely concerned with internal expansion through purchase or conquest. Latin America was mired in internal struggles over the post-colonial direction of its various nations. Divisions over whether to adopt a market or a mercantilist economic system, a monarchy or a republic, and the role of the Catholic Church separated much of the region.

US-Mexico relations have always been challenged by issues of interdependence. A saying by General Porfirio Díaz (1830–1915)—"Poor Mexico!, so far away from God and so close to the United States"—captures the historically ambivalent nature of this relationship. There are five major historical themes in the US-Mexico relationship. First, the theme of foreign wars/occupations dominated the relationship in the half-century after Mexico's independence from Spain in 1821. Second, between 1867 and 1910 the relationship was dominated by Mexico's dependence on American technology and investment, while at the same time Mexico kept American influence at bay through links with Europe. Third, the Mexican Revolution and its long aftermath (1910–1940) opened a new chapter in the relationship, characterized by mutual uncertainty, which was punctuated by political confrontation but eventual accommodation. Fourth, during World War II (1939–1945) and the Cold War (c. 1945–1991) Mexican leaders forged a good working relationship with the United States despite the fact that Mexico was not a liberal democracy. Lastly, economic crisis (1982), the end of the Cold War, and technological developments in transport and communications (since the early 1990s) gave way to a process of globalization, which has affected the US-Mexico special relationship decisively and permanently in the areas of economic integration, mass immigration, cultural and social cross-fertilization, and shared political challenges.

Opinion about the United States has divided Mexican leaders since their country's independence from Spain in 1821. The liberals took the United States as their model, and highlighted the virtue of the republican form of government. The conservatives, on the other hand, supported the creation of a monarchy based on a European model. This foundational split between liberal and conservative elites led to a half-century of civil wars, which were accompanied on several occasions by foreign wars and occupations. The most difficult for Mexico were the secession of Texas (1835–1836) and the Mexican-American War (1846–1848), followed by the French invasion and occupation of Mexico (1863–1867). As a consequence of the first two events, Mexico lost more than half of its original 1821 territory to the United States. This loss remains the deepest historical trauma in Mexican history since independence.

The increased political and economic strength and influence of the United States after its Civil War confirmed Mexican leaders' admiration and wish to emulate the United States as a successful nation (the United States government supported the Mexican government-in-exile against the French occupation of Mexico under Habsburg Emperor Maximilian in 1863–1867). At the same time, however, growing American power increased Mexican leaders' distrust and fear of their northern neighbor. During the long dictatorship of General Porfirio Díaz, Mexico's cultural and economic links were steered closer to European countries to countervail the influence of the United States.

A civilian-led movement under Francisco I. Madero overthrew Díaz's regime in 1910–1911. This overthrow began a long revolution in Mexico. During the most violent phase of this revolution (1913–1920) the United States intervened diplomatically and militarily in Mexico. United States marines occupied the port of Veracruz in 1914, and in 1916 the United States Army sent an expedition into northern Mexico in a vain attempt to capture revolutionary leader Pancho Villa.

In 1917, in what became infamous as the Zimmermann Telegram, the German Empire proposed that Mexico join the Central Powers in the Great War (the pre-World War II name of World War I) in case the United States joined the Allies. The proposal, intercepted by British spies, outraged the American public and was one factor in the popularity of declaring war on Germany, which the United States government did in April of 1917.

During the 1920s, successive governments on both sides of the border engaged in disputes over American investors' rights in Mexican oil and land, as well as mutual recriminations over the Mexican government's suppression of the Catholic church (1926–1929) and the American occupation of Nicaragua, the Dominican Republic, and Haiti. Further clashes were averted in 1938 when Mexican President Lázaro Cárdenas (1895–1970; in office 1934–1940) nationalized the oil industry, partly because Mexico offered compensation to foreign investors, but primarily because United States President Franklin D. Roosevelt (discussed in the World War II section starting on page 100) did not press the issue, wanting Latin American nations to come out strongly in support of the United States in the event of major war in Europe.

In 1898 the United States joined Cuban forces in their fight for independence from Spain. It was victorious American delegates, however, not Cubans, who signed a peace treaty with Spain in December of that year. The United States came away having secured the Philippines, Puerto Rico, and was granted Guam in the Pacific while maintaining informal control over Cuba. Cuba was granted a limited form of independence, with the United States retaining the right to intervene in Cuban affairs. In 1903 the United States constructed the naval base at Guantanamo Bay on Cuba, which nearly one hundred years later became a controversial detention center for suspected terrorists after the September 11, 2001 terrorist attacks on the United States.

Of the territory gained in the Spanish-American War (1898), the Philippines proved the most intriguing. Under the Treaty of Paris, Spain ceded the Philippines to the United States for 20 million dollars. (There have been nearly two dozen Treaties of Paris since the first, in 1229; the 1783 Treaty of Paris officially ended the American Revolution, the 1815 Treaty of Paris ended the Napoleonic Wars, and the 1898 Treaty of Paris ended the Spanish-American War.) Many American officials thought that the Philippines would be a good stepping stone for access to the lucrative Chinese market. But the Filipino people resisted American control and fought the United States for control of the islands in the Philippine-American War (1899–1902). The insurrection collapsed in 1902 with an estimated 200,000 Filipinos dead and over 4,000 American casualties. An American civil government controlled the Philippines until independence was granted in 1946.

These military interventions finished Spain as a colonial power and established the United States as a world power with the military means to intervene beyond the Western Hemisphere. The nation would come to wield that power across the globe in the twentieth century.

CHAPTER FOUR: THE TWENTIETH CENTURY TO TODAY

The United States in 1901 was a transformed nation. Born hugging the eastern seaboard and historically isolationist, it had become by the dawn of the twentieth century a continent-sized nation and a world power. Its Industrial Revolution relied on large factories and brought with it the growth of mammoth corporations and a consolidation of wealth and private economic power. At the same time, the nation underwent significant social change. The population of the United States grew from just over 31 million people before the Civil War in 1860 to over 76 million in 1900. Between 1880 and 1910 the number of Americans working in industry tripled. Increased industrial activity led to increased labor disputes and strikes. The changing nature of employment was combined with the changing face of the American worker. The new immigrants settled in already crowded cities—many living in tenement houses—and staffed the large factories. They brought new languages, religions, and cultures. Their dangerous working and living conditions threatened basic assumptions about the quality of life in the United States. Despite those conditions, the United States at the beginning of the twentieth century was mainly prosperous, although the prosperity was certainly not shared by all.

The Progressive Era

The Progressive Era was a period in American history that lasted from the end of the nineteenth century to about 1920, but the transformations initiated during that period have carried over into the twenty-first century. This was a time when the basic underpinnings of the economy, social structure, and governing institutions were called into question, and leaders sought to redefine the notion of the American community. It was during this era that many of the features of modern American society and politics were born: party primaries, federal regulation of businesses, the environmental conservation movement, and the movement for women's rights. A turn away from the localism of the eighteenth and nineteenth centuries set the Progressive Era apart, and its characteristics came to define twentieth-century American politics and society.

Background: The Depression of 1893

The United States suffered its worst economic depression to date in 1893. The economic downturn was especially severe in rural areas, where the crisis began around 1890, and in cities, where in some cases unemployment reached 20 percent. The massive dislocation caused by the economic hard times presaged great changes in the nation, beginning with the populist movement. This reform movement was based in the Midwest and South, and coalesced around the "People's Party," or Populist Party, which formed in 1892. The party was supported by farmers who, suffering the effects of the depression, criticized railroad owners, bank lenders, and others with whom they conducted business and whom they blamed for their plight. When the depression hit urban areas, industrial workers joined farmers in the movement. With this uneasy coalition, Populists captured nearly 40 percent of the national vote in the 1894 congressional elections by advocating government ownership of the railroads and the telegraph industries, as well as the federal coinage of silver. The movement reached its peak in the mid-1890s. By 1900, with the economy recovered and political disagreement plaguing the Democratic Party, populist strength evaporated, but its call to strengthen the powers of the federal government—and for mechanisms of greater democracy—became hallmarks of the country's next great reform movement.

The greatest symbols of private capitalist power were the corporate trusts: one hundred corporations controlled 40 percent of the nation's industrial capacity. Many Americans began to believe the trusts were uncontrollable; they seemed to threaten equal opportunity and individual control of one's destiny. Trusts, and the corporate bosses who controlled them, successfully sought to control the political system through political contributions and outright bribery.

Facing this economic and social situation was a political movement opposed to a status quo in which party bosses supported by big-city political machines wielded undue influence over national politics. By 1900 both the Democratic and Republican parties had "progressive" elements. Although populism had established a beachhead in the Democratic Party, progressives came in all political stripes: Republicans, Democrats, Socialists, and people unaffiliated with a political party. Progressives attacked political corruption and agitated for change. At the national level the Progressive Era's central characters were two presidents of opposing political parties, both of whom took on progressive causes: Republican Theodore Roosevelt (1858–1919; served

A cartoon from c. 1890 by A. C. Hutchison titled "Man Poking Fat Man" illustrates the widening income gap in the United States of the late nineteenth century. Source: Caroline and Erwin Swann Collection of Caricature and Cartoon, Library of Congress.

1901–1909) and Democrat Woodrow Wilson (1856–1924; served 1913–1921). Their electoral battle in 1912 was the zenith of progressive politics in the United States.

The Roosevelt, Taft, and Wilson Presidencies

Theodore Roosevelt assumed the presidency after the assassination of William McKinley by an anarchist in Buffalo, New York, in September 1901, becoming, at 42, the youngest president in history to assume office. Roosevelt brought to prominence many social movements during his presidency, among them civil rights, women's rights, environmental conservation, prohibition, and the rights of labor. He was aided in his endeavor by another great change in American politics and society, the rise of a mass media that had begun to expose and sensationalize the sins of big business and politics. These "muckrakers," as they were called, had a major impact on the thinking (and legislation) of the country. In 1904, muckracker Ida Tarbell (1857–1944) wrote a scathing indictment of industrialist John D. Rockefeller in her book *The History of the Standard Oil Company*. Social reformer Jacob Riis (1849–1914), a native of Denmark, brought the plight of the poor in New York City to the public's attention with his innovative style of photojournalism; his best known work is *How the Other Half Lives: Studies among the Tenements of New York*, from 1890.

Theodore Roosevelt showed that there existed a need for popular leadership to cleanse American politics, with the president acting as the voice of the people. He left office in 1909, making way for William Howard Taft (1857–1930; in office 1909–1913), who is mainly remembered, perhaps unfairly, for his girth: weighing in at 340 pounds (154 kg), he was the nation's portliest president. Roosevelt then launched an insurgent reform campaign in 1912, on the Progressive ticket, newly renamed the Bull Moose Party.

The "Genesis of the Tenement"

In 1890 Danish-born social activist and photojournalist Jacob Riis, among the first of the "muckrakers," published How the Other Half Lives: Studies Among the Tenements of New York. *The relatively new invention of flash photography allowed Riis to document the dark, overcrowded slums of New York as never before. The following is an extract of that work.*

The first tenement New York knew bore the mark of Cain from its birth, though a generation passed before the writing was deciphered. It was the "rear house," infamous ever after in our city's history. There had been tenant-houses before, but they were not built for the purpose. Nothing would probably have shocked their original owners more than the idea of their harboring a promiscuous crowd; for they were the decorous homes of the old Knickerbockers, the proud aristocracy of Manhattan in the early days.

It was the stir and bustle of trade, together with the tremendous immigration that followed upon the war of 1812 that dislodged them. In thirty-five years the city of less than a hundred thousand souls came to harbor half a million souls, for whom homes had to be found. Within the memory of men not yet in their prime, Washington had moved from his house on Cherry Hill as too far out of town to be easily reached. Now the old residents followed his example; but they moved in a different direction and for a different reason. Their comfortable dwellings in the once fashionable streets along the East River front fell into the hands of real-estate agents and boarding house keepers. . . . And here, says the report to the Legislature of 1857, their ". . . large rooms were partitioned into several smaller ones, without regard to light or ventilation, the rate of rent being lower in proportion to space or height from the street; and they soon became filled from cellar to garret with a class of tenantry living from hand to mouth, loose in morals, improvident in habits, degraded, and squalid as beggary itself."

—Jacob Riis, *How the Other Half Lives: Studies Among the Tenements of New York*, pp. 7–8. New York: Charles Scribner's Sons, 1914.

Roosevelt lost the race to Woodrow Wilson, but his successor echoed Roosevelt's faith in the cleansing role of popular leadership. Wilson, the former president of Princeton University and governor of New Jersey, advocated primary elections and constitutional amendments to guarantee the direct election of senators, and for women's suffrage.

The 1912 election has been called the first modern presidential election. It earned this distinction for many reasons: it signaled a rebellion against party leaders and conventions; it heralded the use of primary elections; and it witnessed campaigning by presidential candidates.

Some historians have argued that the Progressive Party lies at the very heart of fundamental changes in American politics, changes that were initially (and partially) negotiated during the Progressive Era. The personality-driven quality of Roosevelt's campaign, a feature of all modern presidential campaigns, was only one aspect of these changes. The Progressive Party, with its leadership-centered organization, embodied the aspirations of an array of reformers—insurgent Republicans, disaffected Democrats, muckrakers, environmentalists, academics, social workers, feminists, and civil-rights activists—all of whom hoped the new party would realize their common goal of making federal and state governments more responsive to the economic, social, and political demands of the people. Their reformist effort aimed specifically at the concentration of wealth in a few hands, which caused social unrest and was seen as a threat to democracy. Progressives hoped to combine social reform with direct democracy and energetic popular leadership. It was Wilson, not Roosevelt, who initiated the final series of progressive reforms.

The final verdict on the accomplishments of the Progressive Era is mixed. Many of the changes progressives pressed for did not come to pass in their time. It was not until the New Deal of Franklin Delano Roosevelt (a distant cousin of Theodore Roosevelt) in the 1930s that a general system of welfare was instituted, and it was not until 1972 that primary elections truly replaced the grip of party bosses in presidential campaigns. Though progressives raised the issue of civil rights for African Americans and equal rights for women—especially with the Nineteenth Amendment—those social movements did not begin to achieve true success until the 1960s and 1970s. Nonetheless, the era witnessed a flowering of direct democracy, national regulation, and a concern for social welfare. The changes brought by this unique period continue to shape the United States today.

Labor Movements in the Twentieth Century

An integral part of the Progressive Era, the labor movements that began in the nineteenth century continued unabated into the twentieth, a century that would see membership in the American Communist Party (ACP) and its rival the Socialist Party of America (SPA) reach all-time highs. During both the 1904 and 1908 presidential elections, Socialist Party candidate Eugene Debs won over 400,000 votes. By 1912 the SPA's journal *Appeal to Reason* was selling a half million copies a week.

The opening of the new century witnessed a flurry of strikes. In 1902, coal miners in northeastern Pennsylvania called for a strike. Under the leadership of John L. Lewis, their union, the United Mine Workers (UMW), mobilized some 100,000 coal miners, who shut down the coal mines in which they worked. When the owners of the mines turned down a UMW proposal for arbitration, President Roosevelt intervened, appointing a commission for mediation and arbitration. Five months later, the commission awarded the workers a ten percent increase in wages and a shortened workday, but it denied the union's demand for formal recognition, which was a precondition for arbitration; in its absence, workers faced loss of wages and the possibility of starvation.

In 1908, twenty thousand women garment workers in New York and Philadelphia walked off their jobs to protest harsh working conditions. It was only after 146 young female workers died when a fire broke out at the Triangle Shirtwaist Company on New York's crowded and impoverished Lower East Side in 1911 that the government finally acted to remedy hazardous working conditions in New York factories. Many of the women at the Triangle Shirtwaist Company had been forced to jump out of windows when the fire broke out because the owners had insisted on keeping the doors of the building locked from the outside to prevent "loss of goods." An outraged public helped pave the way for the enactment of industrial safety reforms, beginning with the targeting of sweatshop conditions in the garment industry. As is often the case, it took an industrial catastrophe to spur the enactment of workplace safety regulations. A catastrophic building collapse in Bangladesh that killed over 1,100 garment workers in 2013 showed the tragic results of such a lack of government oversight, combined with rampant corruption.

Favorable public sentiment played an important role in the growth of labor unions. In 1912, the Industrial Workers of the World, a militant multiracial union whose members were known as "Wobblies" for obscure reasons, led a strike of fifty thousand workers in the textile mills of Lawrence, Massachusetts. When striking women and their children were attacked by police, a large public protest ensued; the textile workers' pay was eventually restored and then increased. An important victory for the broader American labor movement was won two years after the Lawrence strike when Congress passed the Clayton Antitrust Act (1914), which legalized strikes, boycotts, and peaceful picketing. Referred to as the "Magna Carta" for labor, the Clayton Act also limited the use of injunctions to halt strike actions. But another generation would pass before unions were fully recognized.

World War I (1914–1918)

Labor disputes at home would soon take a back seat to international affairs. World War I, fought from July 1914 to November 1918, was one of the most cataclysmic events in modern history. Known at the time as the Great War (or the "war to end all wars"), it badly weakened the great powers of Europe, introduced the world to the horrors of mechanized trench warfare, and resulted in roughly twenty million deaths. It led to the era of Modernism in arts and literature, where artists, writers, and musicians such as Ernest Hemingway, Virginia Woolf, T. S. Eliot, Alban Berg, Igor Stravinsky, and Pablo Picasso upended centuries of Western tradition in their respective spheres as they grappled with the sweeping societal changes wrought by the war.

The Great War also had the unanticipated effect of vaulting the United States into a leadership role in global affairs. As a neutral power in the first three years of the war, the United States enriched itself by trading with the warring European nations. Woodrow Wilson, like Theodore Roosevelt and Taft before him, believed that capitalism, not traditional imperialism, leads to the greatest wealth and power and would promote peaceful relations between nations. Countries that traded, these presidents reasoned, would be less likely to fight. In 1914, as the European powers went to war, the United States was the greatest industrial power in the world, but had limited military capabilities. Wilson would thus use the power of capital to extend American influence, conducting vitally needed trade with Britain and France, and brokering loans to the allies to keep them afloat and fighting. Wilson's involvement paid off: by 1919 the United States, which had entered the war as a debtor nation, had $11.7 billion in credits, and the seat of global economic power had moved from London to New York's Wall Street. As a combatant from April 1917 to November 1918 the United States had a decisive impact on the outcome of the war, turning the tide against Germany and

Something to think about:

What does it mean for a nation to remain neutral during times of war? Many nations continue to have profitable economic dealings with other, warring, nations, as the United States did in the early years of World War I. Switzerland was later accused of profiting from its neutrality during World War II. Is real neutrality ever possible given these economic realities?

in favor of Britain and France. The United States emerged from World War I as an economic colossus and a proven military power. This shift caused a major rethinking of global perspectives toward the United States, which had previously been dismissed by European leaders as little more than a distant regional power.

The origins of the First World War were complex and remain hotly contested; there is no meaningful scholarly consensus on its cause. At heart was the imperialist competition of all the great European powers, an accelerating naval arms race between Britain and Germany, and rigid alliance systems. The immediate spark was the June 1914 assassination of the heir to the throne of Austria-Hungary, Archduke Franz Ferdinand, as he visited Serbia. This assassination set in motion a full-scale confrontation between the Triple Entente (Britain, France, and Russia) and the Central Powers (Germany, Austria-Hungary, and the Ottoman Empire). Vast armies were mobilized across the continent, with leaders making the mistaken assumption that the war would be short and glorious.

At first the war had little to do with the United States. Not until the casualties in Europe began to mount, and the immense economic and human sacrifices needed to wage modern war became painfully clear, did the particulars of American neutrality become crucially important. The basic problem with "strict neutrality" was that in practice it heavily favored the Entente powers of Britain and France. The United States had always exported more to them than to Germany, but this disparity was made more pronounced during the war, especially after the British blockade that prevented Germany having access to American markets of any kind.

Wilson often spoke with a moralistic tone that irritated the warring European nations. He also tried to play the role of impartial mediator, urging both sides to state their war aims and attempting to bring them to the negotiating table. This was a noble effort, but it was not appreciated by European leaders. They resented his pious attitude and doubted that the United States acted only for selfless reasons. Eventually the Germans, suffering from the British naval blockade, decided that they had little to lose by declaring unrestricted submarine warfare, which was almost certain to bring the United States into the war. In 1915, German submarines were let loose on all Atlantic shipping, declaring the seas around the United Kingdom a war zone.

The most notorious result of this style of warfare was the May 1915 sinking of the British ship RMS *Lusitania*, for a brief time the largest ship in the world, resulting in the deaths of nearly 1,200 passengers. While Germany had posted warnings in American newspapers on the day of the vessel's departure from New York, bound for Liverpool, most Americans considered them to be idle threats.

The sinking of the British ship the RMS *Lusitania* by a German submarine off the Irish coast in 1915, resulting in the loss of nearly 1,200 lives (including 128 Americans), was one factor in the United States's entry two years later into World War I. Source: *New York Times*. Images copyright © 2000 by Cartography Associates; licensed under a Creative Commons License.

In March of 1917, Czar Nicholas II of Russia (1870–1918) was deposed by a democratic uprising. The czar and his family were placed under house arrest; the following year, they were shot by the Bolsheviks under Lenin, ending the over 300-year reign of the Romanov dynasty.

Germany's unrelenting submarine warfare, combined with the interception of the Zimmermann Telegram from Germany to Mexico, discussed in the previous chapter, further convinced Wilson that the Entente occupied the moral high ground. Now able to justify American entry as part of a historic campaign to "make the world safe for democracy," on 6 April 1917 Wilson declared war on Germany with the overwhelming support of Congress. The question in the spring of 1917 was whether the Americans could get their forces into the field fast enough to make a difference before Britain and France were starved into submission by unrestricted submarine warfare.

Although the American infantry troops known as "doughboys" (another term with uncertain origins) were initially slow to arrive, by May 1918 one million American troops were on the Western Front to help block the last German offensive. Two million American troops had reached Europe by 11 November 1918, when an armistice brought hostilities to an end.

The United States had played a critical role for the Entente, but the British and French were not entirely thrilled with their ally. In January of 1918 Wilson had unilaterally introduced his "Fourteen Points of Light," a plan for the postwar peace that embraced political and economic liberalism, the League of Nations to enforce collective security, and "self-determination" as a basic right of nationalities around the world: an unpopular suggestion for nations with large overseas empires. Wilson also promised "peace without victory," implying that a peace settlement should treat all sides fairly. This

> **Mr. Wilson bores me with his fourteen points; why, God Almighty has only ten!**
>
> —FRENCH PREMIER GEORGES CLEMENCEAU

development frustrated Britain and France, neither of which had agreed to Wilson's forgiving approach beforehand. Wilson did get his League of Nations—a weak predecessor of the United Nations—but this body failed to prevent Germany from resurrecting itself and seeking retribution in World War II two decades later.

The war and the Paris Peace Conference that ended it—another conflict ended in Paris—dramatically increased the power and prestige of the United States. Wilson was the central figure at the conference. His nation had benefited greatly from its period of neutrality, becoming a leading creditor and expanding the most dynamic and productive economy in the world. The United States had also proven itself capable of mobilizing vast armies, even if it did not maintain them in peacetime.

Americans generally enjoyed good relations with most nations after the war, especially with wartime allies. Canada and the United States, for example, drew closer together because of their shared sacrifices. Britain and France became more intimate friends of the United States because of the war, largely because of their shared democratic values and desire to build a safer world order. The Anglo-American relationship, which had been improving, blossomed into what was termed "the Great Rapprochement" as a result of the First World War, laying the basis for the "special relationship" and pillar of each nation's foreign policy following the Second World War. The British and French did harbor some ill-will toward the United States, however. Neither nation agreed wholly with the Fourteen Points, which seemed tailored to serve American interests. As an example of French and indeed British views of Woodrow Wilson's diplomatic evangelism, a frustrated Georges Clemenceau, the French Premier, is supposed to have remarked: "Mr. Wilson bores me with his fourteen points; why, God Almighty has only ten!" The issue of war debts poisoned relations for years, as the United States government insisted on repayment, and the British and French replied that they had already paid a high enough cost in human lives for the Entente victory.

The Germans, not surprisingly, adopted a negative view of the United States after the war. Germans were bitter about the one-sided character of American neutrality and, of course, about the eventual entry of the United States into the war against them. Oddly, however, German leaders continued to think little of Americans as major players in world affairs. Nazi leader Adolf Hitler dismissed the United States in the 1930s as a "mongrel nation." He would come to regret that assessment during World War II, much as he would underestimate the ability of the Soviet Union (and its fierce winters) to repel his invasion of the USSR during that conflict.

Perhaps the most lasting damage to America's image was done in Russia, after 1922 known as the Union of Soviet Socialist Republics. There Lenin and the Bolsheviks saw American foreign policy at its most hypocritical. American troops backed the anti-communist White Russians from 1918 to 1920 at the same time that the president was preaching the universal right of "self-determination." (The anti-communist effort ultimately failed, as the Bolsheviks prevailed in Russia's civil war.) That intervention was an unmitigated disaster, earning the United States the lasting hatred of the Soviet Union. This hatred was unfortunate because of the critical importance of US-Russian relations into the twenty-first century.

Overall, the rest of the world keenly felt the sudden increase in American power that resulted from World War I. American culture also spread abroad in the 1920s as Ford cars and Hollywood movies proliferated across Europe, and "Americanism" came to stand for progress, technological innovation, and popular culture.

The Interwar Period: Prohibition, Flappers, and the Great Depression

The interwar period following the Great War was marked by extremes. On the one hand, there was until 1929 an economic boom premised primarily on recovery after World War I. Untouched by the physical devastation of the war and with an economy flush from wealth garnished as a neutral country trading with belligerents, the United States became the world's bank, a new "consumer society" quickly emerged, and the war empowered women, who gained not only the right to vote (from the Nineteenth Amendment, ratified in August 1920) but also economic and political power in running farms and factories while men were overseas. Many women began to challenge social norms and class structures by adopting "radical" lifestyles that included various degrees of sexual liberation, smoking, drinking, and experimentation. Known as "flappers" (a name thought to derive from the loose, flapping galoshes that were favorite footwear among the fashionable), they were in effect rebelling against the Victorian mentality prevalent before 1914. American culture spread throughout the world with the export of Hollywood movies, jazz,

Flappers, known for various degrees of sexual liberation, smoking, and drinking, were in open rebellion against the Victorian mentality of the nineteenth century. Source: "Where There's Smoke There's Fire," by Russell Patterson. Library of Congress.

and literature, and in some ways the United States became the focal point of the world and the cultural model upon which many Europeans based their own rebellions against the old order.

Temperance and Prohibition (1920–1933)

Two related movements during the interwar period were the temperance (from alcohol) and women's suffrage movements. The temperance movement was related to the old abolitionist movement; many abolitionists had been supporters of temperance, and vice-versa. A common complaint among those in favor of women's suffrage was that a hardworking citizen who happened to be a woman could not vote, while a man who spent his days drinking in a saloon could. The temperance movement started in the nineteenth century and was, from the beginning, mostly popular with women. Temperance leader Carrie Nation (1846–1911; sometimes spelled Carry), a radical member of the Woman's Christian Temperance Union, gained notoriety for entering a saloon in Kiowa, Kansas, in 1900 and destroying the bar's array of liquor bottles with rocks. A subsequent tornado that hit the state seemed to Nation to be a sign of divine approval of her actions, and so she

> At one time it was quite apparent that no real effort was being made to put an end to such open defiance of our laws. Liquor runners operated off Florida practically in the open, in broad daylight, with little or no interference. There for years the prosecuting office and the prohibition agents engaged equally in the game of evasion of responsibility.
>
> —US ASSISTANT ATTORNEY GENERAL MABEL WALKER WILLEBRANDT

continued in her crusade against what she saw as the country's rampant alcoholism and related immorality. She would go on to gain fame for smashing taverns with a hatchet, getting arrested roughly thirty times in the process; the prize-fighter John L. Sullivan is reported to have hid when Nation burst into his New York saloon. Although she would not live to see it, the efforts of Nation and other reformers would lead eventually to passage of the Eighteenth Amendment prohibiting the sales and distribution of alcoholic beverages, which took effect on 17 January 1920. (Notably, the consumption and personal possession of alcohol were still legal.) Later that year, women gained the right to vote. Prohibition would prove to be an almost unmitigated disaster on many levels.

Prohibition would lead to unprecedented levels of smuggling and the illegal distilling of alcohol, enjoyed in thousands of illegal bars known as "speakeasys." Moonshiners had been distilling tax-free liquor, and bootleggers distributing it widely, long before the Eighteenth Amendment took effect, however. When the country instituted prohibition, it merely enhanced the vast potential for profit. During the late 1920s, Al Capone (1899–1947), known as "Scarface," became the most notorious crime boss of the time, consolidating all forms of commercialized vice and gambling in Chicago. Prohibition Agent Eliot Ness (1903–1957) assembled a team of Bureau of Prohibition agents known as "the Untouchables," famous in television and film, to crack down on the activities of Capone and others. Capone would eventually get sent to Alcatraz Prison in San Francisco Bay on tax evasion charges—the only crime the authorities could pin on him—thanks to the efforts of US Assistant Attorney General Mabel Walker Willebrandt (1889–1963), the most prominent woman in the United States government at the time.

Illegal liquor production and distribution remain significant criminal operations wherever taxes on liquor are high and in "dry" jurisdictions where the sale of alcohol is restricted or prohibited. Prohibition, which had been tremendously popular among the many Americans who saw alcohol as the root of many of the plagues of society, was finally repealed in 1933 by the Twenty-first Amendment. The popular vote for repealing what President Franklin Roosevelt would later call "the damnable affliction of Prohibition" had been three to one.

Repercussions of the Great War

Despite the terms "Progressive Era" and "Roaring Twenties," in many respects the interwar period was anything but roaring or progressive. The Great War had been so destructive that many people around the world were left with nothing. With millions suffering from the war, communism seriously threatened already shaky governments throughout Europe. The Soviet Union became the world's first communist state, utterly transforming international relations in the process.

World War I also gave life to extreme forms of nationalism that took root in the devastation that followed. In Germany and other nations that had lost the Great War, resentment over the war and the peace that followed spawned radical movements that were built upon the anger and frustration of millions. Many of these radicals blamed both the war and its aftermath on particular groups: Jews, Catholics, immigrants, and others. Fascist movements in Italy and Germany depended on nationalist sentiments to exclude such people, ultimately dehumanizing them. In the United States organizations such as the Ku Klux Klan, which had first emerged during the Civil War, enjoyed a huge surge in new membership, in part as a reaction to the changes that war had brought, and in part stemming from the popularity of the D. W. Griffith silent film *The Birth of a Nation* (originally titled *The Clansman*), controversial for its positive portrayal of the Klan and negative portrayal of African Americans, who were played by white actors in blackface.

Extremists gained even more strength after the collapse of the global economy, beginning in the United States with the stock market crash of October 1929 that precipitated the Great Depression (1929–1940). With the apparent failure of both capitalism and democracy, many people turned to radical solutions. It was in this context that dictators such as Benito Mussolini and Adolf Hitler, discussed below, came to power in Italy and Germany respectively, and that militarists took over the government of Japan in 1940—developments that ultimately paved the way for World War II.

The Great Depression and Renewed Isolationism

On 29 October 1929, known as "Black Tuesday," the American stock market crashed, sending shock waves throughout the world economy. By the mid-to late 1920s the consumerism of the Jazz Age that had led to greater production had begun to decline, and prices had begun to fall. Furthermore, wobbly governments deeply indebted from the war, as well as small investors, together had begun to default on their loans from the United States. As a result, federal managers raised interest rates, and financial institutions began to collapse. The panic spread to the world market, where investors had been investing in speculative ventures for a quick profit. The crash led to the rise of tariff borders and hence a contraction in world trade. Everywhere people suffered from unemployment and hunger. What would soon become known as the "Great Depression," to differentiate it from earlier bad economic times, caused people to further question the liberal doctrine of free markets, and states began to intervene more heavily in economic affairs.

To many people around the world, American-style *laissez-faire* democracy seemed to have failed to provide the prosperity it had promised, and people began welcoming authoritarian solutions to poverty and mass unemployment. Soviet Russia, fascist Italy, Nazi Germany, and militaristic Japan mobilized against the liberal democracies whose "moral decay" and "decadence" they claimed to oppose. Leaders such as Joseph Stalin (1879–1953) of the Soviet Union, Benito Mussolini (1883–1945) of Italy, and Adolf Hitler (1889–1945) of Nazi Germany promised to deliver all of modernity's benefits without side effects such as class division, urban-industrial squalor, or moral and social decay. In order to enact their programs, however, the authoritarian leaders of both the right and the left first identified scapegoats upon whom they could place the blame for the adverse economic and social conditions, and then advocated violence to dispense with their "enemies" in the name of national progress. Stalin identified the "wealthy peasants" (*kulaks*) as the primary enemies of the state and proceeded to intern them in work camps. The Nazi Party blamed Jews for all of modernity's evils. Hitler railed against both "Jewish capitalism" and "Jewish bolshevism," and when he came to power in 1933, he immediately devised a number of plans to take care of the "Jewish problem"— plans that would lead to the Holocaust.

On the home front, labor agitation, not surprisingly, reached new heights in the United States during the Great Depression. Such agitation included pressure by the International Ladies Garment Workers Union, whose members were predominantly Jewish and Italian immigrants, and from A. Philip Randolph's (1889–1979) black-led Brotherhood of Sleeping Car Porters. Beyond government recognition, other important demands gained during the 1930s by labor unions were the long fought-for minimum wage, the reduction of working hours, child labor laws, and welfare programs. The rising tide of labor union agitation in the 1930s culminated in the formation of the Congress of Industrial Organizations (CIO), which brought millions of unskilled workers from the rubber, steel, and other industries under a single umbrella.

In 1935, Congress passed the Social Security Act and the Wagner Labor Relations Act, which created the National Labor Relations Board. While labor unions thereby gained increased power, the federal government's concessions set the stage for the co-optation of the movement and its leadership under President Franklin D. Roosevelt, who is discussed in more detail under the section on World War II that follows.

By the mid-1930s the international order was in a state of decline, and nations everywhere began the process of rearmament. A civil war raged in Spain between the left and the right from 1930 to 1939; this brutal war is the subject of Ernest Hemingway's *For Whom the Bell Tolls*. Furthermore, Mussolini invaded Ethiopia in 1931, and Japan invaded Manchuria (northeastern China) in 1932. The League of Nations stood by helplessly. By 1936 Hitler had sent soldiers to occupy the Rhineland, and by 1938 Nazi Germany had absorbed Austria. Wanting to avoid a repetition of the horrors of World War I, France and Britain sought a peaceable solution with Germany and made several concessions to Hitler, a solution termed "appeasement." (Although the term "appeasement" now has a negative connotation, considering the effect this strategy had, at the time it had no such negative associations: it was simply a way of giving someone something they wanted in order to keep the peace.) In defiance of all agreements, Hitler invaded Poland on 1 September 1939.

Despite all the expectations that people had for a new order based on greater freedom at home and greater collaboration abroad, World War I had left too many wounds, ambiguities, and unresolved disputes. During the 1930s the conflicts between empires and their colonies, between democracy and authoritarianism, and between nationalism and internationalism played out on a world stage. By 1939 these conflicts seemed destined to be resolved by yet another war, a world war that would be even more destructive than the first. By 3 September the world was once again at war.

World War II (1939–1945)

When World War II erupted in September 1939 the United States once again remained neutral. Just as it had during the first three years of World War I, the United States watched as much of Europe, Asia, North Africa, and the Middle East were consumed by the largest and deadliest war in history: a war even more horrifying than the "war to end all wars." By the war's end sixty-one countries had been involved in the fighting and an estimated 72 million people had lost their lives. Only after the Japanese surprise attack on Pearl Harbor, Hawaii, on 7 December 1941 did the United States join the conflict, fundamentally changing the war and again emerging as the most powerful nation the planet. In many respects World War II was one of the biggest turning points in history in ushering in a new global era that was dominated by American military, economic, and political influence that still exists today, although some would say to a diminishing degree.

War Breaks Out in Europe

When another war in Europe erupted, most Americans sympathized with the Allies, which primarily consisted of Britain and its Commonwealth and France and its colonies. Few Americans were willing to fight foreign wars, however. By the summer of 1940 by means of the "blitzkrieg" or "lightning war" (an overwhelming mechanized assault), Germany had in rapid succession taken Belgium, the Netherlands, Luxembourg, Denmark, Norway, and France, putting most of Europe under Hitler's control. Only Britain and its Commonwealth stood in the way of total victory. Confronted with the likely defeat of Britain, President Roosevelt finally responded by beginning to refurbish the United States military, and implemented the first peacetime conscription in American history. Most important, in September 1940 he transferred fifty destroyers to the British Navy in exchange for rights in British possessions, including Jamaica, the Bahamas, Trinidad, and Newfoundland. (Now the easternmost province of Canada, Newfoundland at the time was its own nation within the Commonwealth; it would not join Canada until 1949.)

Roosevelt extended American support in March 1941 with the controversial Lend-Lease Act. Between 1941 and 1945 more than $50 billion worth of military goods made its way to the Allies, mainly by ship. Lend-Lease proved critical to the success of Allied military efforts. From the German perspective the program, in effect, brought the United States into the war.

Roosevelt followed up the Lend-Lease Act with the Atlantic Charter, devised in August 1941 during a secretive shipboard meeting in Newfoundland (Roosevelt was supposedly on a long fishing trip in New England) with British prime minister Winston Churchill (1874–1965). The two leaders agreed to like-minded principles that would govern the postwar order, including the right of self-determination, disarmament, and increased international trade and cooperation. Most important, the Atlantic Charter called for the defeat of Nazi Germany and other Axis powers.

The United States Enters the War

By the summer of 1940 it was clear to Roosevelt that American interests in the Pacific were seriously threatened by Japan. Soon that threat would be realized. For the United States the problem was how to prevent Japanese expansion without risking war. Events in Japan made a peaceful settlement almost impossible. In October 1941 the ostensibly civilian government in Tokyo fell, and the military under General Hideki Tojo (1884–1948) came to power. Japanese leaders prepared to attack.

At 6 A.M. on Sunday, 7 December 1941, the Japanese launched a massive aerial assault against the American Pacific naval base at Pearl Harbor, Hawaii, resulting in the deaths of 2,300 people and the destruction of eight battleships and numerous smaller ships. Nearly simultaneously the Japanese attacked American bases at Guam, Wake Island, and the Philippines; invaded Thailand; and assaulted British positions in Hong Kong and Malaya. In just over three hours the Japanese succeeded in taking out the American battle fleet at Pearl Harbor and thus won a strategic battle.

In the long term, however, the attack was a catastrophic failure as the core of the US Pacific fleet—most importantly, the three carriers—was not in the harbor, and facilities at Pearl Harbor were still operable. Moreover, the attack galvanized American public opinion like never before. Although in retrospect the attack seems like a colossal miscalculation, at the time the Japanese leadership was fully confident that it could decisively eliminate the United States as a threat with a swift blow. Rallying the nation in response to what he called "a day of infamy," on 8 December President Roosevelt asked Congress for a declaration of war, which passed with only one dissension. (The one dissenting vote was cast by pacifist Jeanette Rankin of Montana, the first woman to be elected to Congress.)

Still, the United States took time to fully wake up. Providing the necessities of war was a monumental challenge after a decade of depression. Similarly, building the military to fight the war was no small task.

In what some experts consider another of the worst mistakes of the war, on 11 December Mussolini and Hitler responded to the attack on Pearl Harbor by

"A Date Which Will Live in Infamy"

The surprise attack on the US Pacific naval base at Pearl Harbor catapulted the United States into entering the war on the side of the Allies. The Japanese military command had hoped that the assault on the Pacific Fleet would knock the United States out of commission, although that was not to be. The following is part of President Roosevelt's declaration of war on Japan.

Yesterday, December 7, 1941—a date which will live in infamy—the United States of America was suddenly and deliberately attacked by naval and air forces of the Empire of Japan.

The United States was at peace with that nation, and, at the solicitation of Japan, was still in conversation with its government and its emperor looking toward the maintenance of peace in the Pacific. . . .

It will be recorded that the distance of Hawaii from Japan makes it obvious that the attack was deliberately planned many days or even weeks ago. During the intervening time the Japanese government has deliberately sought to deceive the United States by false statements and expressions of hope for continued peace.

The attack yesterday on the Hawaiian Islands has caused severe damage to American naval and military forces. I regret to tell you that very many American lives have been lost. In addition, American ships have been reported torpedoed on the high seas between San Francisco and Honolulu.

Yesterday the Japanese government also launched an attack against Malaya.

Last night Japanese forces attacked Hong Kong.

Last night Japanese forces attacked Guam.

Last night Japanese forces attacked the Philippine Islands.

Last night Japanese forces attacked Wake Island.

And this morning the Japanese attacked Midway Island.

Japan has, therefore, undertaken a surprise offensive extending throughout the Pacific area. The facts of yesterday and today speak for themselves.

The people of the United States have already formed their opinions and well understand the implications to the very life and safety of our nation.

As commander in chief of the Army and Navy I have directed that all measures be taken for our defense. But always will our whole nation remember the character of the onslaught against us.

No matter how long it may take us to overcome this premeditated invasion, the American people in their righteous might will win through to absolute victory.

I believe I interpret the will of the Congress and of the people when I assert that we will not only defend ourselves to the uttermost, but will make very certain that this form of treachery shall never endanger us again. . . .

Courtesy of the Franklin D. Roosevelt Library, Hyde Park, New York.

---

declaring war on the United States, bringing the United States fully into the European theater of war as well, much to the relief of the Allies. By mid-1942 American soldiers began moving into Britain, and the United States Army Air Force (USAAF) saw action in the systematic Allied bombing campaigns against Germany.

The American war machine as a whole was unquestionably one of the most important factors securing the Allied victory in World War II. The war also changed American society—the unemployment rate dropped to almost nothing; workers moved from rural to urban areas; women, African Americans, the elderly, and youth joined the workforce in unprecedented numbers; and the pressures of war forever changed the dynamics of family, marriage, gender, and class distinctions. Racism and sexism were still widespread, however, and neither minorities nor women were considered the equals of white men. The loyalties of Americans of German, Italian, and Japanese were questioned, and these people were often harassed during the war, none worse than the thousands of Japanese Americans who were forced from their homes along the West Coast and interned in camps.

The United States lost 291,557 dead and 671,846 wounded in nearly four years of war. In comparative terms this was a small number of lives lost compared with the approximately 30 million who perished in the Soviet Union, 20 million in China, or the 6 million European Jews, 5 million Poles, or 7.5 million Germans who died. It was great sacrifice nonetheless. American forces fought in almost every major theater of war and were of critical importance in each.

The War in the Asia-Pacific Theater

The United States bore the brunt of the war against Japan in the Asia-Pacific theater. Just a few days after their attack on Pearl Harbor, Japanese soldiers landed in the Philippines; the American forces stationed there surrendered to the Japanese in early April 1942 after a fierce three-month siege. The surrender led to the infamous 80-mile (130-kilometer) Bataan Death March, during which Filipino and American prisoners-of-war were beaten, and many starved to death after being deprived of food for the first three days of the march.

The fight was long and hard across the Pacific Ocean in what some refer to as a campaign of "island hopping." That required control of the sea, and in the first few months after Pearl Harbor the United States Navy was at a distinct disadvantage against the larger and better-prepared Japanese fleet. In early June the Americans defeated the bulk of the Japanese fleet at Midway in what many historians consider the most important naval engagement of the war. After Midway the Americans went on the offensive with two major thrusts: one in the southwest Pacific through New Guinea to the Philippines, and the other through the north Pacific.

From island bases the Americans could launch long-range bombing missions against Japan and strangle its shipping. From the South Pacific they tightened the noose even further. Fierce fighting throughout the islands dragged out for months, with pockets of Japanese troops holding out until the end of the war. The approach to Japan in early 1945 was marked by key American victories at Iwo Jima and Okinawa. Elsewhere in Asia, American servicemen were vital in British, Commonwealth, and Chinese efforts to dislodge the Japanese. American forces were also instrumental in Allied efforts to push the Japanese out of Southeast Asia and China in 1944–1945.

Africa and Italy

In Africa, American forces saw their first concerted action beginning in November 1942. With a lack of supplies, and the weight of American entry into the war, the Germans were ultimately doomed, and by May 1943 their forces in North Africa had either withdrawn to Europe or had been captured. In July 1943, Allied forces invaded Sicily, less than 100 miles (160 km) from the coast of Tunisia. In less than one month defenders on the island surrendered, and in Rome the fascist government of Benito Mussolini collapsed. In June 1944 Rome was liberated, but not until April 1945 did Allied forces manage to breach German defenses in the north, by which point the war was almost over.

D-Day and the Road to Berlin

On 6 June 1944 the Allies launched their biggest operation of World War II on the shores of Normandy, France. Operation Overlord, better known as "D-Day," saw 160,000 Allied troops landing on the shores of Normandy, under the leadership of future president General Dwight Eisenhower (1890–1969), the supreme commander of all Allied forces in Europe. (The term D-Day is a military term meaning the commencement of any military operation, but this particular D-Day has come to be known as *the* D-Day.) Despite their array of defenses from France to Denmark, the Germans were ill-prepared. Along five major beach sites American, British, and Canadian forces led the assaults. The Americans in particular endured high casualties. By mid-August Allied forces had broken through the last lines of German defenses en route to Paris. On 25 August the French capital was liberated by the Free French forces.

The Germans were, however, not finished. The bulk of their remaining soldiers in the west retreated into Belgium and Holland, where they amassed to protect against an invasion of Germany. In December Hitler ordered the last major German offensive: a drive aimed to break through primarily American lines in the Ardennes region of southern Belgium. The attack was stalled by American forces, however, and in January 1945 the Allies punched through remaining German defenses in various sectors and pushed into Germany itself. In mid-April, American forces met Soviet troops pushing

D-Day was a massive effort to land 160,000 Allied troops on the German-held coast of Normandy, in northern France. The troops arrived in amphibious LCTs ("landing craft, tank") under withering fire. Source: United States Navy.

west at the Elbe River in central Germany. On 30 April, Adolf Hitler committed suicide in his bunker in Berlin, and on 7 May 1945 (known as "V-E Day," short for "Victory in Europe") the last German forces offered their unconditional surrender.

The Atomic Bomb and Its Aftermath

As the Allies celebrated victory in Europe, the war against Japan ground on. Roosevelt died of a cerebral hemorrhage on 12 April 1945. His successor, Harry S. Truman (1884–1972, served 1945–1953), had been vice president for just eighty-two days before Roosevelt's death and knew little about management of the war or foreign affairs.

With the atomic bomb in mind, Truman warned Japanese leaders that unless the Allies received their unconditional and immediate surrender, they would face "prompt and utter destruction." When the Japanese did not heed his warning, Truman followed through on his threat. On 6 August 1945, the city of Hiroshima was destroyed by a single atomic bomb. Approximately ninety thousand people were killed instantly, and up to fifty thousand more died of radiation poisoning and other injuries in the first few months that followed. On 9 August a second atomic bomb was dropped on Japan, at Nagasaki. As many as seventy thousand died instantly in the second blast. Ironically, both cities were centers of Christianity in Japan and thus centers of opposition to the militaristic cult of Shinto.

The decision to use the atomic bomb against Japan remains highly controversial today. Some argue that it was an entirely political, not military, decision aimed at the Soviets—in effect a demonstration of American power calculated for the postwar balance of power. Others object to the timing of the bombs, in particular the one dropped on Nagasaki, pointing out that insufficient time was given the Japanese to respond. Still others consider the decision on more philosophical and moral grounds, accusing the Americans of not only war crimes but also crimes against humanity in unleashing such weapons under any circumstances. Those who defend the decision argue that the Japanese resolutely refused to surrender, and that based on fighting across the Pacific an invasion of the home islands by conventional means would have resulted in dramatically higher death counts on both sides. Defenders also note that the Japanese started the war and were guilty of horrendous war crimes such as the Bataan Death March and the infamous Rape of Nanjing, China. In addition, Japan had threatened to kill more than 100,000 Allied prisoners if an invasion of the home islands was launched. Whether or not the United States should have dropped the atomic bombs on Japan is a question that will never be answered conclusively.

What is certain is that despite its enormous power in 1945 the United States was not simply a military juggernaut. Amid the ashes of World War II the country took the leading role in rebuilding many countries around the world, including Germany and Japan. American values and ideas helped shape post-war institutions like the United Nations, the World Bank, the International Monetary Fund, and others that are still prominent international organizations today. And for many people, even with its inherent flaws and problems, the United States emerged as a symbol of hope, freedom, and progress in a world ravaged by war.

The Role of Franklin Delano Roosevelt (1882–1945)

Franklin Delano Roosevelt, commonly known by Americans by his initials "FDR," was president of the United States from 1933 to 1945: a record four terms. In a poll of historians and other academic experts conducted in 1948 by historian Arthur Schlesinger, Sr., and in similar polls thereafter, Roosevelt is consistently ranked with George Washington and Abraham Lincoln among the most highly regarded of presidents. Tested in crisis, Roosevelt led the United States through the Great Depression and World War II. Roosevelt also established the modern welfare state, and brought to power the "New Deal" voting coalition that shaped national politics to the end of the twentieth century. Students of leadership generally regard Roosevelt as the paragon of democratic statesmanship.

Roosevelt was born to a well-to-do family, a clan of Dutch ancestry that was part of New York's Hudson River gentry. His early life, typical of the American upper class, was filled by private tutoring, trips abroad, and the pursuit of hobbies. Roosevelt somewhat half-heartedly practiced law with a Wall Street firm until 1910, when he won a seat in the New York State Senate. In the election of 1912, FDR was an early backer of Woodrow Wilson. That backing got Roosevelt appointed assistant secretary of the navy.

In the summer of 1921, Roosevelt contracted polio. Despite a strenuous exercise regimen and a two-year period of convalescence, Roosevelt would never regain use of his legs. The disability, in the judgment of his wife, Eleanor, made Roosevelt more compassionate and patient. In 1926, he purchased a resort in Warm Springs, Georgia, that became a rehabilitation center. He mixed with the patients there, who, like him, were stricken with polio, encouraging their recovery.

In the mid-1920s, Roosevelt began his political comeback, becoming active in Democratic Party affairs and winning the New York race for governor in 1928. In 1933, Roosevelt launched his presidential bid as the choice of the progressive wing of the Democratic Party, the only truly national figure in the field. The general election against the widely unpopular President Herbert Hoover (1874–1964; in office 1929–1933), perhaps best remembered for the shantytowns dubbed "Hoovervilles," built by homeless people during the Depression, was an easier contest. (Hoover, however, had been an "uncannily able and insufferably pompous" Secretary of Commerce, in the words of author Bill Bryson, under presidents Harding and Coolidge.)

"There is nothing to fear but fear itself," President Roosevelt announced in his inaugural address, and with those words launched a historic period of legislative innovation and government expansion called the "first 100 days." During this period Roosevelt's landslide election, combined with the sense of despair over the Great Depression, licensed the president to exercise virtually unchecked power. Although some of the policies he enacted were contradictory and failed to help end the economic crisis, for Roosevelt the more important point was that vigorous activity would inspire a worn-out people to no longer despair.

> **There is nothing to fear but fear itself.**
>
> —PRESIDENT FRANKLIN D. ROOSEVELT

Roosevelt's New Deal program consistently made agricultural recovery and conservation top priorities. The Civilian Conservation Corps and other land management agencies restored lands ravaged by erosion and built recreation facilities in the national parks and forests. The Tennessee Valley Authority, which brought cheap electrical power to millions, focused on improving the living and working conditions of people living in that area of the Southeast. In addition, the New Deal sought to rationalize the nation's business system by temporarily ending bitter economic warfare through the National Industrial Recovery Act and its fair practice codes. The New Deal also ended child labor and introduced unemployment insurance and a social security program that guaranteed income for retired Americans. It encouraged the growth of industrial unionism and national legislation to define maximum hours and minimum wages.

Not everyone supported his programs. Emergency expenditures for relief poured millions into the economy, leading to record federal deficits, even though he had promised a balanced budget. If Congress or the courts balked at his programs, he used his executive powers to enact them. Some accused him of introducing a socialist agenda or of undermining free-market capitalism.

The events leading to American entry into World War II in late 1941 are the most controversial aspect of Roosevelt's leadership. In the early years of his presidency Roosevelt largely ignored foreign policy, focusing his attention on reviving the domestic economy. Roosevelt feared that a forceful, confrontational approach with the fascist powers would risk losing support for his New Deal policies. Although Roosevelt abhorred the fascist dictatorships, as late as 1941 he hoped to keep the United States out of war. The Japanese attack at Pearl Harbor in December 1941, of course, forced American entry into the war.

After the United States was committed to the war, Roosevelt's primary leadership tasks were to work in concert with the important Allied powers—Britain and the Soviet Union—as well as to keep up morale on the home front. Roosevelt's overarching goal was to marshal resources for an invasion of Europe across the English Channel, which he would achieve with great success with the D-Day invasion of Normandy.

The defining characteristic of Roosevelt's leadership was the tactical use of political manipulation, feint, and misdirection to serve the strategic goal of allowing him maximum flexibility and freedom to act. This approach was rooted in Roosevelt's personality: he liked practical jokes, enjoyed fooling people, and took particular satisfaction in clever decisions that tied adversaries in knots. All of Roosevelt's political machinations were conveyed with a mischievous humor that many—particularly members of the press—found disarming. Most of the public experienced Roosevelt's charismatic personal leadership through a medium the president exploited well: radio. Roosevelt delivered many informal addresses that were dubbed "fireside chats" because of the great warmth and intimacy that Roosevelt projected to the millions of American citizens who tuned in.

The twelve years of Roosevelt's presidency transformed the American political system. Roosevelt transformed the commitments of the Democratic Party from a states' rights agenda to a liberal party supportive of big government activism. Roosevelt shepherded legislation through Congress that created institutions that are still important today, including the Social Security Administration; the Securities and Exchange Commission (the group charged with preventing investors from engaging in inside trading, among other tasks); the Federal Deposit Insurance Corporation (FDIC), which guarantees the values of bank deposits; and many great public works projects initiated by the Public Works Administration.

Perhaps even more important than the revolutionary changes of the Roosevelt years were the aspects of American life that Roosevelt preserved. In an era when Europe fell under the sway of dictatorships of the left (Eastern Europe and Russia under communism) and right (Germany, Italy, and Spain under fascism), Roosevelt sought to preserve American constitutionalism by expanding the power of the federal government to preserve fundamental commitments to civil liberties, democratic elections, and the separation of powers.

Roosevelt also devoted considerable attention to the postwar international order, a matter that was a central topic of discussion at the Yalta Summit in 1945, held in the resort city of that name on the Soviet Union's Crimean Peninsula, until recently located in Ukraine. (Russia annexed Crimea in March of 2014, bringing up fears of a revival of the Cold War, discussed below, although most experts predicted it would likely be an economic rather than a military war.) There Churchill, Soviet leader Joseph Stalin, and Roosevelt agreed to create the United Nations, and allowed the USSR de facto dominance of Eastern Europe. Although some have condemned Roosevelt for capitulating too readily to Stalin's territorial demands, and view Yalta as Roosevelt's most glaring error of his long presidency, it is clear that Roosevelt had little choice. Soviet troops held the territory, and Stalin was not prepared to negotiate away land that he viewed was vital to the Soviets' military security. Perhaps most importantly, the defeat of Nazi Germany was mostly achieved by the Russians. The Soviets had lost tremendous numbers of troops in what is still called in Russia the "Great Patriotic War"; recent scholarship has calculated that four out of five German casualties in the war were lost to the Russians while fighting on the Eastern Front. Although Roosevelt did not live to see the end of World War II, the stage was set for the Cold War between the United States and the Soviet Union that was to follow.

The Cold War (c. 1945–1991)

The journalist Walter Lippmann coined the term *Cold War* in 1947 to describe the intense military, economic, and political rivalry between the United States and the Soviet Union following World War II. Although scholars generally identify 1945–1950 as the official start of the Cold War, its origins lie in the Russian Revolution of 1917, and it did not end until the collapse of the Soviet Union in 1991.

The 1939 German-Soviet Nonaggression Pact kept the Soviet Union from entering World War II until June 1941, when Hitler broke the pact and invaded, prompting the Soviet Union to enter on the side of the Allies. From the decisive 1943 Battle of Stalingrad onward—during which the Soviet and German armies between them lost roughly three times as many men as the United States would lose in the entire war—the Soviet Union was able to push German forces west and to establish a Soviet presence in Eastern Europe. With the collapse of the Third Reich, Allied occupation of Germany began. American officials considered Germany vital to the economic reconstruction of Western Europe, while the Soviet leader Joseph Stalin was determined to secure the Soviet Union's eastern border against future German threats. Washington moved quickly to enter nations newly liberated from the defeated Axis and retreating colonial powers (the French, Dutch, and British); Stalin similarly sought expansion of the Soviet Union.

The Soviet Union and the United Stated had respective ideological and economic interests in mind as they sought to rebuild parts of Europe and the Pacific. Stalin insisted on securing the USSR's western borders, and as a result, Poland, Finland, Romania, and Bulgaria came under Soviet influence at the conclusion of postwar boundary settlements. On 5 March 1946, Winston Churchill, no longer prime minister, spoke at Westminster College in Fulton, Missouri, of the "iron curtain" that had descended across Europe, referring to the communist presence. (Fulton today is the site of America's National Churchill Museum.)

The Truman Doctrine: American Intervention Abroad

On 12 March 1947, President Truman delivered a speech to a joint session of Congress that came to be known as the Truman Doctrine: a policy of containment directed at the Soviet Union. Truman offered support to any country—specifically naming Greece and Turkey—attempting to resist subjugation by the USSR. The implementation of the Truman Doctrine encouraged American intervention abroad, including the Central Intelligence Agency (CIA)-sponsored coup in 1953 that overthrew the Iranian premier, Muhammad Mosaddeq, as well as Guatemalan president Jacobo Ýrbenz in that same year. The most sustained intervention came when United States military advisors entered Vietnam in the mid-1950s. The American military presence in the region increased to 543,000 troops by 1969, and the United States remained embroiled in war until a cease-fire was agreed upon in 1973.

Although Soviet-American cooperation had led to the creation of the United Nations in 1945, postwar differences remained pronounced. The creation of the US-dominated World Bank (a global body whose presidents have always been American, by tradition, to the consternation of many around the world), the International Monetary Fund (IMF), and the United Nations Relief and Rehabilitation Administration (UNRRA) were intended to provide Western Europe with the stability needed to effectively resist the Soviet Union. In June 1947 the United States began the Marshall Plan (officially titled the European Recovery Program), named for Secretary of State George Marshall, to jump-start the European economy. The Soviet government refused to participate, dismissing the plan as economic imperialism.

Militarily, containment of the Soviet Union took the form of the North Atlantic Treaty Organization (NATO), a North Atlantic defense pact. The treaty, signed in Washington on 4 April 1949, assured collective security for its signatories. The Soviet Union responded to NATO with the Warsaw Pact in 1955, formed partly because of the perceived threat posed by West Germany's joining NATO earlier that year.

The Military-Industrial Complex and McCarthyism

In 1950 the United States National Security Council produced *NSC-68*, perhaps the most important postwar document concerning the growth of American power. In it the NSC urged vast increases in military spending to contain not only the Soviet Union

> In the councils of government, we must guard against the acquisition of unwarranted influence, whether sought or unsought, by the military-industrial complex. The potential for the disastrous rise of misplaced power exists and will persist.
>
> —PRESIDENT (AND RETIRED 5-STAR GENERAL) DWIGHT D. EISENHOWER

but also any country that threatened American interests. This gave great impetus to the so-called military-industrial complex, a term that had been coined in a speech in 1961 by President Dwight D. Eisenhower (1890–1969; held office 1953–1961), commonly known as "Ike." Defense spending and the arms race soared as the United States became involved in commercial and political affairs seemingly everywhere.

At home, this period of economic expansion created prosperity for working people, while the political force of McCarthyism and the "Red Scare" kept critics silent or ineffective. McCarthyism, named for Wisconsin Senator Joseph McCarthy, was a purge of left-wing union leaders and others in which the establishment targeted and attacked any sector of society or individual deemed subversive. Many people, in particular authors, film directors, and other artists, were "blacklisted" by the House Committee of Un-American Activities (HCUA) due to the supposed pro-communist nature of their work, and became virtually unemployable; the baseball team the Cincinnati Reds renamed themselves the "Redlegs" for several seasons in the 1959s, in reference to the color of their socks. (McCarthy was not a member of the HCUA; he was more concerned with security leaks, not Hollywood.)

The Nuclear Arms and Space Races

By 1955, the Cold War was heating up as a nuclear arms race got underway. The Soviets had exploded an atomic bomb in August 1949, and in 1952 the United States tested its first hydrogen bomb. (Hydrogen, or thermonuclear, bombs are roughly 500 times as powerful as atomic, or fission, bombs; the devastating bombs dropped on Hiroshima and Nagasaki were atomic bombs.) The Soviets followed with a hydrogen bomb test in 1953. The proliferation of arms can be attributed largely to a US government decision to maintain the United States' dominant global position and to persuade the American public to support larger defense budgets (and the higher taxes needed to support those budgets). The Soviet Union kept pace militarily and outstripped the United States in the space race. In 1957 the Soviets launched the first artificial satellite and successfully fired the first intercontinental ballistic missile.

The Cuban Missile Crisis of 1962 showed the world the dangers of the Cold War arms race. In 1958–1959, a communist revolution replaced the dictator Fulgencio Batista with Fidel Castro (b. 1926), who looked for support—including military support—from the Soviet Union. In 1962, when the United States discovered that the Soviet Union had placed nuclear missiles on the island, President John F. Kennedy (1917–1963; held office 1961–1963) imposed a naval blockade around Cuba to stop further arms shipments. A tense US-Soviet standoff, during which the fear of nuclear annihilation seemed to be a distinct possibility, lasted for fourteen days, but at last the Soviet Union agreed to remove its missiles and nuclear war was narrowly avoided. The United States made a secret pledge to remove its missiles from Turkey in return, and promised not to invade Cuba again, as it had tried, with spectacular lack of success, in the infamous Bay of Pigs invasion of April 1961. The Cuban Missile Crisis fueled the arms race as the Soviets, exposed as being militarily inferior, became determined to catch up to the United States.

> The most terrifying moment in my life was October 1962, during the Cuban Missile Crisis. I did not know all the facts—we have learned only recently how close we were to war—but I knew enough to make me tremble.
>
> —POLISH-BORN BRITISH PHYSICIST SIR JOSEPH ROTBLAT

President Kennedy made a dramatic announcement to Congress on 25 May 1961, calling for the achievement of landing a man on the moon and returning him safely to the Earth before the end of the decade; this was in response to Yuri Gagarin's becoming the first man in space a month earlier. The National Aeronautics and Space Administration (NASA) accelerated development of its lunar landing program, Project Apollo, to do so. In December of 1961, NASA announced Project Gemini, which would place two men into Earth orbit for extended periods. After a series of historic Gemini flights, *Apollo 8*, launched on 21 December 1968, successfully circumnavigated the moon, albeit after the USSR had managed to orbit the moon with an unmanned spacecraft, *Zond 5*. Satellite photos revealed that the Soviet moon rocket, the N-1, might soon be ready to take men to the moon. Project Apollo culminated in the *Apollo 11* mission, launched on 16 July 1969, with commander Neil Armstrong, lunar module pilot Edwin Eugene "Buzz" Aldrin, Jr., and command module pilot Michael Collins. Two weeks before the launch, a Soviet N-1 moon rocket exploded on its launch pad, effectively ending the moon race. Armstrong and Aldrin touched down on the surface of the moon on 20 July 1969, watched by a television audience of approximately a billion people. NASA had met President Kennedy's challenge, although Kennedy was no longer alive to appreciate the space program's remarkable success.

The Cold War in Asia

In Asia, the United States received a blow in 1949 when Mao Zedong (1893–1976) and the Communists triumphed over Chiang Kai-shek (1887–1975) and the Nationalists in China's long civil war. Mao established the People's Republic of China, but the United States refused to recognize it, continuing to treat Chiang Kai-shek's government, which had fled to the island of Taiwan, as the legitimate government of all China. Although Mao's approach to communism was at variance with Moscow's, the 1950s saw the formation of a Sino-Soviet alliance.

Korea, which had been annexed by Japan in 1910, had been freed from Japanese domination at the end of World War II, but had been divided into two zones of occupation (an American zone and a Soviet zone), with the thirty-eighth parallel as the dividing line. On 25 June 1950, communist North Korea made a bid to reunite the two halves by force, launching an attack on South Korea. In the absence of the Soviet delegate, the United Nations Security Council passed a resolution that called on UN member nations to come to South Korea's aid, and President Truman soon ordered American aircraft and warships into action below the thirty-eighth parallel.

The two sides battled up and down the entire length of the Korean peninsula, with the North first driving US-led forces to the bottom of the peninsula, and the US-led forces then pushing the North Korean forces back almost to the border with China. China then lent its support to North Korea, and the US-led forces were pushed back behind the thirty-eighth parallel. The Korean War—technically the "Korean Conflict," as there was never an actual declaration of war—having become a stalemate, on 27 July 1953 an armistice was signed. Korea remained divided along the thirty-eighth parallel.

The Korean War is often known in the United States as the "forgotten war," as it tends to be overshadowed by World War II and the Vietnam War, although over 36,000 Americans, 58,000 South Koreans, 215,000 North Koreans, and somewhere between 100,000 and 400,000 Chinese soldiers lost their lives in the "conflict." (The lower figure is China's estimate; the higher figure is the US estimate.)

The Vietnam conflict, discussed in more detail in the following section, was a significant example of the Cold War playing out in Asia. After World War II, Vietnam resisted French attempts to return the nation to its colonial status. Like Korea, Vietnam was divided into a communist-controlled northern portion (North Vietnam) and a non-communist southern portion (South Vietnam). Fearing that communist victory in Vietnam would lead to other nations in

Southeast Asia becoming communist—what had become known as the "domino theory" after a 1954 press conference held by President Eisenhower—the United States opposed North Vietnam. In the end, however, the United States withdrew its forces and, in 1976, Vietnam was reunified as the Socialist Republic of Vietnam.

> **Mr. Gorbachev, tear down this wall!**
>
> —PRESIDENT RONALD REAGAN, SPEAKING AT BRANDENBURG GATE, WEST BERLIN, 12 JUNE 1987

Détente and the End of the Cold War

The early 1970s saw Cold War tensions diminishing. Sensing a Sino-Soviet split, President Richard Nixon (1913–1994; held office 1969–1974) sought limited cooperation with the People's Republic of China. Détente led to arms reduction talks between American and Soviet leaders, although they failed to produce lasting disarmament legislation. President Ronald Reagan (1911–2004; held office 1981–1989) condemned the Soviet expansionist strategy and produced unprecedented military budgets and furthered the use of covert operations.

When Mikhail S. Gorbachev (b. 1931) became general secretary of the Communist Party in 1985, he called for a restructuring of the hobbled Soviet economy (called *perestroika*) and the liberalization of authoritarian political systems (*glasnost*). *Perestroika* and *glasnost* soon became two of the few Russian words known to most Americans. In 1986, Gorbachev stopped Soviet deployment of intermediate-range missiles and froze nuclear weapons tests. He withdrew Soviet forces from Afghanistan in 1988 and reduced support for socialist rebels in Nicaragua, and Cuban troops in Angola. Despite the Reagan arms buildup, Gorbachev cut military spending in the interest of economic rebuilding. In 1989, Gorbachev informed East European officials that Soviet forces would no longer intervene in any uprisings. (Several had been put down over the years, notably the Hungarian Uprising, put down in 1956, and the Prague Spring, put down in 1968.) Within a year, popular uprisings in Hungary, Poland, Czechoslovakia, Romania, Bulgaria, and finally, East Germany, ousted communist leaders from power in those former satellite nations.

The Berlin Wall, erected in 1961 to prevent the flight of East Germans to West Germany, came down in November 1989, with free elections promised for 1990. In 1990, Lithuania, Estonia, Latvia, and Ukraine declared their independence, and in the same year Gorbachev was awarded the Nobel Peace Prize. On Christmas Day 1991, the Soviet Union ceased to exist.

The Vietnam War and the Anti-War Movement

The United States's military involvement in the Vietnam conflict that had begun in the mid-1950s did not end until 1973, when the last US troops were pulled out of the country. (South Vietnam did not surrender until 1975; the country was reunited in 1976.) The war called for an enormous investment of personnel, equipment, money, and national prestige. Over the years of American involvement, 2,594,000 military personnel served in Vietnam and a larger number supported the war from bases in the United States, the Philippines, Guam, and elsewhere. Over 1.3 million Vietnamese military personnel died in the war, as did over one million civilians. 58,220 American soldiers were killed and over 600,000 wounded.

The war was controversial among the American public, who could view it up close through coverage on the nightly television news. Opinion polls showed that in 1965 sixty-one percent of Americans supported the war; by 1971 the figure had dropped to twenty-eight percent. The nation was divided between "hawks"—those who were in favor of the war—and "doves"—those who were not. Protestors expressed their opposition during thousands of anti-war and peace marches, rallies, demonstrations, and teach-ins across the nation. It was a tumultuous time in America's civil history. The hawks decried the doves' now-familiar peace symbol, which had been introduced in Britain in 1958 to promote nuclear disarmament, as the "footprint of the American chicken," while returning veterans were often greeted with jeers upon arrival by those opposed to the war.

Two events in particular galvanized public opinion against the war. The first was the anti-war demonstration in August 1968 at the Democratic National Convention in Chicago, which turned into a violent riot when police attacked the demonstrators. The riot was followed by the circus-like trial of the "Chicago Seven," which did little to help the image of the judicial system. The second event was the killing of four student protestors and the wounding of nine others by National Guard troops at Kent State University in Ohio in 1970.

The war had a profound impact on American society. The loss of life and the loss of the war made government officials wary of going to war again, and if they had to go to war, they wanted to be sure they could win. The war also called into question the quality of the policy decision-making at the highest level of government, as well as the ability of military commanders. The war also ended the presidential career of Lyndon Johnson, who chose not to run for reelection in 1968. He was the fourth of five presidents (including Truman, Eisenhower, Kennedy, and Nixon) with a role in the war.

"Ohio"

Tin soldiers and Nixon's coming,
We're finally on our own.
This summer I hear the drumming,
Four dead in Ohio.

Gotta get down to it
Soldiers are cutting us down
Should have been done long ago.
What if you knew her
And found her dead on the ground
How can you run when you know?

—Neil Young, © 1970 Cotillion/Broken Arrow

One of the main objections to the war was that men were drafted to serve in a war they did not support. The war was especially unpopular with African Americans, upset over President Johnson's increases of taxes to support the war and related cuts to anti-poverty programs. The Reverend Martin Luther King, Jr., discussed in the next chapter, wrote, "America would never invest the necessary funds or energies in rehabilitation of its poor as long as Vietnam continued to draw men and skills and money like some demonic, destructive suction tube." The draft was ended in 1973; the United States has had an all-volunteer military since then.

The United States also suffered a long-term loss of political prestige among some allies, particularly Japan and New Zealand, the latter a country that would go on to ban all nuclear vessels, including those of its American ally, from its shores in 1984. The same policies were interpreted elsewhere in the world, including in South Korea, as demonstrating American resolve to support non-communist governments under threat. Beyond intergovernmental relations, however, the conflict had a broad impact in stirring anti-Americanism in Europe, Asia, and beyond. The post–World War II image of American soldiers as liberators was largely displaced by a less favorable image as the United States's involvement in Vietnam produced civilian casualties and incidents of military misconduct, such as the notorious My Lai Massacre of 1968, in which over three hundred unarmed men, women, and children were slain by enraged American soldiers. Together, these developments contributed to emerging popular notions of American military power wielded without mercy or reason.

Many people from both nations were left with long-lasting and devastating physical and emotional scars from the war. As was the case following the Revolutionary War fought against Britain, the former enemies eventually settled their differences. The United States and the Socialist Republic of Vietnam resumed diplomatic relations in 1995, and have enjoyed an amicable relationship since.

Post-Cold War Era

The end of the Cold War was signaled by the fall of the Berlin Wall dividing East and West Germany in 1989 and the collapse of the Soviet Union in 1991. Since then, some would say the United States has been the sole remaining superpower, and although this condition has meant unprecedented political influence by the United States in world affairs in the post–Cold War period, constraints on American power remain.

Is the world a safer place now than it was during the Cold War? On the one hand, the danger of MAD (the aptly titled official military doctrine known as "Mutual Assured Destruction," referring to the equality of US/Soviet nuclear capabilities) has receded, although China remains a nuclear power, and the threat of nuclear weapons being stolen from less stable nations with nuclear arms—particularly Pakistan and Russia—or sold on the black market exists. Generally speaking, however, the threat of massive global destruction has been reduced.

The United States has emerged as by far the greatest military power in the world, with more power than any nation or empire in history. It has the world's largest economy (China is second, and according to some calculations will overtake the United States this year) and spends more on defense than the next ten nations on the list combined. If one supports the American worldview and role in contemporary international relations, then the foregoing figures provide some comfort. If one questions the American worldview, however, the figures indicate something to be feared—a country, in theory, without an external control in international affairs.

What limits American power in a post–Cold War era? One of the most significant factors is the cost of acting as the policeman to the world. In the case of Iraq, for example, the United States government was willing to invade the country without the support of key European allies such as France and Germany. It had the military power to complete the invasion and to remove Saddam Hussein. Even before major hostilities ceased, however, the administration of President George W. Bush (b. 1946; held office 2001–2009) began pressing other countries to support the cost of the war and the continued policing of the country. Although the military power of the

Is the United States the Only Superpower?

What, exactly, is a superpower? Some believe that only the United States qualifies for this status, while others think countries such as Russia, India, Japan, and, especially, China deserve the title. The *Merriam-Webster Online Dictionary* provides two definitions of the word "superpower":

    a. an extremely powerful nation; specifically one of a very few dominant states in an era when the world is divided politically into these states and their satellites

    b. an international governing body able to enforce its will upon the most powerful states

People who believe that the United States is the world's only remaining superpower, following the 1991 demise of the Soviet Union, argue that only countries whose influence is felt in every corner of the globe merit the title "superpower," which is certainly true of the United States. In 1999, French Defense Minister Hubert Vedrine called the United States a "hyperpower," claiming "superpower" was insufficient for a nation with such unprecedented power. China, however, because of its strong economic standing, is a strong contender for the title of superpower, a position that will no doubt grow as China's influence on world affairs continues to strengthen in the course of the twenty-first century.

United States is overwhelming, its capacity to fund major military campaigns and then pay for subsequent operations stretches the nation's budget and risks the support of the American people. One estimate by economists Joseph Stiglitz and Linda J. Barnes put the figure in 2009 at roughly 3 billion dollars per week for the wars in Iraq and Afghanistan. Moreover, given the country's substantial budget deficit, it is dependent on foreign countries to service its debt.

The Rise of Terrorism

The rise of terrorism is also, to an extent, a response to the dominance of the United States in world affairs. Because currently no country can match the United States in military power, the only real way to attack Americans and their allies, according to many enemies, is through acts of terrorism. In this respect the world continues to face danger, but it is more the danger of random acts of violence, and not quite the same level of danger of massive nuclear destruction as was the case during the Cold War. This fact is the underlying reality of the terrorist attacks of September 11, 2001.

> **With the end of the Cold War, international politics moves out of its Western phase, and its center-piece becomes the interaction between the West and non-Western civilizations and among non-Western civilizations.**
>
> —HARVARD PROFESSOR SAMUEL HUNTINGTON

Contemporary terrorism, such as that promulgated by al-Qaeda, is also attempting to promote the concept of a battle of religions, along the lines of Harvard professor Samuel Huntington's article "The Clash of Civilizations." Huntington's basic premise, written before September 11, is that future wars will occur along cultural, rather than economic or ideological, lines, with the Islamic world in conflict with the Russian Orthodox, Chinese, African, and Western worlds; "flashpoints" will occur in such places as Turkey where the Islamic and non-Islamic worlds meet. If Huntington's premise is to be accepted—and there are many who do not accept it—the volatility of the Middle East in particular does not bode well for long-term peace, and because other nations depend on the region's oil, this volatility is a significant problem for the future.

Liberal thinkers saw the immediate post–Cold War period as a time when multilateral approaches to global problems were predominant. The administration of Bill Clinton (b. 1946; held office 1993–2001) generally pursued a policy of inclusion, of discussion over conflict, although Clinton did lead the charge to what is generally seen as a just war in the case of Serbia—a war to stop atrocities that was launched in defiance of the United Nations. Where conflict did occur, as in Somalia and the states of the former Yugoslavia, it was conducted under United Nations auspices.

The Bush administration, however, clearly indicated that American interests came first and that it was willing to make decisions without the support of the United Nations. The clearest example of this policy was the decision to invade Iraq in 2003. This policy is an outcome of the United States being—at least at the time—the only remaining superpower. It may be useful for the United States to have allies, but if necessary the United States has sufficient power to make independent decisions. The Obama administration (2009–present) has sought to create closer ties with allies and to rely on negotiation rather than threats and war. And when war was necessary, as in supporting the overthrow of the Libyan government, it preferred to do so in cooperation with allies. The Obama administration's handling of the Syria crisis, however, confused many around the world. Upon finding that Syrian president Bashar Hafez al-Assad in all likelihood had used chemical weapons to kill hundreds of his opponents in that country's civil war, Obama first threatened immediate strikes by the United States, only to backtrack by asking for Congress to ratify the decision to go to war: a request that was denied to the president by a Congress (and a nation) weary of war and the huge amounts of money necessary to support those wars. The civil war in Syria continues, with no end in sight.

The United States has the world's largest economy (using gross national product as the measure), and Japan and China depend significantly on American consumers for their export success. Although this consumerism may be substantially funded by US debt, a strong belief remains worldwide in the strength of the US economy. The United States therefore remains an integral part of the global economy in the post–Cold War period.

Accompanying the significant role of the United States in global trade is the continuing spread of American culture. With the increase in the ease and speed of communications, American values and customs, as well as films, music, and fashion, are rapidly transmitted around the world. Although this trend produces a degree of backlash in some countries, the influence of the United States in cultural terms is, no doubt, greater than ever before. This is not to say that all countries accept American ideals, however; one need not look any further than the anti-US demonstrations associated with the invasion of Iraq for evidence.

The post–Cold War world in an analytical sense has become a much more complicated place. In a bipolar world, with the USSR on one side and the United States on the other, and various parts of the world cooperating with one superpower or the other, a person could relatively easily understand the motivations and decisions of different countries. Today this is no longer the case. The self-interest of each country might involve decisions that a decade or two ago would have seemed unthinkable; the situation is further complicated by the common practice of putting economic considerations at the forefront of international relations.

The post–Cold War period is an uncertain one. Flashpoints include North Korea and the Taiwan-China relationship in Asia; and Israel and Iran in the Middle East. What part should the United States play in these flashpoints? How should the United States respond to an emergent China as a substantial economic as well as military power; indeed, as some would have it, a superpower? In short, although the post–Cold War period may not be as overtly dangerous as the Cold War period, significant challenges lie ahead for the United States.

September 11, 2001 and its Aftermath

People have said that the world was forever changed on September 11, 2001 by the terrorist attacks on the World Trade Center in New York City and on the Pentagon in Washington, DC, that took the lives of nearly 3,000 people. Jean-Marie Colombanii of France's *Le Monde* newspaper echoed the sentiment of millions around the world when he said, "We are all Americans." (In general, however, *Le Monde* severely criticized US foreign policy and at least partially blamed it for the attacks.) The rest of the world seemed to feel the shock and pain that Americans felt. For a moment in history the terrorist attacks bound the world together in horror as the enormity of the events overwhelmed the public consciousness.

In the immediate aftermath of 9-11, as the date is commonly called by Americans, the world expressed solidarity and support for the United States. Messages of condolence poured in to American embassies and consulates. From Europe to Africa to Southeast Asia, sympathy for the United States as a victim of terrorism manifested itself in tacit support for apprehension of those responsible for the attacks. Suspicion immediately fell on the terrorist network al-Qaeda and its Taliban supporters in Afghanistan. In countries around the world people favored extradition and trial of the suspects rather than military action.

International public opinion was slow to recognize that the United States had decided al-Qaeda and the Taliban were legitimate targets for military retribution. Despite the growing political consensus for the invasion of Afghanistan, public sympathy for the United States did not manifest itself in support of the invasion. In cities as diverse as London, Paris, Berlin, Moscow, Damascus, Islamabad, Tokyo, and Jakarta, thousands of antiwar protesters filled the streets in opposition to the invasion of Afghanistan.

A majority of the world saw the military campaign to oust the Taliban as collective punishment of innocent civilians. Each image of an Afghan child killed by high-altitude bombing reinforced the notion that the United States was punishing innocent Muslims. Resentment spread throughout the world, especially in the Arab world, as increasing numbers of people questioned the persistent use of aerial bombing in a country with no capacity to resist.

Despite the acquiescence of Muslim countries to the attack on Afghanistan, leaders in Muslim countries increasingly faced domestic resistance by allying themselves with the United States. Throughout the Islamic world—from Indonesia to Turkey, from Pakistan to Saudi Arabia—Muslims across the political spectrum, from traditionalist Islamists to secular nationalists, expressed their displeasure with the

American military campaign in Afghanistan because they perceived the attack on Afghanistan as an attack on the *umma* (believers).

In short order the US-dominated alliance attacked al-Qaeda training camps in Afghanistan and quickly toppled the Taliban regime. The job of ridding Afghanistan of enemies was hardly over, however, and in 2009 the Obama administration turned its attention to that country, increasing troop levels and training for the Afghan military and police, winning the allegiance of local leaders, and attempting to stabilize the government. As of 2014 the United States is winding down its involvement in the nation, and the Obama administration has stated that it will withdraw all troops sometime in the near future.

After the ouster of the Taliban regime from Afghanistan, the United States turned its attention to Iraqi leader Saddam Hussein (1937–2006), and began linking al-Qaeda leader Osama bin Laden (1957–2011) and Saddam Hussein's network with Iraq. Despite the repeated denials of Saddam Hussein's regime that it possessed weapons of mass destruction, justification quickly built for the invasion of Iraq. The Bush administration believed that it could invade Iraq, with or without the consent of the United Nations, because the administration expected a replay of Afghanistan: military resistance would dissipate in the face of superior firepower. Iraqis would welcome the Americans and their allies—after all, although many nations expressed their disapproval of invading Iraq, no one claimed that Saddam Hussein was a desirable neighbor or ally—and the US-led coalition would install a regime capable of controlling and rebuilding Iraq. The overthrow of the regime (including the televised death by hanging of Saddam Hussein) was quick and relatively easy, but the rebuilding and stabilization effort that followed was poorly planned and implemented. The job remains unfinished as of 2014 as the United States leaves Iraq to manage its own affairs, with the result that there has been a huge surge in suicide bombings in Iraq: mainly revenge attacks between Sunnis and Shiites, whose sectarian conflict had been kept in check while Saddam Hussein was in power.

In the aftermath of September 11 the subsequent US-led military campaigns in Afghanistan and Iraq altered international relations and redefined global priorities. The United States declared it would make no distinction between suspected terrorists and the country that harbors them. It also declared that the United States was henceforth engaged in a "war against global terrorism" that would last indefinitely. In short, the United States disregarded international laws and norms in its global pursuit of self-defense. The United States would define who "global terrorists" were and would pursue them (and their assets) wherever they might be, in whatever manner was deemed necessary. In essence, the United States would use its global reach and military superiority to launch unilateral, asymmetrical warfare against its enemies, real or imagined. Further damaging the international image of the United States was the perceived double-standard concerning the rule of law and human rights. The United States has long been the defender of human rights around the world, but places such as Guantanamo Bay in Cuba, Abu Ghraib prison in Iraq, and Bagram in Afghanistan became synonymous with the torture and unconstitutional long-term detention of Muslim prisoners, tarnishing the reputation of the United States as well as undermining American standards of judicial fairness.

The Iraq and Afghanistan invasions and wars were just one part of the much larger War on Terror (the Obama administration ceased using the label in May 2009) to protect the United States from future terrorist attacks like those on September 11. Other key components of the war include the detention without speedy trial of suspected terrorists, the "rendition" of suspected terrorists (i.e., sending them to nations where torture might be used to obtain information), military assistance and training in counter-terrorism for allied nations, intelligence-sharing with allies, and the use of drones (unmanned aircraft) to locate and kill known and suspected terrorists. One whole array of activities has focused on enhanced homeland security and includes more stringent entry requirements for foreign visitors, inspections at airports, enhanced border security, and far wider and deeper intelligence gathering and cooperation between agencies to identify terrorists and terrorist plots.

This broader intelligence gathering has proved controversial after the release of classified details of the programs by National Security Agency (NSA) contractor Edward Snowden and Army private Bradley Manning's leak of hundreds of thousands of secret government documents to the anti-secrecy website Wikileaks. Critics charge that the telephone and Internet data gathering activities are too broad and too secretive, and that they infringe on Americans' right of privacy. Supporters, including the Obama administration and most members of Congress, argue that such measures have prevented numerous terrorist attacks and are approved of by a judicial panel. The key question of how effective these methods are is difficult to answer because the information is not made public for security reasons: a "Catch-22" of sorts. The idea of human rights, explored in the next chapter, is an ongoing concern.

CHAPTER FIVE:
THE PURSUIT OF
CIVIL RIGHTS

The American advancement of civil rights over the past two centuries has, in many ways, laid the foundation for equality across the world. Even so, the fight for civil rights and equality continues to be waged on many fronts. The Vietnam War era, in particular, was a time of sweeping change across society as people demanded their rights.

The term *civil rights* has no clear definition in the United States. The American civil rights movement is generally thought of as the movement to gain equal rights for African Americans, but there are also women's rights movements, gay rights movements, workers' rights movements, etc. Generally speaking, civil rights are those privileges given to citizens of a country. Civil rights are not the same as civil liberties—rights that are specifically granted by the Constitution or other legal documents, such as the right to a fair trial in a court or the right to vote—although the terms are often used interchangeably. As an example, a black employee of a company does *not* have the legal right to a promotion, because getting promoted is not a guaranteed civil liberty; that employee, however, *does* have the civil right not to be denied a promotion based on his or her race.

Thomas Jefferson warned that rights must be given to the individual and protected from government intrusion. John Locke suggested that the rights to life, liberty, and property are part of a social contract between the government and its citizens. Throughout history people immigrating to the United States have expected to find a land of freedom and equality. This expectation remains an important part of the civil rights movement.

The United States has an uneven history when it comes to full civil rights for all its citizens. Native Americans were denied basic rights and forced from their lands. Most people of African ancestry were enslaved until 1865 and attained full legal rights only in the 1960s. Women could not vote in national elections until 1920. Jews, Catholics,

A café in Durham, North Carolina, with separate entrances for "White" and "Colored" patrons, 1940. Source: Library of Congress. Photo by Jack Delano.

Muslims, Jehovah's Witnesses, and other religious groups have been discriminated against throughout the nation's history; the Mormon religion of Republican candidate Mitt Romney came under intense scrutiny by many conservative mainstream Christians during his failed bid for the presidency in 2008, over 200 years after freedom of religion was ensured by the First Amendment. Thus, for much of its history the only class of Americans who enjoyed full civil rights were white men, or more precisely, wealthy white men. Groups who were denied civil rights have long fought for full rights, with several of these movements becoming especially active and successful in the last half of the twentieth century and early twenty-first centuries.

The Civil Rights Movement

In theory, the end of slavery in 1865 and the amendments to the Constitution between 1865 and 1870 that afforded African Americans citizenship and the right to vote, in addition to the reconstruction of the South from 1863 to 1877, gave African Americans the same civil rights as white Americans. The reality was that segregation and discrimination in the South, and indifference to inequality in the North, meant that African Americans did not have the equal opportunity guaranteed to all Americans. The civil rights movement was a mass movement led by African Americans, with the support of some whites, meant to remedy this history of injustice. The movement began after the Civil War, but the term "civil rights movement," often capitalized, is usually meant for activities during the 1950s and 1960s, mainly in the South. It involved freedom marches, sit-ins, court cases, negotiation, petitioning of the government, and voter registration drives organized by a number of civil rights organizations, including the National Association for the Advancement of Colored People (NAACP), the Congress of Racial Equality (CORE), the Student Non-Violent Coordinating Committee (SNCC), and the Southern Christian Leadership Conference (SCLC).

The civil rights era of the 1950s and 1960s was launched by the Supreme Court decision in *Brown v. Board of Education of Topeka, Kansas*. The ruling banned racial segregation in public schools, and led to later controversial government actions such as school busing and affirmative action to achieve a racial balance in public schools. Whites, especially in the South, objected to the decision and refused to open schools to black students, and resorted to violence: by individuals, by groups like the Ku Klux Klan, and by law enforcement officials who tried to prevent freedom marches and similar demonstrations. The "freedom fighters" persisted, however, sometimes joined by blacks and whites from the North. The cruel repression of the peaceful marchers forced whites in the North to finally acknowledge the harsh segregation in the South. The violence turned public opinion in favor of the civil rights movement, with Reverend King of Atlanta as its foremost public persona.

In the 1960s real change took place. In 1960 the Supreme Court banned segregation in interstate transport, making it possible and more comfortable for blacks to travel by bus and train. In 1964 Congress passed the Civil Rights Act, which banned segregation in public places and racial and gender discrimination in employment. But the major unresolved issue was voting rights, as most African Americans in the South still were prevented from voting by means both legal and illegal. Various local and state laws in place since Reconstruction known as "Jim Crow laws," discussed in Chapter Three, prevented blacks in the South from being able to vote by, for instance, limiting voting rights to literate property owners. A voting registration drive marred by violence was not especially successful, but it did force Congress to act. In 1965 it passed the Voting Rights Act, which banned Jim Crow-style laws.

As of 2014, the goals of the civil rights movement have not yet been fully met. African Americans do have a far greater role in the political system, although, with the notable exception of President Barack Obama, most African American legislators represent mostly black districts carved out by white-controlled legislatures. Discrimination in housing, employment, health care, and education occurs less than it did before the movement, but African Americans, on average, still earn less than whites, live in lower-quality housing, have a higher rate of infant mortality, and live shorter lives. African Americans are around four times more likely to be murdered than the national average.

President Lyndon Johnson signing the Voting Rights Act in the Capitol Rotunda, as Martin Luther King, Jr. (below and to the left of the portrait on the wall) and other civil rights leaders look on. Washington, DC, 6 August 1965. Source: National Archives.

As with most mass movements, efforts to gain full rights for African Americans have been pursued both by leaders and by many brave but anonymous people whose names have been forgotten to history. Of the many notable figures from the Civil Rights Movement, two of the most influential were the long-lived W. E. B. Du Bois (1868–1963) and the Reverend Martin Luther King, Jr. (1929–1968), gunned down in his prime. Both are profiled below.

W. E. B. Du Bois

William Edward Burghardt Du Bois (pronounced "Due *Boys*") was one of the most important African American leaders in the United States in the first half of the twentieth century. He was a man of many talents who made significant contributions as a journalist, research scholar, sociologist, historian, novelist, pamphleteer, civil rights leader, and teacher. It is almost impossible to undertake a study of African Americans without encountering W. E. B. Du Bois's name at every turn.

He was instrumental in the formation of the Niagara movement, an organization that was the precursor to the National Association for the Advancement of Colored

People. He was also a major promoter of the NAACP's publication program and served as editor of its magazine, *The Crisis*, from 1910 to 1934. As editor of *The Crisis* (the title of which underlines the state of affairs for most African Americans at the time), Du Bois exercised considerable influence on African American politics and thought.

During a long and productive lifetime, Du Bois changed his opinions on issues of the day many times. A complex and unpredictable personality, he could appear as assertive, accommodative, practical, obtuse, an activist, a joiner, and a loner. Despite his many personal and intellectual inconsistencies, Du Bois's thoughts and actions were united by a

Photograph of sociologist, activist, and writer W. E. B. Du Bois, taken in Atlanta, Georgia, in 1900. Source: New York Public Library.

single goal: to achieve what he saw as the betterment of all "people of color"—African Americans and Africans alike.

Du Bois was born on 23 February 1868, in Great Barrington, Massachusetts. In 1884 he graduated as valedictorian of Great Barrington High School. He married (twice) and had two children. In 1888, Du Bois graduated from Fisk College (now Fisk University), a historically black institution in Nashville, Tennessee. Growing up in Great Barrington, he experienced subtle discrimination, but it was in Tennessee that Du Bois first experienced overt racial discrimination. Du Bois earned a second bachelor's degree (1890) and a master of arts degree (1892) from Harvard University in Cambridge, Massachusetts. From 1892 to 1893 he studied at the University of Berlin, where he was greatly influenced by the socialist scholar Edward Bernstein. In 1895 Du Bois was awarded the first doctorate ever to be granted to an African American by Harvard University.

Du Bois championed the power of the ballot, but he also developed a concept of what he termed the "Talented Tenth"—his ideal of an elite group of African American leaders who, he believed, were obligated to lift the illiterate and poverty-stricken African American masses. A number of critics suggested that Du Bois's notion of the "Talented Tenth" could become a limiting, restraining, and subordinating concept for the African American masses.

Du Bois was one of the first advocates of feminism in the early twentieth century. He praised African American women for their great courage in the face of oppression,

Something to think about:

There is great contradiction between the founding fathers' espousal of equality for their countrymen and their simultaneous acceptance of the institution of slavery. What factors led to the civil rights movement taking place in the twentieth century but not the eighteenth?

and in a 1917 essay supporting women's suffrage, he asserted that much of the actual work of the world was performed by women—not men.

Du Bois's views on civil rights clashed with those of another prominent and influential black leader of the period, Booker T. Washington (1856–1915). Washington promoted a philosophy of accommodation to racism, urging African Americans to accept discrimination—at least for the time being. Washington encouraged African Americans to elevate themselves through hard work. He believed that African Americans had to acquire the skills necessary for economic advancement, and that once a genuinely educated, skilled, and relatively prosperous African American people came into existence, political rights would naturally follow. The Tuskegee Institute, founded in Alabama in 1891 with Washington as its first principal, aimed to do just that, and was quite successful in its efforts. Washington, unlike Du Bois, was born a slave and lived in the segregated South; some would argue that he contributed more to the creation of that Southern black middle class that led the civil rights movement in the twentieth century than did Du Bois. Du Bois, along with some other African American leaders, argued that Washington's strategy could only serve to perpetuate the further oppression of African Americans.

Du Bois was a strong advocate of "Pan-Africanism"—the belief that all people of African descent had common interests and should work together in a common struggle for freedom. He was critical of the Jamaican politician, writer, and orator Marcus Garvey (1887–1940) and the "Back to Africa" movement, which advocated the repatriation of African Americans to Africa. It is ironic that of the many prominent African American leaders who actively participated in the Back to Africa debate, only Du Bois—who opposed the Back to Africa movement—actually ever moved to Africa.

In the 1890s, Du Bois had been an outspoken supporter of capitalism. He urged African Americans to support African American businesses. But still he had reservations about the capitalist system. By 1905 he had become thoroughly convinced of the advantages of socialism. He joined the Socialist Party in 1912 and remained sympathetic to Marxist ideals for the rest of his life. After 1948, Du Bois moved further leftward politically. He publicly identified with pro-Russian causes and was indicted in 1951 as an "unregistered agent for a foreign power." Although acquitted of all charges, Du Bois became increasingly disillusioned with the United States. In 1962, he renounced his American citizenship and moved to Ghana, where he died on 27 August 1963. In 2005, in Du Bois's hometown of Great Barrington, the local school board voted to name the new elementary school "Muddy Brook Elementary School" (after a small stream in the area) rather than naming it for Du Bois, as many town residents wanted, in part because of perceived opposition to his association with the Communist Party.

Du Bois possessed an independent spirit. He could never confine himself to any one ideology, party, or organization. Nevertheless, he was both willing and able to compromise his beliefs in order to attain a higher goal: the betterment of all peoples of color. His thoughts and actions would resonate with activists for generations to come.

Martin Luther King, Jr.

In presenting Martin Luther King, Jr. with the Nobel Peace Prize in 1964, Gunnar Jahn, chairman of the Nobel Committee, stated, "He is the first person in the Western world to have shown us that a struggle can be waged without violence. He is the first to make the message of brotherly love a reality in the course of his struggle, and he has brought this message to all men, to all nations and races." King's leadership during the civil rights movement of the 1950s and 1960s was crucial to passage of both the 1964 Civil Rights Act and the 1965 Voting Rights Act, and he remains the figure most identified with the struggles and achievements of the civil rights movement seeking equality for African Americans.

Martin Luther King, Jr.'s family had a long history of Afro-Baptist leadership. His maternal great-grandfather, Willie Williams, was a slave exhorter (a preacher who used biblical exhortations to try to sustain slaves in their labors) on a plantation in Greene County, Georgia. His son, Adam Daniel Williams, had only a few months of formal education when he left the plantations of east Georgia in 1887 for Atlanta. There, he became the pastor of the small Ebenezer Baptist Church. At his death, Williams was succeeded as pastor by his son-in-law, Martin Luther King, Sr., who went on to nurture a congregation of respectable working-class people, many of whom were women working six-and-a-half days a week in the homes of Atlanta's white population.

Born on 16 January 1929, Martin Luther King, Jr. was the second of three children born to the Reverend Martin Luther King, Sr. and Alberta Williams King. He entered Atlanta's Morehouse College at the young age of fifteen, graduating

> **Hold fast by Christ! He is the mighty One! He will help! He will do everything well! Trust in him my sister, my brother. Call upon Him. Yes. Yes. Hold fast by Christ! He is the Lord!**
>
> —WORDS OF ENCOURAGEMENT FROM A "SLAVE EXHORTER"

in 1948 at nineteen. Already ordained in the Baptist ministry, he had begun years of listening and learning how to preach. In 1948, King left Atlanta for six years in northern, predominantly white schools. His three years at Crozer Theological Seminary in Chester, Pennsylvania, and three years at Boston University's Graduate School of Theology produced the first real signs of King's leadership potential among his fellow students. In Boston, King met Coretta Scott (1927–2006), from Alabama. They married in 1953 and were to have four children.

In 1954 he accepted a call to become the pastor of Dexter Avenue Baptist Church in Montgomery, Alabama. When the city's experienced civil rights leaders decided to launch a boycott of the city's buses in December 1955 because of a long series of abuses—which culminated with African American activist Rosa Parks (1913–2005) famously refusing to give up her seat to a white passenger—King was an inexperienced, but unanimous, choice to become the boycott's spokesperson. Even at the boycott's beginning, King proved to be an eloquent public speaker. He believed that its success depended on a militant nonviolence that would become a hallmark of his career. By March 1956, the Montgomery bus boycott had won national attention, and King spent increasing amounts of time away from the city to raise moral and financial support for the local struggle. In December 1956, federal courts ordered the desegregation of Montgomery's city buses.

In January 1957, Martin Luther King, Jr. and others met in Atlanta to organize the Southern Christian Leadership Conference (SCLC). In 1960, King moved to Atlanta to become co-pastor, with his father, of Ebenezer Baptist Church. It was a propitious time in the civil rights movement. Black college students launched the sit-in movement as King settled in Atlanta. Although King did not participate, the Congress of Racial Equality (CORE) initiated the "Freedom Rides" a year later, during which activists challenged the segregation of interstate buses by riding between Washington, DC, and Jackson, Mississippi, where the riders were met with violence.

Between 1961 and 1965, SCLC became the center of a broad coalition of organizations at the heart of the civil rights movement. To its right, the older NAACP and the Urban League were firmly based in the black middle class and pursued their goals largely through litigation and lobbying. To its left, CORE and the Student

Nonviolent Coordinating Committee (SNCC), organized by young leaders of the sit-in movement, were more volatile.

In the summer of 1963, Martin Luther King Jr. delivered his best-known public address, "I Have a Dream," to an estimated 250,000 people at the March on

---

"I Have a Dream"

. . . . I am not unmindful that some of you have come here out of great trials and tribulations. Some of you have come fresh from narrow jail cells. Some of you have come from areas where your quest for freedom left you battered by the storms of persecution and staggered by the winds of police brutality. You have been the veterans of creative suffering. Continue to work with the faith that unearned suffering is redemptive.

Go back to Mississippi, go back to Alabama, go back to South Carolina, go back to Georgia, go back to Louisiana, go back to the slums and ghettos of our northern cities, knowing that somehow this situation can and will be changed. Let us not wallow in the valley of despair.

I say to you today, my friends, so even though we face the difficulties of today and tomorrow, I still have a dream. It is a dream deeply rooted in the American dream.

I have a dream that one day this nation will rise up and live out the true meaning of its creed: "We hold these truths to be self-evident: that all men are created equal."

I have a dream that one day on the red hills of Georgia the sons of former slaves and the sons of former slave owners will be able to sit down together at the table of brotherhood.

I have a dream that one day even the state of Mississippi, a state sweltering with the heat of injustice, sweltering with the heat of oppression, will be transformed into an oasis of freedom and justice.

I have a dream that my four little children will one day live in a nation where they will not be judged by the color of their skin but by the content of their character.

I have a dream today. . . .

—Dr. Martin Luther King, Jr., Washington, DC, 28 August 1963.

Washington. Here, perhaps most effectively, his leadership as orator was manifest. He invoked biblical and national values and embodied the civil rights movement in the first-person "I" of his speech. His speech was a ringing declaration of hope for all humanity. Martin Luther King, Jr. knew that his vocation was to preach. He was, occasionally, awkward when cast in other roles.

The Selma to Montgomery march, during which hundreds of marchers attempted to travel from one city to the other, only to be met with authorities wielding tear gas and billy clubs, was eventually successful. By the time the marchers reached the state capital of Montgomery on 25 March 1965, after walking twelve miles (twenty kilometers) a day, the number of marchers had swelled to 25,000 people. President Johnson signed the 1965 Voting Rights Act into law five months later.

King died, the victim of an assassin's bullet, on 4 April 1968, at the Lorraine Motel in Memphis, Tennessee, now the site of the National Civil Rights Museum. Two months later, on 5 June, the nation again mourned the loss of a prominent leader when Senator Robert F. Kennedy, charismatic younger brother of President John F. Kennedy, who had himself been assassinated in 1963 in Dallas, Texas, met the same fate as his brother.

Martin Luther King, Jr. was the greatest preacher in twentieth-century America. More than anyone else, he demonstrated the power of the proclaimed word and moved a nation to confront racial issues that it had mishandled or avoided for a century before his death. In his embrace of nonviolence as a powerful tool for social change, King owed much to the life and work of the Indian activist Mohandas Gandhi (1869–1948), of whom King wrote in 1958, ten years after Gandhi's assassination by a Hindu nationalist:

> Gandhi was probably the first person in history to lift the love ethic of Jesus above mere interaction between individuals to a powerful and effective social force on a large scale. Love, for Gandhi, was a potent instrument for social and collective transformation. It was in this Gandhian emphasis on love and nonviolence that I discovered the method for social reform that I had been seeking for so many months. . . . I came to feel that this was the only morally and practically sound method open to oppressed people in their struggle for freedom.
>
> —Martin Luther King, Jr., "My Pilgrimage to Nonviolence," 1 September 1958

Feminist Movement and Women's Rights

Many people in the United States assume that American values have been in the forefront of the struggle for women's equality internationally, and that American women have been leaders in that struggle. Although those assumptions contain some truth, it is equally true that American values and American women have been both an inspiration to and a constraint on the international women's movement.

The earliest efforts of women to organize internationally for their rights were inspired by the French Revolution and by the principles found in the earliest feminist writings, the first being the treatise *A Vindication of the Rights of Women* (1792) by the British activist Mary Wollstonecraft (also well-known as the mother of Mary Shelley, author of *Frankenstein*). Some historians say the women's rights movement was actually sparked by the refusal to seat women delegates from the United States at the World Anti-Slavery Convention held in London in 1840. A decade later the American suffragists Elizabeth Cady Stanton (1815–1902) and Lucretia Mott (1793–1880) organized the first women's rights conference in the United States, with three hundred men and women meeting in Seneca Falls, in the Finger Lakes region of New York; today Seneca Falls is the site of the National Women's Hall of Fame.

The conference sought to apply principles of the Declaration of Independence to women. The conference's *A Declaration of the Rights of Women* reads, "We hold these truths to be self-evident: that all men and women are created equal." The National Women's Rights Convention, held in October 1850, representing women from nine states, endorsed "equality before the law without distinction of sex or color" and made news in Europe. Black women leaders such as Sojourner Truth (1797–1883) and Harriet Tubman (1820–1913) made significant contributions to antislavery efforts and to women's equality, although tensions existed between the American abolitionist movement and the women's movement. The National Women's Suffrage Association (now the League of Women Voters) pushed for suffrage, a move that resulted decades later in the Nineteenth Amendment to the United States Constitution. This fight for the right to vote was the focus of American women's efforts for many decades.

As with the movement to gain full civil rights for African Americans, efforts to gain full rights for women have been pursued by many brave but anonymous people—men and women—whose names are no longer remembered to posterity. Of the many notable figures from the women's rights era, one of the most influential reformers was Susan B. Anthony, profiled below.

Susan B. Anthony (1820–1906)

One of the key figures in the early women's rights movement was Susan B. Anthony, a trailblazer for women's rights who spent her life working for positive social change. Anthony dedicated her life to various reform movements, including abolition of slavery and temperance, which eventually gave way to her leading the fight against society's overall oppression of women. Anthony sought legal reforms of the restrictive marriage and divorce laws of the nineteenth century that left divorced women without property or a means of support. Likewise, nineteenth-century laws denied divorced women custody of their children, and afforded women little or no legal recourse over domestic disputes. Along with other like-minded early feminists, Anthony appealed to local and state legislatures of the Northeast to consider the plight of women, especially the most vulnerable, who had little or no means of support or way of seeking restitution in a society favoring men and restricting the lives of women. Anthony led the way for general social reforms and fought for equal voting rights for women against opponents who supported disenfranchisement of women. She demonstrated a tenacity and commitment to improving women's lives not typical of most nineteenth-century women, although throughout her long life Anthony did share the limelight with many notable figures, such as Elizabeth Cady Stanton.

Anthony believed that obtaining voting rights would be the best first step in eradicating other oppressive conditions for women, and that women's public activism would help level the playing field in the domestic, social, economic, and political arenas. Everything she did was deemed to be for "the cause," which she regularly referenced as being the central force of her being—to gain the vote so that future generations of women could break free of the chains of oppression and openly participate in public life.

Susan Brownell Anthony was born to Daniel and Lucy Read Anthony, in Adams, Massachusetts. Theirs was a typical working-class household. Her father was a devout Quaker, and her mother was a Baptist. Anthony's father, like other Quakers, based his beliefs on egalitarian principles and valued education as a worthy endeavor for both boys and girls. With their father's guidance, the Anthony children briefly attended public school and then were home-schooled. As a young girl attending a public school, Susan was denied the opportunity to learn long division because the schoolmaster did not believe that girls should learn mathematics. At this point in her life, Anthony's outraged father removed her from public school and began the process of home schooling under the tutelage of Mary Perkins.

Although the nineteenth century has been referred to as the "Era of the Common Man," the common woman gained little for her commonness. Economic dependency and restrictive marriages dictated the common woman's role in society, which led to Anthony's challenging the status quo at an early age. By the time Anthony finished seminary, she had met Lucretia Mott, who had spoken at the seminary in 1837. Mott, a Quaker and an avid abolitionist, was one of the founders of the Philadelphia Female Anti-Slavery Society. She spoke with a passion that stirred Anthony's soul and solidified her conviction.

Anthony's father's cotton mills went bankrupt during the Panic of 1837 (a financial crisis that led to a deep recession that lasted into the 1840s), and by 1839 Daniel Anthony had moved his family to the impoverished town of Hardscrabble, New York (later renamed Center Falls). At this point Susan B. Anthony took up teaching and severed the close bonds she had enjoyed with her parents and siblings.

Teaching was one of the few professions available to nineteenth-century women. Susan B. Anthony vowed never to marry and to encourage women to shun the social institution of marriage until full rights of citizenry were granted to women.

The Susan B. Anthony dollar coin, introduced in 1979 to honor a woman who worked tirelessly for the cause of women's rights, was the first circulating United States coin to bear a woman's image. Much like the Sacagawea dollar coins issued in 2000, the coins never caught on with the public and are mainly kept by collectors. Source: United States Mint image. Designer: Frank Gasparro.

Through teaching, Anthony gained a sense of autonomy and independence that she would have never realized as a married woman. By 1845 she had carved out a life as a teacher and reform activist and had broadened her circle of friends to include many abolitionists and temperance reformers. During the 1840s Anthony was involved with abolition and the Daughters of Temperance, which effectively placed her in the spotlight. Anthony became acquainted with many prominent leaders. One such person was Stanton, who became a lifelong friend and partner in the fight for equal rights. The duo attended temperance, abolition, and women's rights conventions together, and by 1855 Susan B. Anthony had become one of the nation's most outspoken leaders in the reform arena.

Until 1854, Anthony's work had been conducted in New York. As Anthony became more active in the public sphere, her connection to the prominent literati and reformers became extremely important to her leadership development. For example, prominent abolitionists William Lloyd Garrison and Samuel May sought her out as a traveling agent for their abolition society, which led her to widespread speaking engagements and national fame. Likewise, Anthony continued to work for temperance and women's rights, with women's suffrage at the center of her work. Her leadership captured the attention of the nation, with many newspapers expressing opinions ranging from praise for her activities to condemnation that a woman would speak so forcefully in the public arena.

Anthony remained single her entire life, feeling that marriage would interfere with her beloved reform work. At times she became frustrated with the women around her, and often expressed deep regret when one by one most of her female friends married and had children. Married women such as Stanton aided Anthony's rise to prominence as a leader, however. Many historians have noted that Stanton was an eloquent writer, whereas Anthony became a dedicated orator. Both women wrote and gave speeches. By 1900, Anthony's leadership came full circle as she stepped down from her post as leader of the National American Woman Suffrage Association (NAWSA), which began in 1848 and lasted until 1921. Anthony quietly died in 1906 as her friend Anna Howard Shaw held her hand, but not before her leadership had inspired a nation of women to press on in order to gain the vote in 1920.

The International Women's Movement

The first *international* women's congress was held in Paris (1878) in connection with the World Exposition. Issues included abolition, nationalist and revolutionary strategies, liberal to radical social reform, and often conflicting national agendas.

The first wave of the international women's movement was based on a web of international feminist connections inspired by socialist struggles in Europe and abolitionist efforts in the United States, as well as by temperance and moral reform movements in many countries. Although the role of American women leaders in these first-wave international organizations was significant, American interests tended to be more narrowly focused on suffrage rather than on the wider range of issues held by the European constituents.

In the United States, after securing the right to vote in 1920, many middle-class women moved into medical, educational, government, and legal professions. By 1945, motivated by world-changing events such as the Great Depression and World War II, during which women moved into many jobs previously closed to them, women's activism took on issues such as peace and disarmament. In the 1960s the civil rights movement inspired a renewed struggle for women's rights as well. Students on college campuses criticized the materialism of American culture and the hypocrisy of the nation's foreign policy. A new and vocal women's movement arose in the United States. Groups such as Women's Strike for Peace and the League of Women Voters found new voice. The publication of Betty Friedan's *The Feminine Mystique* in 1963 and the founding of the National Organization for Women (NOW) in 1966 addressed middle-class women's frustrations and their struggle for equal political and economic rights.

The Feminine Mystique

The following is an excerpt from Betty Friedan's influential 1963 book The Feminine Mystique, *chapter one: "The Problem That Has No Name."*

In the fifteen years after World War II, this mystique of feminine fulfillment became the cherished and self-perpetuating core of contemporary American culture. Millions of women lived their lives in the image of those pretty pictures of the American suburban housewife, kissing their husbands goodbye in front of the picture window, depositing their station-wagonsful of children at school, and smiling as they ran the new electric waxer over the spotless kitchen floor. They baked their own bread, sewed their own and their children's clothes, kept their new washing machines and dryers running all day. They changed the sheets on the beds twice a week instead of once, took the rug-hooking class in adult education, pitied their poor frustrated mothers, who had dreamed of having a career. Their only dream was to be perfect wives and mothers; their highest ambition to have five children and a beautiful house, their only fight to get and keep their husbands. They had no thought for the unfeminine problems of the world outside the home; they wanted the men to make the major decisions. They gloried in their role as women, and wrote proudly on the census blank: Occupation: housewife.

Betty Friedan (2013). *The Feminine Mystique*, 50th Anniversary Edition. New York: W. W. Norton & Co.

NOW presumed a model of political activity that was essentially individualist, recalling the early suffragists' focus on the relationship between the individual citizen's rights and the state. Many women could not identify with the dilemmas of the middle-class professional woman, however. Challenges arose both internationally and domestically, with more radical women's organizations taking on issues that fundamentally challenged the nation's economic and political status quo.

Feminism's Second Wave: Post-1975

The period after 1975 brought growth in women's movements worldwide. The United Nations International Women's Year (1975) and the subsequent United Nations Decade of Women (1976–1985) were major factors in stimulating local activities in countries in both the Northern and Southern hemispheres, as well as spawning international connections, shared resources, active networks, and global conferences.

What made this second-wave international women's movement so much more diverse and complex than the first was the multiplicity of women's issues. The second-wave international women's movement reflected a multiplicity of global experiences and perspectives. The leadership roles of American and European women and of Western values, as witnessed in the first wave, were questioned. Whereas American women tended to focus on electoral politics and individual human rights, many women in the developing world focused on poverty, health, disease, and other issues that affected women, children, and men alike. Women more concerned with women's equality were often viewed as agents of Westernization and "modernization," privilege, and individualism. Western ideals of modernity and progress were often dismissed, and "feminism" was stigmatized and resented as the unpopular outgrowth of Western cultural imperialism. These were often difficult times for American women involved in international women's organizations.

One of the major focuses of the international women's movement since the Decade of Women has been passage of the Convention on the Elimination of All Forms of Discrimination against Women (CEDAW), adopted in 1979 by the United Nations General Assembly. It is often described as an international bill of rights for women. The convention defines what constitutes discrimination against women, and sets up an agenda for action to end such discrimination. The United States is not one of the ratifying countries. The proposed Equal Rights Amendment (ERA) to the US Constitution, ratified by Congress in 1972, failed to gain the necessary votes when it was sent to the states. The ERA, which would have guaranteed women pay and status equal to those of men, would have been the Twenty-seventh Amendment had it been ratified by the states. (As it happened, the actual Twenty-seventh Amendment—the most recent to date—was passed in 1992; first proposed in 1789, the amendment has to do with salaries of representatives in Congress.)

There are many (often contradicting) theories about why the ERA did not pass; some of these include:

1. the seven-year timeline given to the states to ratify the amendment was too short, given the somewhat radical nature of the amendment, especially in the more conservative states;
2. states were hesitant to hand over power to the federal government, especially since many of the rules for protecting women's rights were already in place in most state constitutions;
3. some people were afraid that giving fully equal rights to women would extend to the draft, and that women would then get drafted into the military and shipped off to fight in Vietnam; there was also a fear that the ERA would lead to enforced unisex bathrooms, among other issues both real and imagined;
4. many public figures, notably conservative lawyer-activist Phyllis Schlafly (b. 1925), campaigned for the ERA's demise on the basis that it would radically change American society.

The real reason for the ERA's demise is likely a combination of these factors. Whatever the exact reason, the fact remains that a differential in pay between men and women remains: according to *The Atlantic* magazine, in 2012 American women made approximately 77 cents for every dollar made by an American man. This figure—which is often disputed for various reasons—is up from roughly 60 cents per dollar in the 1950s, but still quite a bit short of equality in pay.

In 1973 the Supreme Court legalized a woman's right to choose abortion in *Roe v. Wade*; nonetheless the issue remains deeply divisive—gun rights and abortion are among the two most heatedly debated topics in modern American life—and some states have enacted laws that limit women's access to abortion, and limit the time period during pregnancy in which they may have one. Women's rights continue to be an object of frequent and heated discussion in modern America.

Gay and Lesbian Rights Movement

Although the United States was certainly not the first Western country in which an organized movement to secure legal, political, and economic rights for gays and lesbians developed, the country's large population, its influential civil rights movement, and its tradition of democratic self-expression combined to make the United States a leader in rights for gays and lesbians. A major conservative upsurge in the late twentieth and early twenty-first centuries undermined the American gay and lesbian rights movement, however, leaving it well behind similar movements in other Western countries.

By the early twentieth century in larger American cities, notably in the New England states, California, and the upper Midwest, secretive gay and lesbian networks were giving rise to more developed gay and lesbian communities. By the 1920s gays and lesbians were the targets of prohibition enforcement, "blue" laws, anti-gay violence, and police raids at a time when a shift in medical opinion ascribed homosexual desire and activity to pathology and mental disease. (Blue laws are laws of a religious nature, such as those that prohibit selling alcohol on Sundays, or that prohibit certain sexual acts.)

By midcentury, gay activism in the United States had begun to focus on legal issues, in part because of the experience of World War II: during the war the American armed services maintained racial segregation in housing and unit assignments, tolerated race-based and anti-gay violence within the ranks, and imposed sanctions on gay and lesbian service personnel. Many gays received administrative discharges, also known as "blue tickets" or "blue discharges."

In 1948 the widely publicized *Kinsey Report* on adult sexual behavior in the United States revealed the wide experience of homoerotic and homosexual activity. Thus, even at the height of McCarthyism, the American gay rights movement continued to grow. In 1951 San Francisco nightclub owners prevailed in litigation establishing the right of businesses to cater to a gay and lesbian clientele, and in Los Angeles a new organization, the Mattachine Society, advocated for personal rights and liberties of gays, educated potential political allies, and defended its right to use the United States Postal Service for delivery of its newsletter. By 1953 Mattachine had some one hundred chapters in Southern California, and a lesbian counterpart organization, the Daughters of Bilitis (DOB), was formed in San Francisco in 1955. (The name Bilitis referred to an obscure nineteenth century erotic poem called the "Songs of Bilitis"; the name was intentionally obscure to protect women who may have been afraid of the consequences of declaring themselves to be lesbians.) Both Mattachine and DOB adopted cautious tactics, emphasizing small community contacts and relying chiefly on education for eventual improvement in the lives of homosexuals.

For American gays and lesbians, the 1950s was a period of deep distrust by law enforcement, medical professionals, and society at large. In 1952, for example, the American Psychiatric Association issued a policy proclamation that homosexuality is a mental disorder. As a consequence, gays and lesbians were both socially stigmatized and economically threatened: to retain their jobs in the educational, medical, government, and social work fields, gays and lesbians had to avoid disclosure of their personal lives to co-workers, superiors, clergy, and family members.

A sign in a snowy Philadelphia marks the site of Fourth of July gay rights demonstrations during the 1960s, held outside of Independence Hall, where the Declaration of Independence and the Constitution were both signed. Photo by Bill Siever.

By the early 1960s the American gay rights movement had accelerated, largely because of the accomplishments of the African American–led civil rights movement and the growth of the anti–Vietnam War movement. Bar raids and arrests, first in Hollywood and Los Angeles in 1967 and then in the Greenwich Village section of Manhattan outside the Stonewall Bar in June 1969, provoked resistance by gays and lesbians and opened a new phase in gay rights activism in the United States. Gays, lesbians, and supporters rallied publicly to confront conservatives and anti-gay law enforcement officers. In 1969 a radical organization, the Gay Liberation Front (GLF), was formed in New York City, and affiliated groups formed quickly in California and the Midwest. GLF chapters concentrated on local issues such as discriminatory hiring practices and police entrapment.

The Gay Activists Alliance (GAA), which broke from the GLF in late 1969, was dedicated to gay rights issues only, eschewing broader progressive initiatives. GAA successfully pushed for several concrete legal changes, including decriminalization of sodomy in three states in 1971; in the same year a federal court ruling banned the firing of homosexual civil service employees. In 1973 GAA also successfully pushed the American Psychological Association to repeal its "mental disease" definition of homosexuality in favor of listing it as "a normal variant of sexual behavior."

Backlash, and "Don't Ask, Don't Tell"

Beginning in the late 1970s a popular movement based in conservative churches and social organizations began to react against the successes of the women's and gay rights movements. Local ordinances assuring equal rights were rescinded, notably in Miami, Florida, where entertainer Anita Bryant (b. 1940) developed a national coalition called "Save Our Children" and linked her fight against Miami's equal rights law to the criminal activities of male pedophiles. This theme energized the growing conservative movement in the United States, and in 1978 equal rights clauses that had been adopted in the early 1970s were repealed in Minnesota, Kansas, and Oregon.

In November 1978 in San Francisco—the site of one of the country's largest gay communities—an aggrieved public official shot and killed Mayor George Moscone and a city council member, Harvey Milk, the most widely known openly gay elected official in the United States at that time, months after a citywide Gay Freedom Day event. (The assassination is thought to have been motivated mainly by personal and professional grievances, rather than a particular anti-gay agenda.) Police raids and anti-gay violence increased. Backed by well-funded evangelical organizations, empowered by the failure of the Equal Rights Amendment to the United States Constitution, and reinforced by the candidacy and election in 1980 of conservative Ronald Reagan as president, a resurgent "new right" claimed to defend traditional social conventions and launched a vigorous anti-gay rights campaign.

Harvey Milk's Message to President Carter

Harvey Milk, the country's first openly gay public official, included the following message to President Jimmy Carter as part of the San Francisco Gay Freedom Day's official program, in June 1978.

Supervisor Harvey Milk
City Hall, San Francisco

Gay Freedom? That is a question that Jimmy Carter must answer. We must raise our voices loud and clear until he hears our message. How long, Jimmy, before you speak out for the human rights of all Americans? How much damage must be done and how much violence must take place before you speak to the needs of 10–20 million of your fellow Americans? History tells us that gay people will one day win our freedom. The only question is, when? Jimmy, you can help turn the pages of history faster. Until you do you are just Jimmy Carter; when you do you will be our President and a true leader for human rights.

Source: San Francisco Pride.

Three principal issues came to dominate the fight for gay rights: funding for HIV-related prevention and education initiatives; the inclusion of gays in national military service; and legal recognition of monogamous, long-term gay and lesbian relationships. In the United States, HIV and AIDS were popularly called "the gay plague" during the 1980s, and the emergence of the disease provided new opportunities for both misinformation about homosexuals, particularly men, and anti-gay discrimination and violence. The Reagan administration (1981–1989) was slow to respond, and federal support for clinical research remained limited until the early 1990s, when President Bill Clinton increased funding for HIV/AIDS public education and research. After some 400,000 deaths in the United States, clinical trials finally identified a multidrug "cocktail" that allowed much longer survival for those infected with HIV. Clinton did not, however, fulfill his promise to overturn the ban on homosexuals serving in the United States armed forces. Instead, in 1993–1994 a "don't ask, don't tell" policy was introduced, under which homosexuals could serve, provided they did not explicitly reveal their sexual orientation. There were numerous criticisms about the policy; one was that the military was losing critical personnel, particularly speakers of Persian Farsi and Arabic. Others noted that the partners of gay members of the military who died in combat were not afforded the same rights and respect as heterosexual war widows and widowers. Still others noted that the policy interfered with the First Amendment right of free speech and the Fifth Amendment's insurance against the abuse of governmental authority in citizens' private lives. In 2011 President Obama rescinded the policy and allowed gays and lesbians to serve openly in the military.

In the late 1990s and early 2000s American gay rights activists began calling for legal recognition of same-sex "domestic partnerships" that would provide gay and lesbian couples with the same legal, civil, and economic privileges and responsibilities enjoyed by heterosexual married couples, including access to medical insurance coverage, income tax breaks, legal standing as next of kin, and Social Security benefits. This initiative then transformed into a movement for gay marriage, equal in all ways to heterosexual marriage.

Television has had a major influence on Americans' opinions of gays and gay culture. As George Lange of the *Los Angeles Times* wrote, in 2012:

> When *Will & Grace* premiered on NBC in 1998, few expected it to become a cultural touchstone or a ratings success. *Ellen* [a talk show hosted by Ellen DeGeneres, who went on to host the popular *Ellen DeGeneres Show*] had gone down in flames after blazing a trail for out

gay characters on TV, and there was skepticism that a sitcom about a gay man and his female best friend could speak to the heartland. But the show went on to be a huge hit for much of its eight-season run, winning 16 Emmys, and is often credited with making Americans comfortable with "the gay next door."

This past spring, Vice President Joe Biden told *Meet the Press,* "I think *Will & Grace* did more to educate the American public than almost anything anybody has ever done so far."

—George Lange, "The Will & Grace Effect," *The Los Angeles Times,* 19 July 2012

In 2013 gay marriage achieved a major breakthrough when the Supreme Court ruled that provisions in the Defense of Marriage Act of 1996 (DOMA), which prevented gay couples from receiving the same federal benefits as heterosexual couples, were unconstitutional. Both supporters and opponents agree that the issue will continue to be contested at the state level for years to come. While Americans' differing opinions on gun rights and abortion have tended to stay more or less stable over the years, the idea of gay marriage seems to be steadily gaining acceptance in the United States. As of March 2014, seventeen states and Washington, DC, allow same-sex marriage, while the rest of the states ban it by legislation or in their state constitutions.

These and other issues will be discussed further in the final chapter.

CHAPTER SIX:
THE AMERICAN DREAM

"Rumors of my death have been greatly exaggerated," wrote the author Mark Twain, and it may be that rumors of the declining role of the United States may be exaggerated, too, given that its economy, and its influence in world affairs and culture, remain strong, and also given the fact that no other country seems ready to take on such a role. On the other hand, there are many signs of America's struggle to live up to its avowed position as the "city upon a hill," and troubles at home, combined with troubles abroad, make it harder to justify some of the claims that Americans make. American politicians are fond of saying that the United States is the greatest country in the world, a claim that rankles many people but clearly strikes a chord with the American public at large. The fear of decline is a powerful force in American politics.

American Exceptionalism: Is America One of a Kind?

Americans have always believed that they are a special people with a special destiny. This is the essence of American "exceptionalism," the idea that the United States is set apart from other nations by its unique national character and a global mission to spread the values of freedom and democracy. Americans have embraced this national ethos for more than two centuries. The idea holds that Americans possess trademark qualities of rugged individualism and entrepreneurial spirit, a willingness to fight for democratic principles, and a strong sense of morality and idealism. These qualities are coupled with the belief that the United States is endowed with a special responsibility to serve as a global champion of liberal and democratic values. Understandably, the rest of

> We shall be as a city upon a hill; the eyes of all people are upon us.
>
> —JOHN WINTHROP (1630), FUTURE GOVERNOR OF THE MASSACHUSETTS BAY COLONY

the world has had mixed feelings about American exceptionalism. Americans have always been willing to fight for their freedoms, and particularly since the late 1800s, they have been willing to lend their support to the struggles of other peoples for such freedoms. The global community has often accepted and encouraged that moral and political leadership.

Americans' belief in their own exceptionalism has fostered considerable resentment and frustration around the world. Many people do not accept the premise that the United States is superior to other nations, morally or otherwise; they point out that a lot of nations are exceptional for one reason or another. American leaders tend to present their foreign policies as driven purely by selfless and virtuous motives, but many see these policies as being as self-serving and unscrupulous as those of any other global power. The affected populations have found it galling that American leaders often champion freedom and democracy in their rhetoric, but ignore those ideals when doing so serves their strategic interests. The idea of American exceptionalism has therefore not always been welcomed by the rest of the world.

There is no precise definition of "exceptionalism" and no particular historical moment at which the idea was first conceived, although some would argue the concept originated with Alexis de Tocqueville, who said America is "quite exceptional" in *Democracy in America*. The notion that Americans are a special—and specially blessed—people was prevalent long before the actual foundation of the United States. The Puritans who founded the Massachusetts Bay Colony believed that they were blessed by God with the chance to begin life anew in a promised land. Such religious convictions were common among early New England settlers, and the notion that God literally blessed America—a notion that is likely familiar to anyone who has ever listened to an American political speech—has been an important component of exceptionalist thought.

You may think this a little mystical, and I've said it many times before, but I believe there was a Divine Plan to place this great continent here between the two oceans to be found by peoples from every corner of the earth. I believe we were preordained to carry the torch of freedom for the world.

—PRESIDENT RONALD REAGAN

Religious conviction instilled the idea that Americans occupied a blessed land, but geography helped to make that conviction a believable one. North America is endowed with remarkable geographic advantages. It occupies an enormous physical space. It has ample arable land and natural resources of immense economic value. For early European settlers, it seemed a gift from God for virtually unlimited Christian settlement.

Racial ideology also played a role in exceptionalist thinking. White settlers used the notion of racial superiority to justify their expansion into Native American lands. They presumed that the "savages" were on the losing end of history, destined to surrender their lands to the Anglo-Saxon race. Racial ideology helped American leaders to rationalize egregious policies toward Native Americans, as well as the longstanding practice of African American slavery.

The last formative influence on the development of exceptionalism as an intellectual concept was political philosophy. When it was founded, the United States was conceived as a nation that would cherish individual freedom, political and economic liberalism, and republican democracy. These ideals turned an isolated colonial struggle against Britain into what political philosophers such as Thomas Paine saw as a watershed moment in recorded history. Americans were not just struggling for their own independence, but for the universal principles of freedom and democracy. This assessment of the significance of the Revolution is one of the critical assumptions behind American exceptionalism.

American Progress, by John Gast, commissioned by a publisher of western travel guides, c. 1872. Various methods of travel across the Great Plains appear in an idealized landscape, led by the embodiment of progress: a woman holding a book and telegraph wire.
Source: Library of Congress.

The American Political System as a Model

Exceptional or not, the American system has exerted considerable influence as a model for other nations. There are at least three ways in which this influence has operated: (1) the details of specific features of the system have served as a kind of blueprint for some democratizing states, mostly in Latin America; (2) more generally, the ideas of liberal representative government and national self-determination exemplified in the American system have exerted a more diffuse influence across a broader geographical span; (3) some nations, even those with political institutions quite different from those in the United States, have borrowed from the governing style (idealistic rhetoric and attentiveness to media, for example) associated with American politics.

That the American system should have influenced the rest of the world is perhaps not surprising, since the United States has long aspired to provide an example of a "city upon a hill" in the hope that others would seek to emulate it. One of the long-standing motifs of American foreign policy has been its missionary zeal—its desire to spread American ideas and institutions to other parts of the globe—which has been evident both during its isolationist phases and during its current period of internationalism.

Until World War II, however, American missionary zeal was mostly confined to the Americas. In part as a result, American influence on the actual institutional design of other states has mostly been limited to Central and South America. As a broad generalization, the United States served as the political model for newly democratizing states in the Americas, but elsewhere (particularly in Africa) the Westminster, or parliamentary, model has predominated. Perhaps not surprisingly, many of the Commonwealth states (states that were formerly a part of the British Empire) copied, or have had foisted upon them, a British-style parliamentary system. Except for Asia, where a few presidential systems exist, most democracies have adopted the parliamentary system of governance, and even in Latin America institution builders drew lessons from Europe as well as from the United States.

Nevertheless, we can see the influence of the American model in this direct sense right across the Americas, especially in the prevalence of federalism. The three geographically largest nations in Latin America—Brazil, Argentina, and Mexico—all not only have federal systems today, but have had them for most of their existence. Brazil has had a federal system for most of the period since 1891, when it adopted a system so closely modeled on that of the United States that the writers of its constitution went so far as to use the phrase Estados Unidos do Brasil (United States of Brazil). In Mexico, most of the constitutions under which Mexicans have lived have included a federal system, obviously inspired by that of its neighbor to the north. Except during the regime of Juan Perón (1946–1955), Argentina also has had a federal system since 1853.

Also worth noting is the continuing relevance of the American example in the process of European integration. Winston Churchill's notion of a United States of Europe, and the federalist model generally, continues to exert an impact on those who ultimately matter most in the process of European integration: European politicians themselves. (Curiously, Churchill did not believe that Great Britain should be a part of this United States of Europe.) Although the Swiss and German models were also influential, the American example provided much of the original impetus for the creation of the new postwar Europe. Some students of European integration continue to find the American example instructive; they point out that the United States under the Articles of the Confederation was little more than a loose grouping of national entities (although the articles did provide the thirteen states with a common foreign policy, among other things), but subsequently became and remained a strong and viable entity. Some would point out, however, that the modern European Union, comprised of dozens of countries whose inhabitants speak scores of languages, is in an entirely different league from the fledgling United States under the Articles of the Confederation.

The United States has probably served as an abstract model or inspiration for others—spreading and advocating the democratic idea in a general sense—to a far greater extent than it has been a blueprint as discussed above. The notion of national self-determination enshrined in the Declaration of Independence has provided a source of inspiration for many nationalist movements, starting in Latin America in the early nineteenth century and continuing on throughout the world to the present day. This has not always been done in a manner consistent with the values of the American Revolution. Such was the case in 1965 when Rhodesia, now Zimbabwe, issued a Unilateral Declaration of Independence from British rule in a direct attempt to prevent democracy. Vietnam provides another striking example. In 1945, the communist-nationalist leader Ho Chi Minh (1890–1969) replicated the opening lines of the American document in his own declaration of independence from the French. Ho and the Americans had been allies during World War II against the two nations' common enemy (Japan), and Ho fully expected American support for his declaration. As it happened, the Cold War intervened, political expediency determined the American response, and successive American administrations sided with the French colonialists and then fought Ho directly in the American war in Vietnam.

A third form of influence has been that exerted by the American style of politics. Glamorous and colorful, often identified with Hollywood images and high-sounding, emotive rhetoric—although this is by no means unique to the United States—the American political style is frequently lampooned overseas; its grandiose language and idealistic tone often ring hollow in many peoples' ears and sometimes sounds silly and simplistic.

Forced Adoption of the American Political Model

The previous three mechanisms all involve voluntary compliance with the American model; all are the result of some form of admiration for, or identification with, that model. In assessing the influence of the American political system on others, however, we should consider not only the voluntary adoption of American institutions and ideas, but also the fact that American power in the international system that emerged in the late 1800s afforded the United States the power to forcibly compel other states to adopt its conventions. The United States is not merely a passive participant in the spread of liberal democratic norms. A fourth form of influence, then, is the long-established practice in American foreign policy of forcing other states to adopt democratic forms of governance. According to the political scientist Mark Peceny, the desire to spread democracy has been the primary motivation behind about one-third of all the military interventions the United States has undertaken around the globe since its founding.

The American Dream

Connected to the idea of American exceptionalism is the idea of the American Dream. A term coined in 1931 by the writer James Truslow Adams, the American Dream was made possible by the founding principles of the United States. The first principle was confidence in reason, which was the essence of the eighteenth century Enlightenment; it represented the triumph of reason over centuries of ignorance, superstition, and religious dogma. It was the view that the universe followed natural laws that could be discovered by science. The second principle was Aristotle's philosophy of egoism: the view that man could properly pursue his own happiness. The third principle was a consequence of the first two: that all men were equal in possessing individual rights, that man did not exist to serve governments, but that governments existed to "serve" men—that is, to protect its citizens against coercion and lawlessness. The concept of individual rights was an expression of individualism, the concept that man is an end in himself, not a means to the ends of others, and that each individual is responsible for earning his own living. These revolutionary principles were what prompted Thomas Paine to exclaim, "We have it in our power to begin the world over again."

The American Dream means controlling one's own destiny. Calvin Colton, a prominent journalist, wrote in 1844, "Ours is a country where men start from a humble origin, and from small beginnings rise gradually in the world, as the reward

Xi Jinping's "Chinese Dream"

The American Dream of a better life for its citizens is widely admired around the world. In the spring of 2013, the incoming general secretary of the Communist Party of China, Xi Jinping, delivered a speech that laid out his vision of a Chinese Dream for his nation. Unlike the American version, which stresses the role of individuals in finding success and happiness, the Chinese Dream stresses the power of a united people to create a more successful and just China. The following is an excerpt of his speech.

In November last year, the Communist Party of China held its 18th National Congress, which drew the blueprint for China's development in the years to come. The main goals we set for China are as follows: By 2020, China's GDP and per capita incomes for urban and rural residents will double the 2010 figures, and the building of a moderately prosperous society in all respects will be completed. By the mid-21st century, China will be turned into a modern socialist country that is prosperous, strong, democratic, culturally advanced and harmonious; and the Chinese dream, namely, the great renewal of the Chinese nation, will be realized. Looking ahead, we are full of confidence in China's future. . . .

We need to make relentless efforts in the years ahead to deliver a better life to all our people. We are unwaveringly committed to reform and opening up, and we will concentrate on the major task of shifting the growth model, focus on running our own affairs well and make continued efforts to boost the socialist modernization drive.

As a Chinese saying goes, neighbors wish each other well, just as loved ones do to each other. China will continue to promote friendship and partnership with its neighbors, consolidate friendly ties and deepen mutually beneficial cooperation with them and ensure that its development will bring even greater benefits to its neighbors. . . .

Source: Xi Jinping, speech to the Boao Forum for Asia, 7 April 2013.

of merit and industry, and where they can attain the most elevated positions, or acquire a large amount of wealth, according to the pursuits they elect for themselves. No exclusive privilege of birth . . . stand[s] in their path; but one has a good chance as another, according to his talents, prudence and personal exertions. This is a country of self-made men."

The American Dream was always an aspiration. Americans have traditionally been optimistic, confident that lives could be improved. The Dream, of course, was not a guarantee of success, and not all people achieved it. But, over time the trend in the United States has been for each generation to have more education and material wealth than the preceding generation, as well as higher socioeconomic status: a trend that only recently has begun to reverse its course. And while there have always been clear distinctions in wealth and status between people in different socioeconomic strata, those differences were not especially large, and could be erased by upward mobility.

In the twenty-first century, despite legal limits on immigration and the physical dangers of crossing the country's borders illegally, the American Dream still continues to attract people from all over the world. People from Cuba and other Caribbean nations travel by flimsy rafts and risk drowning trying to make it the 90 miles (150 km) across the Florida Straits. People trek daily through the harsh and mountainous deserts surrounding the United States–Mexico border, risking death by heat stroke, hypothermia, and dehydration. Clearly, the American Dream is still a draw.

The fact that the United States is a free country does not mean that all Americans have been treated justly and had equal opportunity to realize the American Dream. It took a bloody civil war to abolish slavery, and African Americans were still politically disenfranchised for over a century after the war. Asian Americans have often been viewed as second-class citizens; Japanese Americans were placed in internment camps during World War II. Italians have been called demeaning names. Jews have been discriminated against in many professions. Catholics were looked down on by Protestants. (Curiously, the widespread belief that Irish immigrants were confronted with signs saying "Irish Need Not Apply" is most likely a myth, as no evidence exists of such signs.) Latinos from a wide variety of nations—often lumped together indiscriminately as "Mexicans" even if they come from Guatemala—continue to face discrimination as the newer wave of immigrants to the United States. Nonetheless, the prejudices against different immigrant groups have—almost as a rule—gradually broken down as assimilation into American culture takes place over generations. Overall, no other "melting pot" society in history has ever succeeded as well as the United States has.

The economic recession that began in 2007 and the slow recovery in the years that followed have led many in America to question whether the American Dream has become more myth than reality, especially for middle class and poor Americans. One recent survey showed that the socioeconomic structure of American society has become increasingly rigid since the 1990s. The children of sixty-two percent of Americans at the top can expect to remain at the top, while sixty-five percent of children at the bottom can expect to remain at the bottom for their entire lives. These statistics suggest a lack of socioeconomic mobility, and place the United States near the bottom of the socioeconomic mobility scale among

The Revolutionary Dwindling of the Middle Class

In November of 2013, National Public Radio correspondent Kelly McEvers interviewed Richard Longworth, author of Caught in the Middle: America's Heartland in the Age of Globalism. *Their conversation focused on the future of small American towns such as McEvers's hometown of Lincoln, Illinois (population 14,000), where, as McEvers noted in her broadcast, "As we recover from the Great Recession, jobs are coming back. But they are not middle-wage jobs—they are either high-wage jobs or low-wage jobs. The middle class is in serious decline. And that has all kinds of repercussions." The following is an extract of their interview.*

RL: "The earth isn't going to open up and swallow [towns like Lincoln]. They'll survive, but they'll be backwaters, getting ever more what you saw: shrinking in population, population older, young families not moving in, high school grads like yourself moving away to seek their fortune somewhere else. . . . I grew up in a middle-class America where we pretty much knew life was an escalator. You got on the bottom step, and if you behaved yourself, paid your dues, went to work, worked hard—you'd end up at the top of the escalator. And I think that escalator's broken now. It's a tougher scramble."

KM: "How to cover that upheaval?"

RL: "You've covered revolutions before. Treat it like just another damn revolution."

modern, economically developed nations. The American Dream is also threatened by increasing socioeconomic inequality in America. Compared to other nations, the United States, despite being the world's richest nation, has levels of income and literacy inequality, poverty, and infant mortality typical of developing nations such as Mexico and Turkey, and far higher than developed nations such as Germany and Britain. The buying power of American families is decreasing, dropping by four percent from 2000 to 2010. All of these numbers point to a high level of inequality: inequality that hinders people's ability to successfully pursue the American Dream.

Politicians and economists offer various solutions to lessen inequality and increase opportunity. Conservatives believe that the fundamental problem is government—government is too big, too intrusive, and taxes citizens too heavily. A smaller government, lower taxes on the wealthy and on small business owners, and less government regulation will allow the free market to operate, creating and growing businesses and jobs and thereby creating wealth and opportunity. Liberals believe that government is part of the solution and advocate higher taxes on the wealthy; government programs and incentives to stimulate innovation, business growth, and job creation; and lower education and health care costs. Although liberals and conservatives both claim to have the nation's best interests in mind with their differing economic plans, they very seldom agree on even the most basic principles of governance, which has led to increasing legislative gridlock: often stymieing everyone's common goal of improving the economy.

Sports

To further delve into the idea of American exceptionalism we must steer away from politics for a moment and explore an even more passion-inducing topic: sports. Looking into the unique history of American sports allows us to draw a few parallels with America's place in the world in other spheres. Several sports were invented, or at least cohered into their modern state, in the United States, and American sports later displayed a pronounced variance with the international sporting scene. American sports culture differs in many ways from the international sports culture, with greater focus on commercialization, individual rather than team potential, and rivalries between regions or cities, rather than with other nations (one notable exception is the Olympics). Perhaps most noticeable is a widespread lack of interest in what most of the world calls football (known as soccer in the United States), although soccer is an extremely popular youth team sport.

The world's most dominant military and economic power favors a sport—American-style football—that has limited international appeal, while its men's national soccer team could be considered an also-ran in soccer, the world's most popular sport. What seems equally significant is the United States's lack of noted international sporting rivalries, particularly in team sports. Apart from rare moments when the Cold War was played out on the hockey rink, such as the "Miracle on Ice" won by the college athletes of the US hockey team against the vastly more favored Soviet team at the Winter Olympics in Lake Placid, New York, in 1980, the United States's most important sporting competitions have been domestic contests between rivals such as those between the New York Yankees and the Boston Red Sox; there are also bouts, particularly in ice hockey, with teams from Canada. At the college level, basketball games between such rivals as North Carolina State and Duke, and football games between the University of Michigan and Ohio State, are also strikingly intense, and many visitors to the United States are astounded by the record crowds—the University of Michigan's stadium can hold nearly 110,000 fans—and national coverage that these college contests command.

O, we don't give a damn
for the whole state of Michigan
The whole state of Michigan,
the whole state of Michigan
We don't give a damn
for the whole state of Michigan,
we're from O-hi-o

—OHIO STATE UNIVERSITY SONG

Oh how I hate Ohio State!

—UNIVERSITY OF MICHIGAN
EXPRESSION

At the same time, the United States has a marked lack of success or involvement in many of the major international team sporting events. In male sports the United States is underwhelming in the world cup competitions for the three major sports of soccer, cricket, and rugby. Such national sporting differences, particularly in nations such as Great Britain and France, give us an insight into the inward-oriented nature of American culture and nationalism. This argument nonetheless holds more credence in team sports than in individual sports. Further, the dominance that the United States enjoys in the medal tally at the Olympics every four years mirrors the global power of the United States. American success at the Olympics is largely the result of individual triumphs on the track or in the gymnasium or in the pool.

One cannot deny the global reach and cultural impact of basketball, a sport invented in Massachusetts by a Canadian that grew out of YMCA culture to become a global sport and fashion phenomenon. It is undoubtedly still the most significant

American contribution to international team sports. The stars of the National Basketball Association (NBA) are outsized global icons, recognized as much for the clothes and shoes they wear and promote as for their abilities on the court.

The historical remembrance of American sporting icons is also the product of the strong culture in the United States of sports writing—a culture that could rightly be called "literary sports journalism." Great American writers have often turned their pen to portraying boxers and boxing bouts: Norman Mailer on the "rumble in the jungle" (the 1974 Muhammad Ali–George Foreman bout that took place in Zaire, orchestrated by promoter Don King), David Remnick on Mike Tyson, and Joyce Carol Oates on boxing. Many of the great essays about the stars and "wannabes" of the full panoply of American sports have been collected every year since 1991 in Glenn Stout's series *The Best American Sports Writing*. These essays offer insight into American culture and set a standard of popular sports writing that is rarely met in other English-language nations. This is somewhat ironic, given the impact that US-styled commercialism has had at times on the integrity and wonder of modern sports.

America and Its Firearms

Yet another way America is exceptional is in the number of firearms owned by individuals and the number of deaths caused each year by those firearms. Although gun rights advocates say that people, not guns, kill people, there is no doubt that the more guns there are, the more people will die from gunshots, by suicide, homicide, accidents, or from clashes with law enforcement.

Although statistics on firearms are not especially trustworthy, Americans own more firearms per capita and America has more firearm-related deaths each year than most other nations, and more than any other developed nation. Recent data suggest that there are over 300 million privately owned firearms in the United States; there are, therefore, nearly as many firearms in America as there are Americans, although the common stereotype that all Americans own a weapon is most certainly not true. In 2010, the United States had a firearm murder rate of about 3.2 per 100,000 people, according to the United Nations Office on Drugs and Crime: roughly twenty times the rate for other developed nations. (Honduras, in turn—often called the murder capital of the world—has around twenty times the firearm homicide rate of the United States.) Many firearms-related deaths in the United States are linked to the drug trade, alcohol abuse, domestic violence, suicide, and gang violence. Most of the mass shootings in recent decades have been by mentally unstable individuals who had access to automatic weapons.

Gun ownership is a contentious and politically charged issue in the United States. Passion often runs high on both sides of the issue, with little room for compromise. Many gun rights advocates, whose interests are represented by the politically powerful National Rifle Association (NRA), believe that if they give up the right to gun owner- ship, other rights will follow. In some states, especially in the South and Great Plains, failure to support gun rights by voting for restrictions on gun ownership and sales often ends the careers of politicians at all levels of government. The NRA grades politicians on their voting records on gun rights, with grades ranging from A (consistently pro–gun ownership) to F (consistently pro–gun control). The debate over gun rights is complicated and emotional, with relatively little trustworthy information available to policy makers.

At the core of the debate, for many, is the Second Amendment to the Constitu- tion: "A well regulated militia, being necessary to the security of a free state, the right of the people to keep and bear arms, shall not be infringed." Gun rights advocates argue that the amendment makes gun ownership by American citizens a constitution- ally guaranteed right that can be limited only by amending the Constitution. They see gun ownership as an element of the core American values of individual freedom and liberty; as a legal means to protects oneself, one's family, and one's property; and as an insurance policy against tyranny. These advocates believe that they will be safer if they own firearms: indeed, the nation would be safer if there were *more* firearms, not less. A common argument of gun-rights advocates is that if guns are outlawed for ordinary citizens, only criminals will be left owning guns.

It should be noted that only a tiny minority of gun owners obtain guns for the purpose of harming another human being. Most own guns in order to hunt (an American tradition, particularly in rural areas), to target shoot, or for self-defense; many others collect guns. In rural America, learning to shoot and hunt is part of growing up, and shooting one's first game animal is an important rite of passage.

Gun control advocates interpret the Second Amendment differently. They see this amendment as a product of post-revolutionary America when men who were called to serve in local militias were expected to supply their own firearms. Today, these advocates say, those who serve in the American armed forces are supplied with weapons by the government, making the need for individual ownership—especially ownership of high-power, automatic weapons—obsolete. Most gun-control advocates, realizing that the majority of gun owners are responsible owners, wish to ban access to the types of high-power, high-capacity weapons that have been used in a spate of mass murders, while still allowing legal access to weapons such as hunting rifles.

Court cases have not yet fully sorted out these opposing viewpoints. Efforts to control gun ownership and thereby gun violence (according to gun control advocates) have become public issues in the late twentieth and early twenty-first centuries following a number of mass murders of innocent adults and children in public places such as schools, movie theaters, college campuses, and shopping centers. A spate of mass shootings in Columbine and Aurora, Colorado (1999 and 2012, respectively); Blacksburg, Virginia, site of the nation's deadliest rampage, on the campus of Virginia Tech (2007); Fort Hood, Texas (2009 and again in 2014); Binghamton, New York (2009); Tucson, Arizona, where US Representative Gabrielle Giffords and eighteen others (including a federal judge) were shot (2011); and the Washington Navy Yard (2013) only hint at the severity of the problem.

One of the most shocking of many shocking incidents—one that gun control advocates were sure would lead to the widespread enactment of gun control laws—was the killing of twenty young children and six educators at an elementary school in Newtown, Connecticut in December, 2012 by a mentally disturbed young man whose mother (whom he also killed) owned a large collection of automatic weapons.

Efforts to control gun violence focus on restrictions on sales through background checks of buyers to ban sales to those with histories of criminal behavior or mental illness, limiting the types of guns and ammunition that can be purchased, training for gun owners, and buy-backs by local police departments. Following the Newtown massacre, the federal government failed to pass new gun control legislation. Some states, such as New York, California, and Connecticut, did pass new control legislation, while others, such as Texas, Florida, and Kansas, passed new legislation easing restrictions, including allowing the carrying of concealed weapons in public. In the wake of the Newtown tragedy, the nation is more divided than ever over the issue of gun control.

CHAPTER SEVEN: THE ENVIRONMENTAL HISTORY OF THE UNITED STATES

American environmental activists helped found the modern environmental movement in the twentieth century, but the United States has since fallen behind other countries in protecting the environment and fighting global climate change. Whether in absolute or per capita terms, the United States ranks high in most surveys among the world's largest consumers of natural resources, especially oil, natural gas, copper, lead, and zinc: even meat and coffee (but not wine or beer: those titles belong to China and the Czech Republic, respectively). The United States also ranks as one of the world's largest polluters. Whereas the United States accounts for only 4 percent of the world's population, it produces 25 percent of all carbon dioxide emissions.

The same country has also been at the forefront of many global environmental initiatives. Although American environmental philosophy appears compatible with that of the rest of the globe, as seen from numerous laws and international agreements that have been inspired by US laws, the implementation of this philosophy has differed from administration to administration. Those inconsistencies have led to sharp criticism in the global debate. These inconsistencies have a long history, and there are several reasons for them: chief among them are the often tangled roles of science and religion in American society.

In a famous 1967 essay titled "The Historical Roots of Our Ecological Crisis," published in the magazine *Science*, the historian Lynn White, Jr. (1907–1987) concluded that Christianity, particularly Protestantism, bears "a huge burden of guilt" for the environmental woes of the world. Although this essay has been widely criticized, those who agree with White's claim point out that those Western countries—like the United States—that are largely responsible for environmental problems such as climate change, ozone depletion, toxic waste piling, and various forms of pollution, are also countries where Protestantism has historically been influential. As an example, Genesis 1:27–28 (Revised Standard Version), says: "So God created man in his own image; male and female he created them. And God blessed them, and God said to them, 'Be fruitful and multiply, and fill the earth and subdue it; and have dominion . . .'" As a historically Christian nation, this attitude toward the environment as a thing to be subdued and put to good use has had a profound impact on the directions the United States has taken in its environmental history, from the felling of America's forests to make room for agriculture and villages (centered around a Christian church) to the wholesale removal of whole forests to create charcoal for the iron industry.

In the wake of the White essay, more and more modern religious thinkers (Christians as well as others) have used religion to spur ecological improvements, citing other biblical verses that stress the importance of caring for the land. Abraham and Lot, and later Jacob and Esau, dispersed their flocks and herds because "the land could not support both of them dwelling together" (Genesis 13:2–13, 36:6–8). These nomads were exceeding the carrying capacity, ecologists now say. They knew enough to let land lie fallow in the seventh year for its regeneration.

Putting aside questions of how much of an effect religion had on the nation's development, the environmental history of the United States has followed a distinct pattern: natural resource exploitation (mainly forests), which led to the development of the conservation movement, followed by concern about wilderness preservation, before the modern environmental movement appeared in the post–World War II era, mainly credited to two books: Rachel Carson's *Silent Spring* and Aldo Leopold's *A Sand County Almanac*, both discussed below.

Although native peoples had used the land for thousands of years prior to European settlement beginning in the seventeenth century, the rapid growth of population over the first three hundred years of European settlement took a toll on many resources. By the late nineteenth century, resource depletion sparked the conservation and preservation movements, which sought to manage resources—in the words of Gifford Pinchot, the first chief of the US Forest Service—for the "greatest good, of the greatest number, for the longest time," and to set aside lands for national parks and to preserve wildlife and wilderness. (In 1965 Pinchot's hometown of Simsbury, Connecticut dedicated the largest tree in Connecticut in Pinchot's honor; today it is known as the "Pinchot Sycamore.") By the end of the twentieth century the environmental movement was focused on environmental quality and justice, and included the regulation of industrial pollution and urban development.

Over time, science has joined religion in playing an integral role in shaping attitudes and policy toward the environment. Science was initially used to exploit natural resources, but the conservation movement soon engaged science as a tool for developing resources more efficiently. The twentieth-century American environmental movement used the sciences not only to manage resources, but to justify not developing them at all.

Natural Resource Exploitation

Until the 1820s, European settlers looked upon forests as frightening and potentially dangerous places—hindrances to be removed to allow for a more familiar-looking European-style landscape of farms and villages—even though they often provided essential resources settlers needed. In a subtle shift in attitude, the growing demand for wood by the mid-nineteenth century led businesspeople, land speculators, and even the federal government to view forests as just another agricultural commodity to be bought, sold, and harvested. Changes in saw technology and manufacturing made it possible to cut down more trees more quickly. By 1850 the lumber industry had become the second-largest industry in the United States and remained among the top five industries in the nation until 1920.

Forests provided more than just timber. They also provided habitat for essential game animals that provided meat for settlers and Native Americans alike, and valuable skins and pelts for trade with European merchants. As early as 1604, French and British explorers began trading with Native Americans: French and British traded furs for knives, glasses, combs, hatchets, kettles, and food. Between 1700 and 1775, the beaver supplied over half of England's total fur imports, and eight other animals totaled another 40 percent of imports. The beaver and its habitats disappeared from the New England states, as did other associated species. Hunters drove the white-tailed deer out of all of New England except Maine by 1890, along with the buffalo, the American elk, caribou, wild turkey, and moose. Several tribes in New England had become dependent on European traders for food and European tools, which accelerated the rate at which animals were killed. This pattern of exploitation and extermination was repeated in other regions with other animals used for trade purposes, including otter (West Coast), buffalo (the Great Plains), and deer (the Southeast).

Agriculture also contributed to environmental problems. In the South, early dependence on commercial crops created a vicious cycle: because tobacco and cotton quickly rob the soil of nutrients, land had to be rehabilitated by being enriched with fertilizer or by being left fallow for several seasons, or new land had to be acquired.

The American bison, the largest land mammal in North America, once roamed the Great Plains in the millions. The species was virtually exterminated by hunters in the 1800s but today has made a comeback, notably in Yellowstone National Park, pictured here. Photo by Amy Siever.

Impatient growers, who were focused on immediate profits rather than long-term planning, moved on to new land instead of developing environmentally beneficial practices. Commercial production led to the wasteful clearing of forests as farmers continually relocated. Clearing land of ground cover created soil erosion problems: waterways clogged with silt and vital topsoil lost.

The Conservation Movement

Just as forests were the first resource exploited, they were also the first resource protected. The dramatic increase in lumber production during the late 1800s, coupled with the visual evidence of how deforestation altered the landscape, created fear of a timber famine. Modern visitors to the heavily wooded New England states—New Hampshire leads the nation in tree cover at 89 percent, followed closed by Maine (83 percent) and Vermont (82 percent)—are often surprised to learn that the landscape was radically different one hundred years ago, when the ratio was reversed. Today's seemingly endless forests were almost gone, felled for charcoal production, lumber, and paper-making. The conservation movement of the late nineteenth century was a direct response to that fear. In the 1860s and 1870s, a small group of American scientists and political leaders, including George Perkins Marsh, Charles S. Sargent, and Carl Schurz, spoke out against the rapid deforestation, as well as the depletion of water, minerals, and soil that went with the deforestation. Interest groups, often founded and led by the wealthy, such as the American Forestry Association (forests), the Boone and Crockett Club (big game), and the National Audubon Society (birds), were formed to protect specific resources; recreation groups like the Appalachian Mountain Club and the Sierra Club also became involved when industrial activities threatened the places where their members hiked or camped. They deplored the un-regulated exploitation of natural resources and called for government action on public land. Many favored conservation, or the sustained yield of renewable resources, such as water, trees, and game animals, and the careful, scientific management of both

The Appalachian Trail

The entire length of the Appalachian Mountain chain in the eastern United States is threaded by the Appalachian Trail, a 2,181-mile (3,500-km) trail conceived by forester and conservationist Benton MacKaye of Connecticut in 1921 and completed in 1937. The trail, which stretches from Mount Katahdin in Maine to Springer Mountain in Georgia, remains a popular destination for residents and visitors alike. MacKaye conceived of the trail as a "new approach to the problem of living." The National Park Service, which administers the trail, estimates that four million people a year enjoy the trail. Today the "AT" is the nation's longest national park. The trail depends on volunteers for upkeep of the trail itself—clearing away brush and ensuring that heavy rains and flooding don't wash away the surface of the trail or its numerous log bridges—as well as for the rustic shelters that are spaced roughly a day's hike apart for the length of the trail.

Other long-distance trails in the United States include the Pacific Crest Trail, which travels 2,600 miles (4,100 km) from Canada to Mexico along the Cascades and Sierra Nevada ranges in Washington, Oregon, and California; and the 3,100-mile (5,000-km) Continental Divide Trail, a rugged, not always clearly marked trail in the Rocky Mountains that runs the length of the high divide separating the waters of the Atlantic and Pacific oceans. The Continental Divide Trail sees far fewer visitors than its cousins to the west and east due to the rugged nature of the trail: much of the trail is buried in deep snow for a large part of the year.

> God has cared for these trees, saved them from drought, disease, avalanches, and a thousand tempests and floods. But he cannot save them from fools.
>
> —NATURALIST JOHN MUIR

renewable and nonrenewable resources on a permanent basis. They petitioned Congress to take action.

Congress responded by passing first the Forest Reserve Act in 1891 and subsequently the Forest Management Act in 1897; together these laws laid the foundation for federal land management. In 1892 the State of New York created the enormous 48,400 square-kilometer (18,700-square-mile) Adirondack Park, in northern New York State, which is larger than the Grand Canyon, Yosemite, Yellowstone, Glacier, and the Great Smoky Mountains national parks combined.

At the same time these federal and state laws were being passed, government science bureaus, increasingly staffed by graduates of recently formed professional schools, were being established. Decisive action, however, began only during Theodore Roosevelt's presidency (1901–1909). The Roosevelt administration made scientific land management for utilitarian purposes—captured in Pinchot's "the greatest good" phrase—accepted policy. This policy also contributed to a split within the nascent conservation movement in 1906, when the city of San Francisco, in the wake of the Great San Francisco Earthquake and subsequent fires that ravaged the city, applied to the federal government to access the water of the glacially carved Hetch Hetchy Valley of Yosemite National Park. After a protracted legal struggle with environmental groups, led by Scotland-born naturalist John Muir (1838–1914) and the Sierra Club, the federal government eventually approved construction of a dam in 1913, and the valley was flooded. Preservationists who wanted to leave the hitherto pristine valley undeveloped no longer trusted the US Forest Service to protect federal lands, and successfully agitated for creation of a separate national park system and bureau to manage those lands. The National Park Service was created in 1916 in an effort to counter the utilitarianism that had won in the Hetch Hetchy Valley.

Aldo Leopold and "The Land Ethic"

Aldo Leopold (1887–1948) was a forester and wildlife ecologist best known today for his influential 1948 book of nature sketches and philosophical essays, *A Sand County Almanac*, in which he articulated a vision of harmony between people and land and the concept of a land ethic. He is widely considered among the most influential environmental writers in twentieth-century America, as well as the father of the wilderness movement and of the profession of wildlife management.

Leopold was born in Burlington, Iowa, where he developed his acute powers of observation and love of "things natural, wild, and free" along the bluffs and bottomlands of the Mississippi River. After graduating from Yale University with a master of forestry degree in 1909, he joined the US Forest Service, rising to become supervisor of Carson National Forest in New Mexico by age twenty-five, and then to assistant district forester in the Southwest (1918–1924). During those years he organized game protective associations in New Mexico and Arizona; laid the groundwork for a new profession of game management modeled on forestry; made important contributions to the ecological understanding of soil erosion, watersheds, and fire; and developed a rationale for the 1924 designation of the Gila Wilderness in New Mexico, the prototype for the national wilderness system given force of law by the Wilderness Act of 1964 and now totaling nearly 433,000 square kilometers: an area larger than California, with the vast majority of designated wilderness in Alaska.

In the final decade of his career he found his voice as an essayist and further developed his conviction of human responsibility for the restoration of land health, expressed most clearly in "The Land Ethic," the capstone essay of *A Sand County Almanac*: "A thing is right when it tends to preserve the integrity, stability, and beauty of the biotic community. It is wrong when it tends otherwise." The book was accepted for publication only days before Leopold died on 21 April 1948 while fighting a grass fire near the farm along the Wisconsin River that he and his family had restored to ecological integrity.

Leopold's writings won a broad general audience during the ecological awakening of the 1970s, the *Almanac* selling well over 1 million copies, but not until the 1990s was the significance of his ideas of land stewardship, ecological restoration, and ecosystem management acknowledged by the Forest Service and other natural resource agencies and professions among whom he had first articulated them. But even more important is the inspiration that his conviction of individual responsibility as "plain member and citizen" of the land community has provided for conservation efforts on private lands and in local communities, battling the sprawl that has become a common sight in today's American landscape.

National Parks

Most historians credit the establishment of Yellowstone National Park in 1872 as the world's first national park—the first time in history that a large area of land was protected for the benefit of all people—and an important manifestation of conservation and democratic ideals. The historian and author Wallace Stegner (1909–1993) famously wrote that the national parks are "the best idea we ever had." Today there are fifty-eight national parks in the United States, and national parks have been established in nearly all countries around the world.

A number of important national parks were established by Congress in the decades following Yellowstone's creation, but no agency was established to manage these areas until 1916; the US Cavalry had taken care of this duty previously. Congress established the National Park Service in 1916 with the mandate to "conserve the scenery and the natural and historic objects and the wildlife therein, and to provide for the enjoyment of the same in such manner and by such means as will leave them unimpaired for the enjoyment of future generations."

Since the creation of Yellowstone National Park almost a century and a half ago, many more national parks have been established. In 1933, all federally owned parks, memorials, and related historic sites were transferred from other federal agencies to the National Park Service. Beginning in the 1960s, new types of parks were added. Large urban parks were established in several major metropolitan areas, such as Gateway National Recreation Area in New York and Golden Gate National Recreation Area in the San Francisco Bay area of California. The purpose of these parks was to help ensure access to outdoor recreation and national parks for urban residents.

National seashores and lakeshores were also established to address the scarcity of public outdoor recreation areas along the nation's coastlines, including Cape Cod National Seashore on the Atlantic coast, Point Reyes National Seashore on the Pacific coast, Padre Island National Seashore on the Gulf Coast, and Pictured Rocks National Lakeshore on Lake Superior. The newest members of the National Park System are called National Heritage Areas: geographic regions that often include little or no public lands, but where federal, state, and local governments, private businesses, and nonprofit institutions collaborate to ensure conservation of significant natural and cultural resources. The Northern Rio Grande National Heritage Area, in northern New Mexico, where residents speak Spanish, Tewa, Apache, and Tiwa, in addition to English, is one such region.

The National Park System now comprises nearly four hundred areas totaling approximately 340,000 square kilometers (130,000 square miles, or about the size of Finland), in all but two states. Fifty-eight of these areas are official national parks, while the rest are national monuments, historic sites and parks, seashores and lakeshores, national recreation areas, national trails and rivers, battlefields, and a variety of other categories. The National Park System is a principal recreation destination for Americans and overseas visitors, accommodating nearly 300 million visitors annually.

National parks face many challenging management issues, not least of which is funding. (See page 189 for one unfortunate result of this.) The 1916 Organic Act of

America's famous national park system was created to protect the country's unique landscapes, such as the deep canyons found in Zion National Park, Utah, pictured here. The Park System has since expanded to include National Seashores, National Battlegrounds, and other areas of historic and cultural importance. Photo by Amy Siever.

the National Park Service requires that national parks be preserved as well as used for recreation. The popularity of national parks can make it difficult to find the proper balance between these often competing objectives. Snowmobilers in Yellowstone, for instance, have clashed with people who want the park preserved for quieter pursuits such as cross-country skiing and wildlife photography; the snowmobilers counter that they bring much-needed economic input to the communities surrounding the park boundaries. After years of back-and-forth wrangling, in 2013 the Park Service made a compromise, seemingly welcomed by all sides, that allows a certain number of snowmobiles and snow coaches into the park on any given day, but requires users to ride on a new generation of quieter, cleaner machines.

Other challenges to preservation include the limited size of national parks and the evolving meaning of preservation itself. Initial notions of protecting natural features such as forests and iconic wildlife by suppressing fires and eliminating predators such as wolves and mountain lions have given way to the more contemporary idea of ensuring the continuation of natural processes, by allowing forest fires to burn and restoring predators such as wolves to their native habitats, often to the dismay of ranchers in the lands surrounding the national parks.

Federal conservation measures protected only public lands, however, not private lands. Clearing land for agriculture remained the biggest factor in altering the environment.

Forest removal had caused flooding, soil erosion, and loss of wildlife and their habitats on land and in waterways, sometimes causing permanent changes. In 1911, out of concern for watershed protection, Congress passed the Weeks Act, which enabled the federal government to purchase private lands in the eastern United States for incorporation into the national forest system, and to establish a federal-state cooperative framework for fire protection. In the 1920s, automobiles made forests and parks more accessible to more people. The internal combustion engine also helped mechanize farming and logging, although the ramifications of this were not immediately understood.

In the 1930s, President Franklin Roosevelt's administration, faced with the twin crises of the Great Depression and environmental overexploitation (most notably the Dust Bowl, discussed below), expanded state-controlled management. Through programs such as this—as well as the Civilian Conservation Corps and the Tennessee Valley Authority, and agencies like the Forest Service and the Grazing Service—the government tried to use science and commerce to reverse environmental damage on both private and public lands.

The Dust Bowl

Today the term "dust bowl" is applied to any area that is badly affected by wind erosion. Originally, in the 1930s, the term Dust Bowl referred to an area of the Great Plains of North America that experienced huge clouds of blowing dirt, leading to severe economic and social dislocation. A reporter invented the term, but exactly what he meant has never been clear. Perhaps he was thinking of the vast interior of the continent, with the Rocky Mountains as the rim, as a vessel that had been producing cereal grains but now was producing only dust. The US Soil Conservation Service adopted the term officially, designating the western third of Kansas, southeastern Colorado, the Oklahoma Panhandle, the northern two-thirds of the Texas Panhandle, and northeastern New Mexico as the Dust Bowl.

These conditions of severe wind erosion first appeared in the spring of 1934, when a massive dust storm swept eastward out of Montana and Wyoming. As it blew along, it picked up more and more dirt, until giant clouds of airborne dirt were blowing eastward. In early May the storm reached Chicago, then moved on to New York, Boston, and Washington, DC. Ships in the Atlantic, some of them several days' voyage off the coast, found dust on their decks. Later dust storms were mostly confined to the Southern Plains. Some of them were dramatic "black blizzards," rising like a long wall thousands of meters high.

This catastrophic erosion led to a devastating loss of farm income as crops failed and livestock (along with wildlife) died from ingesting the dust. Many people suffered

A farmer in Cimarron County, Oklahoma, raises his fence in an effort to keep it from becoming buried in wind-blown dust. Source: Library of Congress. Photo by Arthur Rothstein, 1936.

from lung damage, or "dust pneumonia," the destruction of their homes and property, and huge financial losses. They also suffered from the psychological trauma of the storms, as it became virtually impossible to do ordinary things like walking outside, hanging laundry out to dry, and even breathing outdoors. Starving families resorted to eating pickled tumbleweed. Recurring years of such conditions turned many people into environmental refugees seeking homes elsewhere: in Arizona, California, or the Pacific Northwest. In the worst-hit Dust Bowl counties, one-third to one-half of the population left during the decade. For those who stayed, bankruptcies were common among both farmers and the townspeople who depended on them. The classic John Steinbeck novel *The Grapes of Wrath* is a tragic tale of one such family of "Okies," the Joads, who migrate to California in search of a better life. ("Okie" was the derogatory term given to Dust Bowl refugees from Oklahoma and other states; the 1969 anti-counterculture song "Okie From Muskogee" by country musician Merle Haggard is a celebration of this heritage.)

The causes of this environmental disaster, the worst in American history, remain a matter of controversy. Some historians, along with many surviving residents of the area, tend to see humans as innocent victims of a natural disaster; without drought, they say, there would have been good crops and no wind erosion. Certainly, the drought experienced in the 1930s was unprecedented for severity and duration in the previous half-century period of white settlement of the Great Plains. But other historians and scientists have argued that the Dust Bowl owed much to human actions, as well as to natural cycles. Agriculture, they say, was largely to blame for its own misfortunes—particularly a system of agriculture that was more attentive to short-term economic gain and distant urban market prices than to long-term ecological patterns and local environmental realities. The main cause was the plowing up of the shortgrass prairie, a perennial plant whose roots had previously held the topsoil in place, in favor of wheat, an annual that must be replanted each year.

During World War I and the 1920s, wheat farming expanded at a phenomenal rate into the windy, drought-prone Plains, driven by the same speculative fever that gripped the whole American economy. The farming that came to the area was commercial, market-driven, characterized by rapid mechanization (gasoline tractors, wheat combines), by a high degree of monoculture specialization, and by heavy borrowing and intense capitalization. As more and more of the prairie was dug up and devoted to wheat, the price of wheat dropped; as the price of wheat dropped, farmers plowed up more and more of the shortgrass prairie to make a profit. Although the typical Plains farm was family-owned and operated, many operators were tenants

Preparing for the Long Journey West

In the little houses the tenant people sifted their belongings and the belongings of their fathers and of their grandfathers. Picked over their possessions for the journey to the west. The men were ruthless because the past had been spoiled, but the women knew how the past would cry to them in the coming days. The men went into the barns and the sheds.

That plow, that harrow, remember in the war we planted mustard? Remember a fella wanted us to put in that rubber bush they call guayule? Get rich, he said. Bring out those tools—get a few dollars for them. Eighteen dollars for that plow, plus freight—Sears Roebuck.

Harness, carts, seeders, little bundles of hoes. Bring 'em out. Pile 'em up. Load 'em in the wagon. Take 'em to town. Sell 'em for what you can get. Sell the team and the wagon, too. No more use for anything.

—John Steinbeck, *The Grapes of Wrath* (1939)

moving from place to place, whereas others were "suitcase farmers"—speculators from town who invested in wheat cropping as others invested in the stock market. Just as Wall Street collapsed in 1929, setting off the Great Depression, so historians have argued, the wheat boom collapsed about the same time. The Dust Bowl, by this interpretation, was a disaster created by modern farming methods and motives, an extreme example of the ecological damage caused by commercial agriculture.

The federal government quickly launched a massive rescue effort in the 1930s, sending over $1 billion into Western counties in an attempt to keep people on the land and in the region. Whether wisely or not, that aid provided a cushion for failure. Federal disaster assistance, soil-saving techniques, and crop subsidies became a permanent way of life. In 1941 the rainfall returned, leading to a long, wet period of recovery and a return to production expansion. Besides government help, farmers came to depend on the new technology of deep-well irrigation—pumping up groundwater from the Ogallala aquifer to supplement the moisture supply. Severe but short-lived droughts continued to occur over the next fifty years, but none had the environmental or economic consequences of the Dust Bowl years, leading many optimists to believe that human ingenuity and improved technology had made another disaster impossible. More realistically, a constant flow of federal dollars, peaking in drought years, along with the mining of groundwater, is why farmers and ranchers have managed to stave off another general catastrophe. Neither panacea is dependable, however, and an agricultural system driven by market opportunism in a highly volatile climate must always face an uncertain future. Meanwhile, in other arid and semiarid parts of the world, similar patterns of desertification and dust bowls have proliferated, raising questions about how agriculture in marginal environments can ever be made safe and reliable.

Wilderness Preservation and Environmentalism

Wilderness preservation and protection had grown along with the conservation movement, in part as a reaction to disasters such as the Dust Bowl and the leveling of the eastern forests, but they largely remained a secondary priority until the 1960s. Until then, scientific research provided a rationale for subduing the wild for the benefit of humankind. Between the two world wars, federal and state governments supported the systematic elimination of wolves and other predators from grazing areas, parks, and forests to increase big game populations for hunters. They built roads and lodging facilities in public parks and forest recreation areas to make wilderness more accessible to more people. During World War II, and into the postwar era, the federal government responded to the unprecedented demands for natural resources by relaxing regulations on public lands and cooperating with industry. The environment suffered proportionate injury from increased extraction activities such as mining and lumbering, from the introduction of chemical pesticides in agriculture, and from the discharge of industrial waste into waterways, landfills, and the air.

The tragedies of the Dust Bowl era had exposed the weakness of unlimited resource exploitation. Conservationists' focus on efficient development of natural resources no longer provided all the answers. Ecologists began explaining to the general public how human activity affects the environment and that humans are part of the environment, not separate from it. In the early 1950s, the public's growing interest in outdoor activity in a more natural environment fused with the science of ecology to create the environmental movement. The unfettered access to public forests and parks allowed private citizens to see how government was managing public lands and led some to begin questioning policies and practices they deemed harmful to the environment.

Environmental consciousness grew exponentially in the 1960s, influenced by concerns such as nuclear radiation from the testing of atomic weapons, an unsustainable increase in the birthrate, and the Santa Barbara, California, oil spill of 1969, which brought environmental disaster to the doorstep of counterculture-era California. The Santa Barbara oil spill was the largest oil spill in American waters at the time, until it was overtaken first in 1989 by the *Exxon Valdez* spill (in Alaska) and then by the larger *Deepwater Horizon* spill in the Gulf of Mexico in 2010. This new consciousness received its greatest expression with the organization of the first Earth Day in 1970, when thousands of people joined in marches across the nation, proclaiming "Give Earth a Chance."

The Legacy of *Silent Spring*

Some historians have stated that the 1962 book *Silent Spring* is responsible for launching the modern environmental movement in the United States. Rachel L. Carson (1907–1964), a government marine biologist with the US Fish and Wildlife Service, had written several environmental books before publishing her most famous one, *Silent Spring*, which decried society's widespread overuse of pesticides. Many people read Carson's work; extensive news coverage about her book led to more widespread concern about science and technology and its unregulated application in addressing various environmental problems. In response to this and other public concerns, the federal government passed a series of laws aimed at cleaning up air and water pollution and protecting wilderness areas and wild and scenic rivers. This culminated in the passage of the National Environmental Policy Act (NEPA) in 1969, whose aim was to promote the enhancement of the environment by establishing a system of procedures and assessments (known as "environmental impact statements") that all federal agencies had to follow; NEPA has since been emulated by numerous nations around the world. From that point forward, government policy evaluated resources for both their aesthetic and commercial value. It is unlikely that the Hetch Hetchy development plan from earlier in the century would have been approved if an environmental impact statement of some sort had been performed on the site. Carson's critique also contributed directly to the establishment of the United States Environmental Protection Agency (EPA) in 1972.

Silent Spring also helped transform the environmental community. Membership in organizations like the Sierra Club, the Wilderness Society, and the National Audubon Society greatly increased during the 1960s. Many housewives in the new consumer- and technology-oriented postwar era took up Carson's arguments, horrified at the hidden dangers they now perceived to be lurking around their homes. These environmental issues particularly attracted young people, many of whom were also involved in the student and/or civil rights movements.

With her 1962 book *Silent Spring,* marine biologist Rachel Carson alerted postwar America to the hazards of synthetic chemical pesticides and established herself as a major intellectual leader of the contemporary environmental movement. Source: National Oceanic and Atmospheric Administration.

All sides in the debate over the environment deployed scientific arguments to support their causes. Some scientists favored responding to ecological problems with increased human intervention, whereas others, like Carson, favored a reduction. Industry used its own scientific findings to support the status quo or the removal of regulations. When information about ecological damage reached the general public, however, it generated a passionate desire to reduce human intervention. Private organizations such as the Wilderness Society and the Sierra Club expressed a desire to limit or halt development in public wilderness areas, and to set them aside for protection on behalf of the general public. Demands to protect nature became a major factor in the debate over the environment. In 1965, only 17 percent of the American public questioned in a Gallup poll said they wanted the government to tackle air and water pollution. By 1970, this figure had risen to just over half the respondents. Between 1972 and 1976, other polls indicated that between 46 and 60 percent of the American public was very concerned about reducing pollution.

The discovery of toxic waste under the Love Canal neighborhood in the city of Niagara Falls, New York, in the late 1970s shifted the focus to urban environmental problems. The neighborhood had been knowingly built over a toxic waste dump site, which caused widespread health problems for residents. After local officials refused to take action, the federal government stepped in and paid to relocate residents; it also passed, in 1980, the so-called Superfund, formally known as the Comprehensive Environmental Response, Compensation, and Liability Act, or CERCLA. This act was introduced to pay for cleanup at sites where hazardous waste had been deposited. Many have described this as the start of the environmental justice movement, which in the 1980s and 1990s was instrumental in working for a safer, fairer, and healthier environment for all.

By the 1980s, more and more environmental organizations were becoming huge, bureaucratic operations (many far removed from local issues) and were increasingly focused on national or international policies. Emboldened, environmental groups pushed for curbs on pollution—first for air and water in the 1950s and 1960s, followed by toxic chemical waste in the 1970s. They sought local, state, and federal laws to protect drinking water, clean up the air and waterways, and contain the spread of toxic chemicals. Environmentalists moved from reacting to a problem to preventing it through government regulation. If the government failed in its duty, environmentalists filed lawsuits to compel enforcement. This shift has left environmentalists at odds with industry leaders and quite frequently with the government agencies in charge of enforcing environmental regulations. Policy makers continually found themselves in a difficult situation: they had to balance the economic needs of industry, and of the local populations dependent upon it, with the ecological requirements of the land and the aesthetic and material needs of taxpayers in mind. Because all involved used scientific research to support their respective arguments, science, which had once provided answers, was now contributing to the confusion over what should be done.

Save a logger, eat an owl

—SLOGAN POPULAR IN PACIFIC NORTHWEST LOGGING TOWNS, C. 1989

Such a scenario helps explain the decline of the timber industry in the Pacific Northwest in the 1990s. When a researcher discovered that the northern spotted owl population was declining to the point that it was declared a threatened species, his research revealed that this was the result of logging the old-growth forests on the federal lands that were the owls' habitat. Environmentalists, loggers, scientists (some working for the government, some not), and government officials became embroiled in a sometimes violent battle that was oversimplified as one of "jobs versus owls." While loggers needed to be able to cut the trees for work, and many forest managers argued that cutting all trees in the area was the best way to manage the land for timber, environmental activists filed lawsuits and staged protests to shut down logging activity and preserve the forests. The situation led the US Forest Service and other agencies to rethink how it managed its lands, and it contributed to its leaders' adoption of an ecosystem-level approach, which required assessing the land for all of its economic and aesthetic values in order to properly manage its forests.

The Case of Detroit

Many people point to the rise and fall of Detroit, Michigan as a stark example of what has gone amiss in America, both with its economy and its environment. Grassroots community-based strategies are leading efforts to rethink the city's future; strategies that others in similarly afflicted cities look to for guidance.

The rapid growth of Detroit—commonly known as "Motor City," a name that spawned the popular 1950s/1960s musical form known as "motown"—in the early twentieth century was largely due to the city's concentration on automotive manufacturing. Although the work opportunities provided by industrialization initially led to the diversification of the city's population by attracting foreign immigrants and African American workers from the South, the decline of the American automotive industry (mainly due to a tradition of building big "gas guzzlers" that has only recently started to change) has since been accompanied by a severe reduction of the city's population. The region's long-standing pattern of racial segregation has led to an isolated black central city surrounded by whiter suburbs and a lack of regional planning. The city, whose population has decreased by more than half since 1950—from almost 1.9 million at mid-century to around 700,000 in 2014—faces major challenges involving regional transportation, vacant property, and air and water pollution.

Although archaeological evidence indicates that indigenous people long frequented the shoreline area that later became Detroit, European settlement of the area dates back to 1701. (The French named it "le détroit du lac Érié, or "the Strait of Lake Erie," for its strategic position on the narrow strait between two of the five Great Lakes—Erie and Huron—and the smaller Lake St. Clair.) By 1810, this early fur-trading post had evolved into a town serving the needs of the surrounding farming communities.

Advancements in water transportation, such as the first steam vessel (1818) and the steam barge (1848), significantly increased activity on the Great Lakes. Detroit's importance as a regional center was strengthened when the Erie Canal opened in 1825. The Erie Canal connected Lake Erie at Buffalo, New York, to the Hudson River and the Atlantic Ocean, and allowed ships for the first time to move gigantic shipments of grain from the Midwest to New York City via the Great Lakes system. This mammoth undertaking allowed ships to avoid having to traverse the Saint Lawrence Seaway, much of which freezes in the winter. The canal's creation, spearheaded by New York Governor DeWitt Clinton (1769–1828), for whom the canal was dubbed by his legions of critics "Clinton's Ditch," was one of the leading factors in New York City's later dominance of the American economy, and New York State's emergence as the "Empire State." It also contributed greatly to the growth of Great Lakes cities such as Detroit and Chicago.

Detroit's Automotive Industry and Immigration

Between 1900 and 1908, over five hundred automotive companies started in the United States; many of these companies, including Hudson, Nash, Fraser, Briggs, Kaiser, Packard, Chrysler, Dodge, Studebaker, and Ford, were located in Detroit. More than 60 percent of these early automotive start-ups failed within several years, however, including the first two efforts by eccentric Michigan industrialist Henry Ford (1863–1947). It was Detroit's higher ratio of truck production that established the city's dominance in automobile manufacturing relative to other Midwestern cities in the 1910s. As the system of railroads in the United States became congested, truck transportation, responsible for moving armaments and munitions to the East, became increasingly important. In 1914, Detroit's 43 car manufacturers built 25,000 trucks per year. By 1918, the last year of World War I, they were producing 227,000 trucks annually.

As the early city experienced explosive economic development, Detroit attracted multiple waves of domestic and international immigrants. The first significant wave comprised foreign-born immigrants from eastern and southern Europe. Beginning in the 1870s, a significant number of Polish, Russian, and Italian immigrants arrived. As automotive production increased in the first two decades of the twentieth century, automakers actively recruited foreign-born immigrants. In 1915, the Ford Motor Company employed workers from forty-nine different countries. In 1925, approximately half of Detroit's over 1.2 million residents had been born outside the United States: the highest percentage of foreign-born residents of any city in the country. Detroit's neighborhoods were divided into ethnic enclaves with utilitarian names such as Poletown, Jewtown, Germantown, Greektown, Hunkytown (inhabited by Hungarians), Corktown (the oldest neighborhood, originally settled by refugees from the Irish potato famine), and Black Bottom, inhabited mainly by African Americans. (The name was not a reference to race; the French originally named the area for its rich black soil.)

The second important wave of immigration to Detroit began in the 1920s when American immigration laws tightened (as discussed in the section on immigration in Chapter Three), thereby making it difficult for foreign-born immigrants to enter the country. With the continuing expansion of local industries, Detroit's employers began recruiting workers from within the United States. It was during this second major wave of immigration that a significant number of African Americans arrived from the South (as part of what was called the Great Migration) and white migrants arrived from the Appalachian Mountains.

World War II created tremendous demand for Allied armaments and munitions. Automakers and their suppliers produced US$30 billion worth of military equipment from 1942 to 1945. But when the automakers built new factories to meet this demand, many were located outside Detroit's boundaries. In the 1950s until the late 1960s, expressways transformed the urban landscapes of American cities and helped trigger the initial stages of the suburban exodus. After the war, in what is termed "white flight," large numbers of predominantly white residents left Detroit for newer and larger homes in the suburbs, relying on cars to commute to work. Undoubtedly influenced by the powerful automobile industry, city leaders saw highways as a method by which to ease traffic congestion, remove "blighted areas," and increase the downtown's competitiveness with the emerging suburbs. The large swaths of land required for highway construction within the city, however, were generally taken from poorer neighborhoods. The construction of highways to the city's downtown and the overdevelopment of highway infrastructure within the city came at the expense of mass transit alternatives.

The Birth of Sprawl

American suburbanization was spurred by a number of social and political factors. Through the Federal Housing Administration (FHA) and Veterans Administration (VA) loan programs, the federal government provided mortgages for 11 million new homes after World War II. With the surge in American population called the "baby boom," a new American ideal was born: a new single-family home in an outlying suburb. Policies of FHA and VA programs discouraged the renovation of existing houses and turned buyers away from urban areas like Detroit.

Planners created home styles that allowed them to develop one site after another, with the automobile linking each one to the outside world. This shift to suburban living became a hallmark of the late twentieth century, with over half of the nation residing in suburbs by the 1990s. The planning system that supported this residential world, however, involved much more than roads. The services necessary to support outlying, suburban communities also needed to be integrated by planners.

Instead of the Main Street prototype, the auto suburbs demanded a new form. Initially, American planners such as Jesse Clyde Nichols devised shopping areas like Kansas City's Country Club District, which appeared as a hybrid of previous forms.

Soon, however, the "strip" evolved as the commercial corridor of the future. These sites quickly became part of suburban development in order to provide basic services close to home. A shopper rarely arrived without an automobile; therefore, the car needed to be part of the design program. Signs were the most obvious architectural development of this new landscape. Integrated into the overall site plan would be towering neon advertisements that identified services. Also, parking lots and drive-through windows suggest the integral role of transportation in this new commerce. In short, sprawl had arrived.

During this period of massive home construction, federal and local subsidies also spurred the construction of roads—including President Eisenhower's 66,000-kilometer (40,000-mile) interstate highway system. The scale of this construction will likely stand as one of the great building feats of human history; some historians have argued that the interstate system was the most far-reaching (some go so far as to say destructive) development, public or private, in US environmental history. Between 1945 and 1954, nine million Americans moved to places such as the Detroit suburbs of Farmington Hills and Grosse Pointe, and became entirely reliant on roadways in their everyday lives. Between 1950 and 1976, central city population in the United States grew by 10 million while suburban population grew by 85 million. Housing developments and the shopping / strip mall culture that accompanied decentralization of the population made the automobile a virtual necessity.

The automobile proved to be the ultimate tool for decentralizing the landscape. With satellite communities constructed far away from downtown resources and shopping, developers seized the opportunity to develop the arteries connecting suburbs to cities. With little thought to livability or other priorities, suburbs incorporated shopping and service areas that would evolve into forms on the American landscape. The common link between each portion of the landscape became the automobile.

These developments culminated in the shopping mall, which quickly became a necessary portion of sprawl. By the 1970s, developers' initiatives clearly included regional economic development for a newly evolving service and retail world. Incorporating suburbs into such development plans, designs for these pseudo-communities were held together by the automobile.

Strip malls, which open on to roadways and parking lots, were installed near residential areas as suburbs extended farther from the city center. Developers then perfected the self-sustained, enclosed shopping mall. Try as they might, such artificial environments could never re-create the culture of local communities. Shopping malls became the symbol of a culture of conspicuous consumption that many Americans began to criticize during the 1960s. Many Americans began to ask: have we given up our ties to genuine community?

Back in Detroit, that city's peacetime automotive manufacturing operations peaked in 1965, when 11.1 million cars, trucks, and buses were built in the United States, and automotive-related parts and products comprised approximately 10 percent of all American manufacturing shipments. Approximately one in every six people employed in the United States at this time had an automobile-related job. The dominance of American manufacturing firms began to fade, however, as foreign manufacturers, often making better (and more fuel-efficient) products, grew. Although specialized manufacturing permitted Detroit to flourish in the first half of the twentieth century, that specialization made the city and region vulnerable to changing world markets in the second half of the twentieth century.

The 2000 census determined that of 951,000 Detroit residents, 81.6 percent were black and 12.3 percent were white; the 2010 census indicated that 10.6 percent of the severely diminished number of residents (713,000) were white. Many of the remaining residents are extremely poor. With the city's financial constraints, community-based organizations are important actors, helping move neighborhoods toward stability and rethinking grassroots approaches to improving residents' quality of life. Improving the public-transportation system is one of the city's greatest challenges; Detroit is the largest metropolitan area in the United States without a regional transit authority.

On the Rebound?

Today, Detroit is more defined by its voids than by a discernible urban fabric of structures. With the loss of more than half of the city's residents since 1960, vacant land and abandoned properties are a problem. The 2009 Detroit Residential Parcel Survey (published in 2010) determined that of the city's 343,849 residential parcels, around a quarter (91,488) were either vacant or contained abandoned structures. The city's physical form, outside the downtown core, always had an open spatial character unlike that of many other cities, but the loss of population has amplified these empty spaces. With little tax base and many poor residents, Detroit took the unprecedented step of declaring bankruptcy in 2013: the first for a major American metropolitan area.

The city's vacant land, inexpensive housing stock, and wide streets have, however, resulted in the rise of urban agriculture, new creative enterprises, and an emerging biking culture. Between 2000 and 2010, the number of college-educated residents under thirty-five increased by 59 percent. Although Detroit was once the symbol of industrial advancement, today the community-based environmental and social justice efforts are rethinking what constitutes community and economic development.

The decline of the US automobile industry led to an enormous decrease in Detroit's population. A 2009 survey found that there were over 90,000 vacant land parcels within Detroit's city limits. One positive result of this decline is that community gardens like this one have sprung up in vacant lots all over the city; one group estimates there are 1,600 such gardens in the city. Photo by Larissa Larsen.

The Greening of Detroit, a local nonprofit organization, estimated that in 2012 there were 1,600 gardens of various sizes within the city. The organization has a strong community development component that sees the establishment of urban gardening, green employment opportunities, and environmental education as key to a better future for the city. The rebuilding of shattered communities has had a tremendous influence on the attempted resurrection of Detroit. Residents of similarly afflicted cities are keeping a close eye on happenings in Detroit.

America's Environmental Future

Many view Detroit—its vigorous automobile manufacturing history and its subsequent decline and, it is hoped, eventual renewal—as symptomatic of America's often rocky adjustment to the new economic and environmental realities of the twenty-first century. Since the end of the last century, the major environmental issue concerning many groups has been another of the unfortunate results of the booming automobile industry, among several other factors: climate change. Carbon dioxide emissions are the single greatest concern. Emission levels in the United States are some of the highest in the world, with approximately 16 to 20 tons of carbon released per person annually: an especially worrisome figure considering the large population of the United States.

Despite America's position as the world's leading emitter of greenhouse gases, the United States and Australia were the only industrialized nations not to ratify the Kyoto Protocol, the internationally binding climate change agreement that went into force in 2005. Australia, under Kevin Rudd's Labor government, eventually signed the agreement in 2007; Canada, however, later abandoned the agreement in 2011 under Prime Minister Stephen Harper, aligning its greenhouse gas emissions goals with those of its powerful neighbor. The United States under President George W. Bush pulled out of the protocol in 2001, in part on the grounds that the American economy would suffer as a result of the protocol's limitations on industrial output. (President Bill Clinton had signed the protocol in 1998, but it was never ratified.)

Energy is an extraordinarily complicated issue. To meet energy demands while also making the United States less dependent on foreign oil, some advocate increasing the use of nuclear power (see the discussion below) or coal, which is used to generate nearly 50 percent of all electricity in the United States, but has a significant environmental impact from the mining and burning of it. Others advocate for boosting domestic production of oil, as well as increasing the flow of oil from Canada, considered to be a safer and more reliable source for oil than Middle Eastern nations. The much-delayed XL Keystone oil pipeline, if approved, would carry up to 830,000 barrels of oil per day from the Canadian province of Alberta through the United States—including many environmentally sensitive areas—to processing sites on the Gulf Coast. As an example of the complications involved in international projects of this nature, many of the people who elected President Obama were liberals who voted him into office under the assumption that he would be a stronger champion for the environment than his predecessor, George Bush, had been. The Canadian government, under the conservative Harper administration, voiced frustration at the ongoing delay, saying that the traditionally friendly US-Canadian relationship was at risk.

Another source of controversy is the process of injecting pressurized chemicals into the ground to force out gas and petroleum through a process called hydrological fracturing (popularly known as "fracking"), discussed below. When in 2010 the *Deepwater Horizon* oil rig exploded and sank in the Gulf of Mexico, releasing millions of liters of oil into the Gulf per day for three months, many asked whether society's dependence on oil had become excessive, and began demanding an increase in the use of renewable energy sources like wood and other biofuels, wind, and solar. But despite the federal government providing research funding and tax incentives to develop and use renewable resources and licensing public lands for drilling and mining, it has yet to formulate a national energy policy.

Climate Change, the Nuclear Question, and Fracking

Increasingly the environment, and especially climate change—whether or not it is a reality, and if so, what to do about it—is becoming a divisive issue in American policy making and politics. Despite overwhelming evidence from all corners of the globe that the Earth's atmosphere is warming, a sizable portion of the American public (and its leadership) remains unconvinced. This attitude may slowly be starting to change as storms of increasing severity sweep across the United States and the rest of the world with greater frequency, and the evidence for climate change becomes increasingly more difficult to ignore or discredit. Changing climatic conditions are thought to have contributed to a spate of unusually severe storms in recent years, from Hurricane Katrina, which devastated New Orleans (much of which is below sea level) in 2005, killing over 1,800 people and causing a record $108 billion in damages, to "Superstorm" Sandy, a hurricane that flooded New York City and much of the East Coast in October of 2012, killing scores of people and causing an estimated $50 billion in damage. Hurricanes Katrina and Sandy were the nation's two most costly storms on record, spurring defensive strategies for the future even from those who don't believe that climate change is a reality. Numerous outbreaks of tornadoes and other forms of severe weather from flooding and droughts to blizzards have also affected virtually every corner of the nation.

Climate change and its potential impact on the environment entered popular American consciousness in 2006 when former Vice President Al Gore (held office under President Bill Clinton 1993–2001) produced an Academy Award–winning film, *An Inconvenient Truth*, which explained for a general audience the dangers and effects of climate change that would occur worldwide if no concerted action was taken to stop it.

As the various energy choices available to humanity, and the downsides inherent in each—from visually obstructive wind turbines to solar panels that depend on sunny skies—mix with the economic realities of a worldwide recession that is only beginning to loosen its grip, the ways in which Americans use and produce energy is transforming in often surprising ways. The fear of the dangers of climate change has caused a phenomena that would have been unthinkable in the 1960s: environmentalists such as Stewart Brand (creator of the *Whole Earth Catalog*, a kind of pre-Internet catalog of environmentally friendly goods and services) speaking publicly in favor of nuclear power as an effective form of power generation that does not emit carbon.

Americans have mixed feelings on nuclear energy. The partial meltdown in 1979 at the Three Mile Island (TMI) nuclear power plant in Pennsylvania fundamentally altered the landscape of American power generation. Although TMI involved a relatively minor release of radioactive gas, panic ripped through the state, and the city of Harrisburg was partially evacuated. The disaster at Three Mile Island was vastly overshadowed by the Chernobyl meltdown in Ukraine (then still a part of the Soviet Union) in 1986. The accident released an estimated thirty to forty times more radiation than the atomic bombs dropped on Hiroshima and Nagasaki. Hundreds of people died in the months after the accident, and hundreds of thousands of Ukrainians and Russians had to abandon entire cities. A large swath of territory has reverted to wilderness and has become home to many rare species of animals, including wolves and lynx.

Accidents such as Three Mile Island and Chernobyl decreased the American appetite for nuclear power generation, although nuclear power continued to grow internationally. Experts debate whether or not the TMI accident killed the nuclear industry in the United States, or if the subsequent decline in support for nuclear energy reflected greater societal fears of nuclear warfare. In any event, no new nuclear power plants have been built in the United States since 1974, although the Nuclear Regulatory Committee (NRC) approved the construction of five reactors at existing nuclear sites in 2013. Aging utilities are frequently closed down, often after public campaigns.

The worldwide energy scene experienced another dramatic change in 2011 when an earthquake off the coast of Japan spawned a tsunami whose tides overwhelmed coastal areas of northeast Japan, killing thousands of people and crippling the nuclear reactors at the Fukushima Daiichi facility. Three of its six reactors experienced full meltdowns. The immediate emergency brought great confusion and, ultimately, the contamination of an 11,580-square-mile (30,000-square-km) area: an area the size of Belgium. In response to the Fukushima disaster, Germany under conservative Chancellor Angela Merkel instituted plans to close all of its reactors by 2022, and Japan took all fifty-four of its reactors out of service.

Only a year before the Fukushima disaster, the prospect of nuclear power offered more energy autonomy for many energy-intensive nations, including the United States. The wild card that could restore nuclear power's promise, according to some, is technological innovation. While engineers very likely may improve their siting of reactors and better prepare for the next tsunami or other natural or human-caused disaster, nuclear energy seems to be stained in the mind of international consumers by its potential—however slight—for cataclysm. Given the increased issues of safety and security, combined with the slow worldwide economy, the cost of new reactors may prove prohibitive for most nations, including the United States.

Another wild card in the American energy scene is fracking, which has seen a boom in recent years, dramatically driving down the costs of natural gas—and thus increasing the technology's acceptability to consumers. Technologies for extracting gas from shale by using high-volume hydraulic fracturing, a process that breaks up the rock and releases the gas, have developed since about the year 2000. Although many see shale gas as a viable alternative to other fossil fuels, especially natural gas from conventional sources, the environmental costs are high. Particular concerns include water and air pollution as well as emissions of greenhouse gases. A natural gas boom in North Dakota has upended many traditional prairie communities, as previously serene small towns have become clogged with the trappings of heavy industry necessary to extract the gas. As a result of the weak economy, many workers commute from surrounding states, often driving hundreds of kilometers, for a natural gas–related job, leaving their families behind for weeks at a time to do so. Because the practice of fracking is banned in large parts of Europe, many European energy companies are relocating to the United States to do business.

The environmental movement in the United States is not constrained to politicians and government agencies. Popular initiatives continue to drive change in the United States, as individuals, businesses, and community groups voluntarily try to reduce their own impact on the Earth's environment and try to challenge environmental injustice when they see it: often to the consternation of those who see an improved economy as the most important component of an improved future for Americans. The debate continues.

CONCLUSION:
UNITY FROM DIVERSITY?

Athread that weaves its way through the American story is a sense of national unity that has developed in the midst of, and perhaps in spite of, American diversity. We have seen how the American colonists overthrew British rule even though roughly a third of colonists remained loyal to Britain, and how slavery finally ended through a bloody and bitter civil war. We have seen how the United States assimilated tens of millions of European immigrants in the late nineteenth and early twentieth centuries. And, finally, we have seen how the United States struggles in the twenty-first century with contentious issues of civil rights and immigration policy. This struggle for unity amidst diversity is so central to the American story that many believe that it is a basic source of American strength and resilience.

As we worked on this book in late 2013, American unity was being tested again. This time the conflict was over the nation's financial management and over the introduction of the Affordable Care Act (ACA), commonly known as "Obamacare," an ambitious and controversial piece of legislation whose introduction was marred by a flawed website for the millions of people lacking health insurance trying to enroll in the new program. While nationalized health care was first proposed in the late 1800s during the Progressive Era, and in 1915 a bill was proposed by the American Association of Labor Legislation with the initial support of the powerful American Medical Association, all subsequent efforts to introduce nationalized health care were ultimately doomed, one of the reasons being the strong anti-communist and anti-socialist feelings of a large part of the American population. This most recent public conflict was over the annual budget and the national debt, and whether the Republican-controlled House of Representatives on one side, and President Barack Obama and the Democratic-controlled Senate on the other, could work out an agreement to fund the national government—most controversially, to fund the ACA—and raise the nation's debt limit so it would have the ability to pay its debts on time.

This public political-financial conflict is a symptom of deeper divisions which, to many observers, seem deeper than in the past, although this view may simply

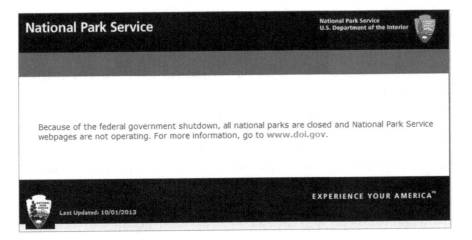

One result of the partial government shutdown of October 2013 was that all national parks and monuments in the United States were closed to visitors. Thousands of federal workers were furloughed, and numerous vacations plans, weddings, and other events had to be cancelled while Congress and the President argued over funding for the federal government. Source: National Park Service.

reflect an ignorance of some of the trends and traumatic events in American history that have been summarized in this book. Nonetheless, there are at least four clear and deep divisions in American society today: wealth distribution, religion, political outlook, and outlook on immigration. These divisions can be briefly framed as follows.

Wealth

The United States is among the wealthiest nations on Earth, with a gross domestic product (based on purchasing power parity, a measure favored by the World Bank for determining buying power) of $52,000, compared with $58,000 in the United Arab Emirates, $35,000 in Japan and Great Britain, $23,000 in Russia, $11,000 in China, and $459 in the Democratic Republic of the Congo (2011 data). Within the United States, as in many other nations, there is a considerable gap between the people who own most of the nation's wealth and the rest of the country. The average US household's wealth has declined and income has been flat for decades. Many economists argue, however, that quality of life for poorer Americans has in fact increased overall, due to the cheapness and ubiquity of consumer products such as flat-screen televisions and smart phones.

One Oxfam report estimated that the 30 richest individuals in the United States owned as much wealth—over $790 billion—as the nation's poorest 157 million people combined. This disparity is increasing: income and wealth disparities in the United States are now more similar to those in Russia and China than its historical peers in Western and Northern Europe, such as France, Denmark, and Finland. According to Thomas Piketty's 2014 book, *Capital in the 21st Century*, this is a matter of simple economics: as long as the income an individual can collect from his or her wealth is a higher percentage than the percentage growth of the economy, the larger this gap will become. In a time of slow growth, the wealthy will take an increased share of national income.

The disparity in wealth in the United States was brought to the public eye in 2011 by the Occupy Wall Street movement. One of the movement's principles was that the "one percent" was controlling too much of the nation's wealth, to the detriment of the other "ninety-nine percent" of the population. This, in turn, led to accusations that the wealthy did not pay their fair share of taxes, because they had the means to pay skilled tax accountants and tax lawyers, and capital gains tax rates can be half that of normal income taxes. The wealthy countered that increasing their already high income tax burden would only serve to drive down the nation's economy; they also argued that wealth distribution is not a matter of fairness or unfairness but rather is a reflection of global economic realities.

One common criticism of the Occupy movement was that it did not have goals or leaders and did not offer much in the way of practical solutions, and while some believe that income disparity goes against the very idea of the American Dream, others argue that the American Dream is, in fact, the market at work. The founding fathers did not have wealth in mind when they spoke of all men being equal.

One result of this growing disparity that is not up for debate is that Americans now have a lower level of economic mobility than do people in most developed nations. In other words, those who are born wealthy are likely to remain so, and if an American is born poor, he or she is far more likely to remain poor than someone who lives in Canada or the Scandinavian nations. This fact is at odds with the United States's image as the "land of opportunity."

> **I refuse to believe corporations are people until Texas executes one.**
>
> —BUMPER STICKER

A related issue is that of political spending. In 2010, by a five-to-four margin, the Supreme Court overturned its own twenty-year-old ruling that barred corporations from unlimited spending on political campaigns, sparking widespread controversy. As a result of this decision, corporations and non-governmental organizations have begun spending money on political activities at a greatly increased rate, and often anonymously. The question of how much money individuals and corporations can shower on political parties is one of the more controversial issues in modern American politics.

Religion

Contrary to popular belief, the United States is not strikingly diverse in terms of religion. A 2014 Pew study places the US 68th out of 232 nations in its Religious Diversity Index. There is, however, no national religion as there is in many nations, and many of the early immigrants during the seventeenth century were fleeing religious persecution in Europe. The First Amendment to the US Constitution, in fact, guarantees religious freedom along with freedom of speech. While the majority of Americans are Christians, with Americans belonging to all major and many smaller churches, every religion on the planet has adherents living in the United States; there are also sizable populations of atheists and agnostics, as well as a growing number of people (especially among the young) who do not identify with any one organized religion. Most Americans belong to religions brought to America by their immigrant ancestors, although America also developed some religions, a few of which have now spread beyond its borders and have been successful globally. These include Seventh-Day Adventists, Jehovah's Witnesses, Scientologists, and Christian Scientists. The Pentecostal and Charismatic movement, which blurs the line between Catholicism and Protestantism, is considered the fastest-growing religious movement in the world; it has seen explosive growth especially in developing countries that have experienced internal conflict in recent years, such as Nigeria, Kenya, Brazil, and Vietnam.

Religion in America has often butted heads with science. A notable example was the 1925 Scopes "Monkey" Trial. Formally known as *The State of Tennessee v. John Thomas Scopes,* this was a small-town trial of high school teacher (and part-time football coach) John Scopes, who was accused of violating Tennessee's Butler Act by teaching evolution in a state-funded school. The trial drew two of the most famous lawyers in the nation at the time: three-time Democratic presidential candidate William Jennings Bryan on the side of the state, and the outspokenly agnostic Clarence Darrow, picked by the American Civil Liberties Union (ACLU), on the side of Scopes. (Curiously, Bryan, the "Great Commoner," may have been motivated to get involved against the teaching of evolution because he was afraid that Social Darwinists would disseminate the concept for unsavory practices such as racial selection; the practice of eugenics was quite popular at the time.) Bryan died six days after the case was decided against the state. The Tennessee Supreme Court eventually dismissed the case, describing it as "bizarre."

Another religion, the Latter Day Saints (also known as the Mormons), received much attention during the 2010 presidential elections, as was discussed in Chapter Five. Mitt Romney, the Republican candidate who lost to Barack Obama, was the first Mormon to win the presidential nomination for a major political party.

Fundamentalist Christians (mainly Pentecostal and Evangelical Protestants), who make up about a quarter of the voting population, disagree with other Americans on a wide range of social issues: gun control, abortion, gay rights, women's role in society, immigration, and whether or not climate change is a reality. Religion is a complicated issue: there are many Catholics, for example, who are socially conservative—opposed to abortion, for instance—but otherwise liberal in their political views. Other people are fiscally conservative but socially liberal. For instance, they might favor gay (same-sex) marriage but oppose high levels of government spending on social programs that they think could lead to an increase in national debt. Because peoples' religious convictions tend not to change much over time (although of course that is a generalization), there is often not much room for debate on issues such as abortion, same-sex marriage, and capital punishment.

Regional Politics and the Urban/Rural Divide

There are also large differences between the so-called red (Republican/conservative) states, located mainly in the Deep South and the Great Plains, and the blue (Democratic/progressive) states, located mainly in the Northeast, the upper Midwest, and the West Coast. In addition to regional differences there is also a deep urban/rural divide; for example, between the blue Philadelphia area of eastern Pennsylvania and the more red-leaning rural regions of the state, or between deeply blue Austin and much of the rest of Texas.

Some states defy geographical conventions. Florida, for instance, is red in the northern part of the state abutting the Deep South, and blue in the southern, Miami-dominated and Latino-influenced part of the state. The bluest state is probably Vermont, often jocularly referred to as the "People's Republic of Vermont," while its next-door neighbor, New Hampshire, is quite conservative, with a sizeable population of libertarians, many of whom moved there in order to have an out-sized political influence in a state with a small population. (It should be noted that some libertarians—people who believe in minimal or no government—are left-leaning. They may favor same-sex marriage and the legalization of all drugs, believing that government has no place regulating these things, or they may oppose government spending on the military and public schooling. The majority of libertarians, however, are on the right of the political spectrum.) New Hampshire is an anomaly in otherwise blue New England.

Oklahoma, where Republican nominee John McCain won every county in the state in his failed 2008 bid for the presidency, is often cited as the reddest state. Others nominate sparsely populated Wyoming, in the northern Rockies, as the reddest state in the union. Interestingly, the "Cowboy State" was the first state to elect a female governor: Nellie Tayloe Ross, in 1925. In between are the so-called purple states, also called "swing states" or "battleground states," such as Colorado, Virginia, Ohio, Nevada, and Florida, which have large populations of both Democrats and Republicans, with much of the blue population living in urban areas and much of the red population living in rural areas.

Some suggest there is a trend of people moving to states (or parts of states) that are blue or red, thus concentrating political opinions in different regions, and furthering the breakdown of communication between people who hold different opinions. A similar trend caused by the proliferation of modern media is that people tend to pick their news sources based on what they want to hear, with the result that bloggers and other online news sources have tended to solidify over time into a "red" or "blue" perspective, thus coloring the news they deliver. Liberals look to the Huffington Post, the Daily Kos, Rachel Maddow, and Bill Moyers for their news, while conservatives look to RedState, the Drudge Report, Peggy Noonan, and Bill O'Reilly for theirs. This too, has contributed to a lack of engagement with those who hold differing opinions, and thus to the recent trend towards polarization in Congress and elsewhere.

Illegal Immigration

A final major issue is the issue of illegal (undocumented and unauthorized) immigration. In 2013, the Pew Research Hispanic Trends Project estimated that there were 11.7 million unauthorized immigrants in the United States. Of this number, just over half were from Mexico, most of the rest from elsewhere in Latin America, and about ten percent from Asia. The number of illegal immigrants peaked around 2006 at 12.2 million, and then declined during the Great Recession as jobs in the United States became increasingly scarce. The number is increasing again, despite a rise in the number of deportations under the Obama administration and new, restrictive laws in states such as Arizona, Alabama, and Georgia. In early 2014, Janet Murguía of the National Council of La Raza (NCLR), a leading Latino advocacy group, described President Obama as the "deporter-in-chief" for the record two million people who have been deported from the country under his administration. This number may be misleading, however, as the definition of the term "deportation" has evolved to include people stopped and turned back at the border.

Illegal immigrants are most heavily concentrated in Nevada (where they make up an estimated 7.2 percent of the population, according to the Pew Hispanic Center), California, Arizona, Texas, and New Jersey, with heavy concentrations (more than 3 percent by population) also found in New Mexico, Colorado, Utah, Washington State, Florida, Illinois, Georgia, New York, Oregon, and North Carolina. They come to the United States mainly for jobs. Some employers desire them because they can be fired easily, they cannot unionize, and they can be paid wages substantially lower than the minimum wage—currently $7.25 an hour, although some states have higher minimum wages and President Obama is attempting to raise the minimum wage for federal employees.

Illegal immigration is a contentious political issue, with the nation divided—and not always along Democratic/Republican lines—on what to do about the many illegal immigrants already living in the country, many of them working on the nation's farms. New controls that have been instituted in recent years continue to be controversial: enhanced patrols, often by armed anti-immigrant groups such as the Minuteman Project; a massive fence on the US/Mexico border, similar to the one dividing Israelis and Palestinians; raids on employers of illegal immigrants; and a web-based program called "E-Verify," co-run by the Department of Homeland Security and the Social Security Administration, that allows employers to "e-verify" the legitimacy of the records of their employees with the government.

The number of minorities holding elective office has grown substantially since the 1990s, although their influence is to some extent limited by the fact that many represent minority communities rather than a broader population. In 2013 the Senate fashioned bipartisan immigration legislation to overhaul what all agree is a broken system, but the future of the legislation is uncertain. The major objection of conservatives to the proposed legislation, which aims to put illegal immigrants on the "path to citizenship," is granting what they see as amnesty to those who have broken the law. (The path to citizenship would entail a series of hurdles and conditions, such as waiting periods, background checks, financial penalties for paying back taxes not paid while living in the country illegally, etc.) They argue that undocumented immigrants are in the country illegally and should return home and then wait in line to enter the United States legally. What kind of citizens will these people make, they wonder, if they broke the law to get into the country in the first place? The opposing argument is that illegal immigrants are already a reality in the American socioeconomic landscape. They would be productive, law-abiding citizens if only they had the chance, and the sooner they can be made fully contributing (i.e., tax-paying) citizens of the United States, the better. Another common myth is that illegal immigrants don't pay taxes; they do. Exact figures are difficult to assess, for obvious reasons, but the IRS estimates that illegal immigrants contribute over $9 billion in Social Security taxes alone each year. The debate serves to illustrate how much importance people attach to the notion of American citizenship.

The Final Word

These domestic debates affect diplomatic relations, the global economy, and the perceptions of the United States held by people around the world. The United States, being a world leader, pulls a lot of weight globally, and when Americans can't agree on things, the effects are felt everywhere, in everything from the economy to the global environment.

While the United States continues to lead the world in its enactment of various environmental policies, for example, domestic disputes over issues such as climate change continue to bedevil efforts to organize effective global action. Many people around the world would argue that the reality of climate change should not be open to debate, while fully sixty percent of Americans do not believe climate change is a major threat to their country.

Contradictions like this—innovative air and water pollution policies on one hand and a perceived lack of commitment to a long-term energy policy on the other—are an essential part of global perceptions of the United States. This is nothing new. As we have seen, people outside the United States have had ambivalent opinions of Americans throughout its history. British ambivalence toward the presence of American troops in the United Kingdom after World War II was expressed in the witticism that American GIs were "overpaid, oversexed, and over here." The United States is a land of contrasts and that shows in its dealings with the outside world.

While people around the world are doubtful about preemptive war, globalization, and Americanization, there is much that people appreciate about the United States, not only its movies and music but its intervention in World War II, the rights accorded the individual by American laws and institutions, the academic rigor of its universities, and the actions of organizations such as the Peace Corps and the Gates Foundation. People see the United States as the most influential and powerful nation on Earth, with a reputation for innovation and creativity, and as the place to go to become educated and wealthy. It is a place where one may live among people with different views on the world. The fact that there are healthy differences in opinion is part of what makes the United States an attractive place for so many, either people who emigrate there or who simply admire it from afar.

The eminent African American intellectual and activist W. E. B. Du Bois, a native of Great Barrington, Massachusetts, commended that virtue in the context of one of the United States's greatest democratic traditions—the town meeting. He wrote, "From early years, I attended the town meeting every Spring . . . . Gradually as I grew up, I began to see that this was the essence of democracy: listening to the other man's opinion and then voting your own, honestly and intelligently."

For all the animosity that makes its way to the airwaves, conservatives and liberals live on the same streets, go to the same baseball games, and send their children to the same schools. Political power is transferred at regular intervals without violence. As world historian William H. McNeill puts it, "What unites us is greater than what divides us." McNeill is referring to US citizens as well as to the global community, people of all nations and beliefs, who face common challenges and share many basic values.

This book will, we hope, help global readers (wherever they live, and whatever their religion or political beliefs) to see the United States and its history more clearly, and as a result to work toward a world in which Americans both lead and learn from others.

APPENDIX A: TIMELINE OF MAJOR EVENTS IN AMERICAN HISTORY

The following is a selection of major events in American history. As with any timeline, countless events have been omitted here; this timeline serves to give the reader a general sense of how America's history fits in with the rest of the world.

c. 15,000 years ago: first humans arrive in the Americas, likely via the Bering Strait land-bridge (time and method of arrival debated; may have been many thousands of years earlier)

c. 10,000–11,000 years ago: agriculture is invented in various parts of Asia

c. 5,000–6,000 years ago: agriculture is independently invented in the Americas

6,000 BCE sugarcane first known in New Guinea

200 CE tobacco is introduced from Mesoamerica to North America

c. 600 CE city of Cahokia founded in the American Bottomlands region, near present-day St. Louis

1368 Ming dynasty takes power in China

1492 Christopher Columbus, thinking he has found India, arrives in the Caribbean; origin of term "Indians" for Native Americans

1493 Columbus brings sugarcane to island of Hispaniola

1519–1685 Texas under Spanish rule

1587 "Lost Colony of Roanoke" founded on Roanoke Island, Virginia; birth of Virginia Dare, the first English child born in the Americas; fate of colonists remains a mystery

1598 Spanish expeditions establish settlements in Florida and the American Southwest

1600s tobacco use spreads throughout most of South America, Europe, the Caribbean, and the North American colonies

1602 founding of the Dutch East India Company

1604 French and British explorers begin trading with Native Americans

English (British After 1707) Colonial Period: 1607–1776

1607 English colonists establish first permanent American settlements at **Jamestown, Virginia**

1612 John Rolfe cultivates first successful commercial tobacco crop, in Virginia

1619 Britain's first black slaves arrive in America

1620 Plymouth, Massachusetts is established on site of abandoned Wampanoag village

1620s tobacco has become Virginia's major crop

1622–1675 uprisings and minor wars with native tribes in Virginia

1632 birth of English philosopher John Locke

1634 small groups of English Catholics settle in Maryland

1635 English Protestant theologian Roger Williams, forced to leave the Massachusetts Bay Colony, founds Rhode Island

1637 Puritan Anne Hutchinson is forced to leave the Massachusetts Bay Colony, flees to Rhode Island

1642–1651 English Civil War

1644 Ming dynasty ends in China

1660 slave codes enacted in the South

1664 English take New Amsterdam from the Dutch, rename it New York

1667 Dutch agree to exchange Manhattan Island for the colony of Suriname in South America

1675–1678 King Philip's War in New England; several allied Native American tribes nearly drive out English settlers

1680 successful uprising of Pueblo nation against the Spanish in present-day New Mexico

1685–1690 Texas under French rule

1687 Spanish start offering English slaves freedom in Florida if they convert to Catholicism and give the Spanish crown four years of service

1688 Pennsylvania Quakers pass **first anti-slavery resolution** in North America

1688 England's Glorious Revolution

1689 John Locke's *Second Treatise of Civil Government* published in England

1690 Texas under Spanish rule

1692–1693 Salem witch trials in Salem, Massachusetts; 20 suspected witches executed

1700 Spanish re-occupy Pueblo territory; Spanish settle present-day Arizona; use of slaves for tobacco plantations begins in the South

1700–1775 population of 13 British colonies increases from 300,000 to 2.5 million

1706 birth of Benjamin Franklin, inventor, philosopher, publisher, diplomat, founding father of the United States

1707 Act of Union between England and Scotland

1716 Spanish settle present-day Texas

1722 Daniel Defoe publishes *Moll Flanders,* about an indentured servant

1730–1743 the "Great Awakening" of religious feeling in the American colonies

1732 birth of George Washington, first President of the United States

1735 birth of John Adams, second President of the United States

1738 first settlement of free blacks established in North America, at Fort Mose, Florida

1739 Stono Revolt in South Carolina causes great concern among Southern slave owners

1743 birth of Thomas Jefferson, third President of the United States

1750–1800 native peoples in North America's Great Plains take to the horse

1750s George Washington leads several militia units in battles against the French in Ohio and Pennsylvania

1751 birth of James Madison, fourth President of the United States

1755 French-speaking Acadians are expelled by the British from Canadian Maritimes region and migrate to Louisiana; become known as "Cajuns"

1756 start of Seven Years' War

1757 birth of Marquis de Lafayette in France; American Revolutionary War general

1758 birth of James Monroe, fifth President of the United States, last founding father to become president; French and Indian War shifts to Britain's favor

1759 British take Quebec City from France; France gives up claims to North American territories

1763 France loses Canada to Britain; end of French and Indian War / Seven Years' War; increased British efforts to control overseas colonies

1765 birth of Eli Whitney, inventor of the cotton gin that will revolutionize agriculture and inadvertently lead to the extension of slavery

1769 Spanish settle present-day California; Thomas Jefferson begins serving as a member of the Virginia House of Burgesses

1772 *Somerset v. Stewart* court case in Britain rules slavery to be illegal in England, alarming Southern American slave owners

1774 George Washington becomes Virginia's representative in the Continental Congress; **Continental Congress** assembles in Philadelphia

American Revolution: 1775–1781/1783

1775 start of the American Revolution with the battles of Lexington and Concord, Massachusetts, between British troops and American minutemen: "the shot heard around the world"; revolutionary armies invade Quebec under command of General Benedict Arnold (invasion fails)

1776 (Fourth of July) signing of the **Declaration of Independence in Philadelphia**; birth of the United States

1781 fighting between the British and American colonists is concentrated in Virginia; George Washington is victorious over British in Yorktown, Virginia, effectively ending the American Revolution

1782 Loyalists flee to Canada and Britain

1783 American Revolution officially ends with the Treaty of Paris

1785–1789 Thomas Jefferson serves as US minister to France

1787 drafting of the **United States Constitution**

1787 and 1788 publication of *The Federalist Papers,* a series of 85 essays written to promote the ratification of the Constitution

1789 start of the **French Revolution**, inspired in part by the American Revolution; **Bill of Rights** (first ten amendments to the Constitution) written

1790 more than 650,000 slaves are working on tobacco plantations at this time

1791 ratification of the Bill of Rights

1792 publication of *A Vindication of the Rights of Women,* by British feminist Mary Wollstonecraft

1793 invention of the **cotton gin** by Eli Whitney

1796 Washington refuses third term as President

1797 birth of Sojourner Truth, African American abolitionist and women's rights activist

1799 death of George Washington

19th Century: The Era of Expansion

1800 Thomas Jefferson and Aaron Burr tie for presidential campaign; House of Representatives settles the tie in favor of Jefferson

1801 Thomas Jefferson becomes third President

1803 Jefferson secretly arranges the **Louisiana Purchase**; area three times the size of France bought from Napoleon Bonaparte

1804 Lewis and Clark expedition begins exploration of the West

1805 Supreme Court Justice Samuel Chase is impeached; first and only Supreme Court Justice to be impeached in US history

1806 Lewis and Clark return to Jefferson with their findings

1807 birth of Confederate general Robert E. Lee

1809 birth of Abraham Lincoln, sixteenth President of the United States

1810 United States acquires portion of the Gulf Coast from Spain

1811 birth of abolitionist and author Harriet Beecher Stowe, author of *Uncle Tom's Cabin*

1812–1815 War of 1812 between United States and Great Britain; British invade new US capital city of Washington, DC, and burn White House; Francis Scott Key composes what will become the National Anthem in response to the unsuccessful British assault on Baltimore; Andrew Jackson defeats the British in one of the last major engagements of the war at the Battle of New Orleans, paving the way to the presidency and the era sometimes referred to as "Jacksonian America"

1813 United States acquires another portion of the Gulf Coast from Spain

1815 (November) Treaty of Paris ends Napoleonic Wars; (December) Treaty of Ghent ends War of 1812

1818 birth (into slavery) of African American orator Frederick Douglass, in Maryland; United States acquires the Red River Basin (present-day North Dakota and Minnesota) from Britain but gives up territory from the Louisiana Purchase in exchange

1819 United States acquires Florida from Spain; Illinois enacts Black Laws requiring black residents to carry "free papers"

c. 1820 birth (into slavery) of Harriet Tubman, "Underground Railroad" conductor

1820 the **Missouri Compromise** prohibits slavery in the northern portion of the Louisiana Territory, permits it in Missouri and Arkansas, and admits Maine (previously a part of Massachusetts) as a free state

1821–1836 Texas under Mexican rule

1821 Mexico gains independence from Spain

1822 birth of Ulysses S. Grant, Civil War general (Union side) and 18th President of the United States

1823 President James Monroe gives congratulatory speech to newly independent nations of South America; policy of US sphere of influence over the Americas later called the **"Monroe Doctrine"**

1825 completion of the **Erie Canal** linking the Great Lakes with the Atlantic Ocean via the Mohawk and Hudson river valleys

1826 (Fourth of July, 1 pm) death of Thomas Jefferson; (Fourth of July, 6 pm) death of John Adams; both former presidents die on the fiftieth anniversary of the signing of the Declaration of Independence

1830 Congress passes Indian Removal Act

1831–1839 Cherokee people are forced to relocate from the East to Indian Territory in the West via the **"Trail of Tears"**

1831 (Fourth of July) death of James Monroe; third founding father to die on the Fourth of July

1832 Alfred Vail and Samuel Morse invent Morse Code; newspaper editor William Lloyd Garrison starts New England Anti-Slavery Society

1833 William Lloyd Garrison starts American Anti-Slavery Society; United States starts to take control of the Southwest from Mexico

1836 Samuel Colt invents the revolver; (February) siege of the Alamo in San Antonio, Texas; (March) Texas becomes an independent republic; (June) death of James Madison, last of the founding fathers

1837 number of Supreme Court Justices increases to nine (from seven)

1839 Charles Goodyear invents vulcanized rubber

1840 refusal to seat American women delegates at the World Anti-Slavery Convention in London; Irish potato famine fungus *Phytophthora infestans* arrives in Ireland, killing potato crops

1842 US acquires disputed territory in Maine from Britain

1845 Texas becomes the 28th state of the US; *Narrative of the Life of Frederick Douglass* is published; organized play of baseball begins

1846 US acquires Oregon and Washington from Britain; start of **Mexican-American War**

1847 United States forces take Mexico City; birth of inventor Thomas Edison

1848 end of Mexican-American War

1850 National Women's Rights Convention held in Worcester, Massachusetts; **Fugitive Slave Act** is passed

1851 Congress passes the Indian Appropriations Act that allows for the creation of **Indian reservations**

1853 Gadsden Purchase: the United States acquires southern Arizona and New Mexico from Spain

1855 birth of American socialist leader Eugene V. Debs

1856 **baseball** becomes the country's national pastime

1857 *Dred Scott vs. Sandford* Supreme Court case declares that African Americans are not American citizens and do not have the right to sue in federal court

1858 birth of Theodore Roosevelt, 26th President of the United States; Abraham Lincoln runs for senator of Illinois against Stephen A. Douglas; their debates draw huge crowds

1859 "Know Nothings" political party begins advocating against immigration

1860 Abraham Lincoln is elected Republican Party presidential candidate; (November) Abraham Lincoln is elected 16th president; (December) southern states, led by South Carolina, secede from the Union

Civil War: 1861–1865

1861 start of the Civil War

1862 Union victory at Antietam, Maryland, is turning point in war

1863 (January) Abraham Lincoln issues the **Emancipation Proclamation**; (November) Lincoln delivers the **Gettysburg Address** after the Battle of Gettysburg sees the largest number of casualties in the American Civil War

1864 the fall of Atlanta, Georgia

1865 14th Amendment is enacted, stating that all people born in the United States are citizens and giving all people equal protection under the law; **end of the Civil War**; **Abraham Lincoln assassinated**

Post-War Reconstruction: 1865–1877

1860s Reconstruction starts to rebuild the defeated South under supervision of the North

1866 Ku Klux Klan is founded; National Labor Union forms

1867 Secretary of State William Seward **purchases Alaska from Russia**, which becomes known as "Seward's Folly"; Lucien B. Smith invents barbed wire, changing Western landscape; J. B. Sutherland invents the refrigerator car

1868 Ulysses S. Grant is elected the 18th President of the United States; birth of civil rights activist W. E. B. Du Bois

1869 the Knights of Labor forms to promote the social and cultural uplift of the workingman; professional baseball begins

1870 15th Amendment is enacted, giving **African Americans the right to vote**

1870 birth of Tsar Nicholas II of Russia; birth of Russian Communist Party leader Vladimir Ilyich Lenin

1871 Congress passes anti-Klan bill to give the president emergency powers to deal with the threat of the Ku Klux Klan

1876 Alexander Graham Bell invents the **telephone**; Thomas Edison opens his "invention factory" in Menlo, New Jersey

1877 Reconstruction ends; national railroad strike takes place

1878 first international women's congress held in Paris

1879 birth of Soviet leader Joseph Stalin

1882 Chinese Exclusion Act prohibits the immigration of Chinese laborers birth of 32nd President Franklin D. Roosevelt

1883 birth of Italian Fascist Party leader Benito Mussolini

1884 birth of 33rd President Harry S. Truman

1885 George Eastman invents **photographic film**

1886 industrialist Andrew Carnegie publishes *Triumphant Democracy*; France gives the **Statue of Liberty** to the United States; American Federation of Labor forms

Progressive Era: 1890s–1920s

1890 economic crisis begins in the United States; Jacob Riis publishes *How the Other Half Lives: Studies among the Tenements of New York*

1891 Brazil adopts a similar federal system to the US; 1891 Congress passes Forest Reserve Act

1892 Andrew Carnegie forms the Carnegie Steel Company; Carnegie crushes the Homestead strike; "People's Party" forms; New York creates the Adirondack Park

1893 United States in the worst economic depression until surpassed the Great Depression in the 1930s

1894 progressive Populist Party gains 40 percent of the national vote; American Railroad Union leads a strike at the Pullman manufacturing plant

1895 W. E. B. Du Bois receives first doctorate to be granted to an African American, from Harvard; death of Frederick Douglass; birth of Nazi Party leader Adolf Hitler in Germany

1896 death of abolitionist and author Harriet Beecher Stowe

1897 Congress passes Forest Management Act to help protect and manage forest reserves

1898 Hawaii becomes a territory of the US

1898 Spanish-American War

1899 start of Philippine-American War

1901 United States Steel is formed; assassination of 25th President William McKinley

1902 end of Philippine-American War; coal miners in Pennsylvania call for a strike

1903 US constructs naval base at **Guantanamo Bay** on Cuba; border dispute over Alaska with Canada

1904 Ida Tarbell writes scathing indictment of industrialist John Rockefeller

1907 birth of environmentalist Rachel L. Carson

1908 20,000 women garment workers in New York and Philadelphia walk off their jobs to protest harsh working conditions

1910 (May) Korea is annexed by Japan; (November) start of Mexican Revolution

1911 (February) birth of 40th President Ronald Reagan; (March) deadly Triangle Shirtwaist Company fire in New York City spurs calls for workplace safety standards

1913 death of former slave and Underground Railroad "conductor" Harriet Tubman

World War I: 1914–1918

1914 (April) US marines occupy the port of Veracruz, Mexico; (June) **assassination of Archduke Franz Ferdinand sparks World War I**; (August) Panama Canal, begun in 1881, officially opens to ship traffic; (October) Congress passes the Clayton Antitrust Act

1915 sinking of the passenger British ship **RMS *Lusitania*** by Germany

1916 US Army sends an expedition into northern Mexico to capture Pancho Villa; Congress establishes the National Park Service to care for the national parks

1917 (January) German **Zimmermann Telegram** asking Mexico to join the Central Powers in World War I intercepted by British spies, leading to outrage in the US; (March) Tsar of Russia is deposed by a democratic uprising; (April) **US declares war on Germany**; (November) **Russian Revolution**

1918 (January) Woodrow Wilson's "Fourteen Points of Light" plan to offer peace after the war; (May) one million US infantry troops are on the Western Front; (November) **end of World War I**; Allies victorious

1918–1919 influenza pandemic kills between 20–40 million people worldwide: the deadliest disease outbreak in recorded history

Prohibition: 1920–1933

1920 Prohibition: Eighteenth Amendment passes, prohibiting the production, transport, and sale of alcohol; Hollywood, California, emerges as the film capital of the world; US troops leave Russia; Nineteenth Amendment passes, giving US **women the right to vote**

1921 Benton MacKaye conceives of the Appalachian Trail

1922 Union of the Soviet Socialist Republics (USSR) is formed

1924 Immigration Act limits the number of immigrants allowed into the US

1925 Nellie Tayloe Ross of Wyoming becomes **first female governor**

1927 *The Jazz Singer* is the first full-length film to feature synchronized sound, ushering in a new era

1928 Franklin D. Roosevelt wins campaign for New York governor

Great Depression: 1929–1939

1929 (January) birth of civil rights leader Martin Luther King, Jr.; (October) start of the **Great Depression**

1930 start of Spain's Civil War

1931 the term "The American Dream" is coined; Italy invades Ethiopia

1932 Japan invades Manchuria (northeastern China)

1933 Franklin D. Roosevelt launches presidential bid; all federally owned sites are transferred to the National Park Service; **Hitler comes to power** in Germany; **Prohibition ends** with repeal of the Eighteenth Amendment by the Twenty-first Amendment

1933–1945 record four-term presidency of Franklin D. Roosevelt

1935 Social Security Act and Wagner Labor Relations Act pass

1936 Hitler occupies Rhineland

1937 Appalachian Trail finished

1938 Germany absorbs Austria

World War II: 1939–1945

1939 (April) end of Spain's Civil War; (August) German-Soviet Nonaggression Pact agreeing to avoid war or armed conflict; (September) **start of World War II when Germany invades Poland**

1940 (May) Germany takes Belgium, the Netherlands, Luxembourg, Denmark, Norway, and France; (September) Franklin D. Roosevelt exchanges fifty destroyers to the British Navy for rights in British possessions; militarists take over Japan; end of Mexican Revolution; end of the Great Depression

1941 (March) Lend-Lease Act states that the US will supply Allies with supplies; (June) breaking the German-Soviet Nonaggression Pact, Germany invades the USSR in the largest operation of the war; (August) Atlantic Charter defines the Allied goals for the post-war world; (October) civilian government in Tokyo falls; (December) **attack on Pearl Harbor by Japan; US entry into World War II**

1942 (April) US forces surrender to Japan in the Philippines; Bataan Death March of US and Filipino prisoners of war; (May) US forces in Africa see first action

1943 (May) German forces withdraw from Africa; (July) Allied forces invade Sicily; (August) Battle of Stalingrad between USSR and Germany

1944–1945 US pushes Japan out of Southeast Asia and China

1944 (June) Rome is liberated by Allies; (June) **D-Day invasion** of German-held Normandy by Allied forces

1945 (February) Yalta Summit; (March) Allied forces breach German defenses in the north; (12 April) death of Franklin D. Roosevelt; (28 April) death of Benito Mussolini; (30 April) death by suicide of Adolf Hitler; (May) German forces surrender; (August) **US drops atomic bombs on Hiroshima and Nagasaki**, Japan; (September) **World War II ends**; (October) **creation of the United Nations**

Cold War: c. 1945–1991

1946 (March) Winston Churchill speaks at Westminster College in Fulton, Missouri; speaks of an "**iron curtain**" across Eastern Europe; (June) The Philippines gains independence from the US

1947 (March) **Truman Doctrine** states that the US will support Greece and Turkey with economic and military aid to prevent them from falling into the Soviet sphere; (April) the Marshall Plan (European Recovery Plan) allows the US to give post-war Europe economic support

1948 segregated units in the military ends

1949 (March) Newfoundland joins Canada; (April) **North Atlantic Treaty Organization** (NATO) is formed; (August) Soviets explode atomic bomb; Mao Zedong and Communists triumph over Nationalist leader Chiang Kai-shek in China

1950 North Korea bids to reunite the two halves of Korea by force; **US enters Korean War**; National Security Council produces *NSC-68*, outlining Cold War strategy

1951 San Francisco nightclub owners prevail in litigation establishing the right of businesses to cater to a gay and lesbian clientele

1952 US tests **first hydrogen bomb**

1953 (March) death of Soviet leader Joseph Stalin; (July) armistice is signed keeping North and South Korea separated; (August) Soviet Union tests hydrogen bomb

Civil Rights Era: 1950s–1960s

1954 *Brown v. Board of Education* court case states that separate public schools for black and white students is unconstitutional

1955 Daughters of Bilitis (DoB) (lesbian rights group) is formed in San Francisco; **boycott of Montgomery, Alabama, city buses over segregation**; (May) **Warsaw Pact** signed to counteract power of NATO; labor unions American Federation of Labor and Congress of Industrial Organizations merge into AFL-CIO; start of nuclear arms race

1956 Montgomery bus boycott wins national attention; federal courts order the desegregation of Montgomery's city buses; Hungarian Uprising is put down by USSR

1957 USSR launches first artificial satellite and successfully fires first intercontinental ballistic missile

1958 birth of early form of the **Internet** with the establishment of the Advanced Research Projects Agency (ARPA) to research and develop new technology for the US military

1959 Hawaii becomes the 50th **and last state of the US**

1960 Supreme Court bans segregation in interstate transport

1961 (January) President Dwight Eisenhower warns of **"military-industrial complex"**; (April) Bay of Pigs invasion of Cuba; (August) **Berlin Wall** is erected, dividing East and West Berlin

1962 W. E. B. Du Bois renounces his US citizenship and moves to Ghana; (September) *Silent Spring* is published by Rachel Carson; (October) **Cuban Missile Crisis**

1963 (February) publication of *The Feminine Mystique* by Betty Friedan; (August) **"I Have a Dream"** speech by Martin Luther King, Jr.; (September) **bombing of 16th Street Baptist Church** in Birmingham, Alabama; (November) **assassination of President John F. Kennedy** in Dallas, Texas

1964 (July) Congress passes the **Civil Rights Act** of 1964, banishing discrimination based on race, color, religion, sex, or national origin; (October) Martin Luther King, Jr. receives the Nobel Peace Prize

US Involvement in Vietnam War: 1965–1973

1965 (March) first US troops enter Vietnam; (August) Congress passes **Voting Rights Act**, banishing discrimination in voting

1966 founding of the National Organization for Women (NOW)

1967 bar raids and arrests start new phase in gay rights activism; influential essay "The Historical Roots of Our Ecological Crisis" published by Lynn White, Jr.

1968 (March) My Lai Massacre in Vietnam; (April) **assassination of Martin Luther King, Jr.** in Memphis, Tennessee; (June) **assassination of Robert F. Kennedy** in Los Angeles; (August) Prague Spring put down by USSR

1969 (February) oil spill in Santa Barbara, California is nation's worst until *Exxon Valdez*; (June) Neil Armstrong and Edwin "Buzz" Aldrin, Jr. become **first men to walk on the moon**; National Environment Policy Act (NEPA) enacted

1970 National Guard troops in Ohio kill four anti–Vietnam War demonstrators at **Kent State University**; first **Earth Day**

1971 federal court ruling bans the firing of homosexual civil service employees

1972 primary elections replace the grip of party bosses in presidential campaigns; formation of **Environmental Protection Agency** (EPA)

1973 (January) *Roe v. Wade* court case states that women have the right to an abortion; (March) last US troops pulled out of Vietnam

1975 South Vietnam surrenders to North Vietnam

1976 Vietnam reunified as the Socialist Republic of Vietnam

1978 assassination of nation's first openly gay official, city council member Harvey Milk (as well mayor of San Francisco George Moscone)

1979 (March) partial nuclear meltdown at **Three Mile Island** plant in Pennsylvania causes widespread panic; (November) Iran hostage crisis begins when 52 Americans taken hostage at US embassy in Tehran for 444 days

1980 (February) "Miracle on Ice" hockey game: US amateur/collegiate team defeats vastly favored Soviets in Olympics; (May) explosion of Mount St. Helen in Washington State; (Summer) President Jimmy Carter orders boycott of 1980 Olympics (held in Moscow) in protest of Soviet invasion of Afghanistan; (November) election of Ronald Reagan

1981 Sandra Day O'Connor becomes **first woman nominated to the Supreme Court**

1982 economic crisis

1984 Soviet Union and its allies ban the Los Angeles Olympics in the US, in retaliation for the US boycott of 1980 Olympics in Moscow

1985 Mikhail S. Gorbachev becomes general secretary of the Communist Party in the Soviet Union

1986 (January) Gorbachev stops Soviet deployment of intermediate-range missiles and freezes nuclear weapons tests; (April) **Chernobyl nuclear meltdown** in Ukraine

1988 Gorbachev removes Soviet troops from Afghanistan and reduces support for socialist rebels in Nicaragua and Cuban troops in Angola

1989 (March) *Exxon Valdez* oil spill in Alaska; (November) **Berlin Wall** is torn down

1989 Gorbachev informs Eastern European officials that Soviet forces would not intervene in any uprisings

1989–1991 end of the Cold War

1990 Lithuania, Estonia, Latvia, and Ukraine declare their independence from the Soviet Union

1990–1991 Gulf War, also known as First Iraq War

1991 collapse of the Soviet Union

Post–Cold War Era: 1991–Present

1993–1994 "Don't Ask, Don't Tell" policy allows gays to enter the military as long as they keep their sexual orientation to themselves

1993 Hawaii first state to propose same-sex marriage; siege and bombing of Branch Davidian compound in Waco, Texas by federal and state law enforcement agencies; first bombing of the World Trade Center in New York City

1995 US and Vietnam resume diplomatic relations; bombing of the Alfred P. Murrah Federal Building in Oklahoma City

1999 Columbine shooting in Columbine, Colorado

2000 controversial election results after narrow race between Al Gore and George W. Bush; Supreme Court gives victory to Bush

Post–9/11 Era: 2001–Present

2001 (September 11) terrorist attacks on the World Trade Center in New York City and the Pentagon in Washington, DC; fourth hijacked airplane brought down by passengers, landing in rural Pennsylvania; US hunts Al Qaeda terrorist network in Afghanistan; US abandons Kyoto Protocol

2003 Second Iraq War begins

2004 (June) death of 40th president Ronald Reagan; (December) **Indian Ocean tsunami** kills nearly a quarter of a million people in Southeast Asia

2005 Kyoto Protocol international climate agreement goes into force (US not a signatory); **Hurricane Katrina devastates New Orleans** and Gulf Coast; deadliest storm in US history

2006 former Vice President Al Gore produces climate change film *An Inconvenient Truth*

2007 worldwide economic recession begins; (April) Virginia Tech shooting is deadliest in US history

2009 Barack Obama takes office; **first African American to win presidency**

2010 Deepwater Horizon oil spill in the Gulf of Mexico is the worst in nation's history, although clean-up proves to be more effective than the 1989 *Exxon Valdez* spill in Alaska

2011 (May) Al Qaeda leader **Osama bin Laden**, mastermind of September 11 terrorist attacks, killed in compound in Pakistan by Navy SEALS; (June) "Don't Ask, Don't Tell" military policy rescinded; (September) Second Iraq War ends; (September) Occupy Wall Street movement begins, protesting wealth inequality; (October) **earthquake and tsunami off the coast of Japan** devastates Fukushima Daiichi nuclear plant; (December) Canada abandons Kyoto Protocol

2012 200th anniversary of War of 1812; many Americans unsure of what war was

2012 (July) Aurora, Colorado shooting at movie theater; (December) Newtown, Connecticut school shooting of young children leads to widespread outrage and renewed gun rights debates

2013 (March) Nuclear Regulatory Committee (NRC) approves the construction of five reactors at existing nuclear sites; (April) Boston Marathon bombing; US considers withdrawing all troops from Afghanistan by 2014; Supreme Court rules that Defense of Marriage Act (DOMA) is unconstitutional

2014 (March) Russia annexes Crimea, leading to international sanctions

APPENDIX B:
SELECTED SOURCES FOR
FURTHER READING

Below is a selection of key readings—primary documents, notable books, novels, plays, history, and humor—that will help the reader to gain a better understanding of the United States. This list is meant to serve as a starting point: it is not by any means a comprehensive list. Entries are listed in chronological order within each section to give a sense of the progression of American writing and thinking in history.

Primary/Key Documents and Speeches

John Winthrop—*A Model of Christian Charity* (1630)

Roger Williams—*A Plea for Religious Liberty* (1644)

Thomas Jefferson, et al.—*Declaration of Independence* (1776)

James Madison, John Jay, and Alexander Hamilton—*The Federalist Papers* (1787–1788)

James Madison, et al.—*The Constitution of the United States* (1788)

James Madison—*The Bill of Rights* (1791)

George Washington—*Farewell Address* (speech) (1796)

James Monroe—*Monroe Doctrine* (speech) (1823)

David Walker—*David Walker's Appeal* (1829)

John O'Sullivan—*Manifest Destiny* (1845)

Elizabeth Cady Stanton and Lucretia Mott—*Declaration of Sentiments*, Seneca Falls Conference (1848)

Abraham Lincoln—*Gettysburg Address* (speech) (1863)

Ida B. Wells—*Southern Horrors: Lynch Law in All Its Phases* (1892)

Frederick Jackson Turner—*The Frontier in American History* (1893)

Williams Jennings Bryan—*Cross of Gold* (speech) (1896)

Woodrow Wilson—*Fourteen Points* (speech) (1918)

Franklin D. Roosevelt—*First Inaugural Address* (speech) (1933)

Henry Luce—"American Century" (editorial in *Life*) (1941)
Dwight Eisenhower—*Farewell Address* (speech; "military industrial complex") (1961)
John F. Kennedy—*Inaugural Address* (speech) (1961)
Tom Hayden, et al.—*Port Huron Statement* (1962) (Students for a Democratic Society manifesto)
Martin Luther King, Jr.—*I Have a Dream* (speech) (1963)
Ronald Reagan—*Tear Down This Wall* (speech) (1987)

Notable Books

Cotton Mather—*The Wonders of the Invisible World* (1693)
Benjamin Franklin—*Autobiography* (1771–1790)
Thomas Jefferson—*Notes on the State of Virginia* (1781–1785)
Alexis de Tocqueville—*Democracy in America* (1835 and 1840)
Frederick Douglass—*A Narrative of the Life of Frederick Douglass: An American Slave* (1845)
James Bryce—*The American Commonwealth* (1888)
William James—*The Varieties of Religious Experience* (1902)
Henry Adams—*The Education of Henry Adams* (1907)
John Rawls—*A Theory of Justice* (1971)

American History

T. R. Fehrenbach—*This Kind of War: The Classic Korean War History* (1950 / 2000 50th anniversary edition)
Shelby Foote—*The Civil War: A Narrative* (1958–1974)
William Appleman Williams—*The Tragedy of American Diplomacy* (1959)
Richard Hofstadter—*Anti-intellectualism in American Life* (1963)
Roderick Nash—*Wilderness and the American Mind* (1967)
Dee Brown—*Bury My Heart At Wounded Knee: An Indian History of the American West* (1970)
Angie Debo—*A History of the Indians of the United States* (1970)
Michael Herr—*Dispatches* [Vietnam War] (1977)
Howard Zinn—*A People's History of the United States* (1980)
Joel Garreau—*The Nine Nations of North America* (1981)
John G. Neihardt—*Black Elk Speaks: Being the Life Story of a Holy Man of the Oglala Sioux* (1988)
David Hackett Fischer—*Albion's Seed* (1989)
David Herbert Donald—*Lincoln* (1995)

Seymour Martin Lipset—*American Exceptionalism: A Double-Edged Sword* (1997)

Studs Terkel—*The Good War: An Oral History of World War II* (1997)

Paul Johnson—*A History of the American People* (1999)

Louis Menand—*The Metaphysical Club* (2002)

Mark A. Noll—*America's God: From Jonathan Edwards to Abraham Lincoln* (2002)

Jim Cullen—*The American Dream: A Short History of an Idea that Shaped a Nation* (2004)

Joseph J. Ellis—*His Excellency: George Washington* (2005)

Peter L. Bernstein—*Wedding of the Waters: The Erie Canal and the Making of a Great Nation* (2006)

Charles Mann—*1491: New Revelations of the Americas Before Columbus* (2006)

David McCullough—*1776* (2006)

Jay Winik—*April 1865: The Month That Saved America* (2006)

Bill Bryson—*One Summer: America 1927* (2013)

Simon Winchester—*The Men Who United the States: America's Explorers, Inventors, Eccentrics and Mavericks, and the Creation of One Nation, Indivisible* (2013)

Literature

Washington Irving—*The Legend of Sleepy Hollow* (1820)

James Fenimore Cooper—*Last of the Mohicans: A Narrative of 1757* (1826)

Edgar Allen Poe—*The Masque of the Red Death* (1842) (short story)

Nathaniel Hawthorne—*House of Seven Gables* (1851)

Herman Melville—*Moby-Dick; or, The Whale* (1851)

Harriet Beecher Stowe—*Uncle Tom's Cabin* (1852)

Louisa May Alcott—*Little Women* (1868–1869)

Henry James—*The American* (1877)

Mark Twain—*Huckleberry Finn* (1885)

Stephen Crane—*The Red Badge of Courage* (1895)

Sarah Orne Jewett—*The Country of the Pointed Firs* (1896) (short story)

Kate Chopin—*The Awakening* (1899)

L. Frank Baum—*The Wizard of Oz* (1900)

Jack London—*The Call of the Wild* (1903)

Edith Wharton—*The House of Mirth* (1905)

Gertrude Stein—*Three Lives* (1909)

Willa Cather—*My Ántonia* (1918)

F. Scott Fitzgerald—*The Great Gatsby* (1925)

Ernest Hemingway—*The Sun Also Rises* (1926)

Willa Cather—*Death Comes for the Archbishop* (1927)
William Faulkner—*The Sound and the Fury* (1929)
William Faulkner—*As I Lay Dying* (1930)
Margaret Mitchell—*Gone with the Wind* (1936)
John Dos Passos—*The USA Trilogy* (1936)
John Steinbeck—*The Grapes of Wrath* (1939)
Walter Van Tilburg Clark—*The Ox-Bow Incident* (1940)
Carson McCullers—*The Heart is a Lonely Hunter* (1940)
Richard Wright—*Native Son* (1940)
Betty Smith—*A Tree Grows in Brooklyn* (1943)
Robert Penn Warren—*All the King's Men* (1946)
Norman Mailer—*The Naked and the Dead* (1948)
J. D. Salinger—*The Catcher in the Rye* (1951)
Ralph Ellison—*Invisible Man* (1952)
Herman Wouk—*The Caine Mutiny* (1952)
Jack Keroauc—*On the Road* (1957)
Vladimir Nabokov—*Pnin* (1957)
Harper Lee—*To Kill a Mockingbird* (1960)
John Updike—*Rabbit Angstrom: The Four Novels: Rabbit, Run* (1960); *Rabbit Redux* (1971); *Rabbit Is Rich* (1981); *Rabbit at Rest* (1995)
Joseph Heller—*Catch-22* (1961)
Ken Kesey—*One Flew Over the Cuckoo's Nest* (1962)
Sylvia Plath—*The Bell Jar* (1963)
Chaim Potok—*The Chosen* (1967)
Tom Wolfe—*The Electric Kool-Aid Acid Test* (1968)
Joyce Carol Oates—*them* (1969)
Kurt Vonnegut—*Slaughterhouse-Five* (1969)
Jerzy Kosinski—*Being There* (novella) 1970)
Thomas Pynchon—*Gravity's Rainbow* (1973)
Robert M. Pirsig—*Zen and the Art of Motorcycle Maintenance: An Inquiry into Values* (1974)
E. L. Doctorow—*Ragtime* (1975)
Toni Morrison—*Song of Solomon* (1977)
John Irving—*The World According to Garp* (1978)
Marilynne Robinson—*Housekeeping* (1980)
John Kennedy Toole—*A Confederacy of Dunces* (published posthumously, 1980)
Alice Walker—*The Color Purple* (1982)

Mark Helprin—*Winter's Tale* (1983)

Don DeLillo—*White Noise* (1985)

Cormac McCarthy—*Blood Meridian* (1985)

Larry McMurtry—*Lonesome Dove* (1985)

Toni Morrison—*Beloved* (1987)

Amy Tan—*The Joy Luck Club* (1989)

Larry Watson—*Montana 1948* (novella) (1993)

Richard Ford—*Independence Day* (1995)

Jane Smiley—*Moo* (1995)

Don DeLillo—*Underworld* (1997)

Philip Roth—*American Pastoral* (1997)

Edward P. Jones—*The Known World* (2003)

Philip Roth—*The Plot Against America* (2004)

Joseph O'Neill—*Netherland* (2008)

Books To Discover America

Urbanization and Immigration

Jacob Riis—*How the Other Half Lives: Studies among the Tenements of New York (1890)*

Upton Sinclair—*The Jungle* (1906)

Henry Roth—*Call It Sleep* (1934)

Jane Jacobs—*The Death and Life of Great American Cities* (1961)

Maxine Hong Kingston—*The Woman Warrior: Memoirs of a Girlhood Among Ghosts* (1975)

Elizabeth Ewen—*Immigrant Women in the Land of Dollars: Life and Culture on the Lower East Side, 1890–1925* (1979)

Sandra Cisneros—*The House on Mango Street* (1984)

Robert A. Slaton—*Back of the Yards: The Making of Local Democracy* (1986)

Michael Patrick MacDonald—*All Souls: A Family Story from Southie* [South Boston] (1999)

Gary Shteyngart—*The Russian Debutante's Handbook* (2002)

Jhumpa Lahiri—*The Namesake* (2003)

Junot Diaz—*The Brief Wondrous Life of Oscar Wao* (2007)

Francine Prose—*My New American Life* (2012)

Karolina Waclawiak—*How to Get Into the Twin Palms* (2012)

Culture and Society

David Potter—*People of Plenty* (1958)

Betty Friedan—*The Feminine Mystique* (1963)

Philip Slater—*The Pursuit of Loneliness* (1970)

Armistead Maupin—*Tales of the City* (series) (first novel 1978)

Beth L. Bailey—*From Front Porch to Back Seat: Courtship in Twentieth-Century America* (1989)

Stephanie Coontz—*The Way We Never Were: American Families and the Nostalgia Trap* (1993)

Robert D. Putnam—*Bowling Alone: The Collapse and Revival of American Community* (2000)

Eric Schlosser—*Fast Food Nation: The Dark Side of the All-American Meal* (2001)

Stephanie Coontz—*American Families: A Multicultural Reader* (2008)

Elaine Tyler May—*Homeward Bound: American Families in the Cold War Era* (2008)

Barbara Ehrenreich—*Nickel and Dimed: On (Not) Getting by in America* (2011)

Karen Sternheimer—*Celebrity Culture and the American Dream: Stardom and Social Mobility* (2011)

Race in America

Richard Wright—*Black Boy* (1945)

Ralph Ellison—*Invisible Man* (1952)

James Baldwin—*The Fire Next Time* (1963)

Maya Angelou—*I Know Why the Caged Bird Sings* (1969)

Toni Morrison—*The Bluest Eye* (1970)

David M. Oshinsky—*Worse than Slavery: Parchman Farm and the Ordeal of Jim Crow Justice* (1997)

Allen M. Hornblum—*Acres of Skin: Human Experiments at Holmesburg Prison* (1999)

Alfred Blumrosen—*Slave Nation: How Slavery United the Colonies and Sparked the American Revolution* (2006)

James W. Loewen—*Sundown Towns* (2006)

Ronald Takaki—*A Different Mirror: A History of Multicultural America* (2008)

N. Scott Momaday—*House Made of Dawn* (2010)

Charles Preston—*Nobody Called Me Charlie: The Story of a Radical White Journalist Writing for a Black Newspaper in the Civil Rights Era* (2010)

Environment and Nature

John James Audubon—*The Birds of America* (1827–1838)

Ralph Waldo Emerson—*Nature* (essay) (1836)

Henry David Thoreau—*Walden; or, Life in the Woods* (1854)

John Muir—*My First Summer in the Sierra* (1911)

Aldo Leopold—*A Sand County Almanac: And Sketches Here and There* (1949)

Rachel Carson—*Silent Spring* (1962)

R. Buckminster Fuller—*Operating Manual for Spaceship Earth* (1968)

Edward Abbey—*The Monkey Wrench Gang* (1975)

Annie Dillard—*Pilgrim at Tinker Creek* (1979)

Donald Worster—*Dust Bowl: The Southern Plains in the 1930s* (1979)

Edward Abbey—*Desert Solitaire: A Season in the Wilderness* (1985)

Bill Bryson—*A Walk in the Woods: Rediscovering America on the Appalachian Trail* (1998)

Diana Muir—*Reflections in Bullough's Pond: Economy and Ecosystem in New England* (2000)

William Cronon—*Changes in the Land: Indians, Colonists, and the Ecology of New England* (2003)

Richard Louv—*Last Child in the Woods: Saving Our Children from Nature-Deficit Disorder* (2006)

Humor

Erma Bombeck—*Life Is Always Greener Over the Septic Tank* (1976)

Woody Allen—*Side Effects* (1980)

Berkeley Breathed—*Bloom County Babylon* (1986)

Matt Groening—*The Big Book of Hell* (1990)

Molly Ivins—*Nothin' But Good Times Ahead* (1993)

David Sedaris—*Me Talk Pretty One Day* (1999)

Robert Mankoff (Ed.)—*The Complete Cartoons of the* New Yorker (2004)

Jon Stewart, et al.—*America (The Book): A Citizen's Guide to Democracy Inaction* (2004)

The Onion—*Our Dumb World* (2007)
Stephen Colbert—*I Am America (And So Can You!)* (2007)
Garry Trudeau—*40: A Doonesbury Retrospective* (2010)

Plays

Lillian Hellman—*Children's Hour* (1934)
Thornton Wilder—*Our Town* (1938)
Richard Rodgers and Oscar Hammerstein II—*Oklahoma!* (1943)
Tennessee Williams—*The Glass Menagerie* (1945)
Eugene O'Neill—*A Moon for the Misbegotten* (1947)
Tennessee Williams—*A Streetcar Named Desire* (1947)
Arthur Miller—*Death of a Salesman* (1949)
Arthur Miller—*The Crucible* (1953)
Tennessee Williams—*Cat on a Hot Tin Roof* (1955)
Eugene O'Neill—*Long Day's Journey Into Night* (1956)
Lorraine Hansberry—*A Raisin in the Sun* (1959)
Leonard Bernstein—*West Side Story* (1961)
Edward Albee—*Who's Afraid of Virginia Woolf?* (1962)
Neil Simon—*The Odd Couple* (1965)
Neil Simon—*Lost in Yonkers* (1990)
Tony Kushner—*Angels in America: A Gay Fantasia on National Themes*, Parts
   One and Two (1991)

ABOUT THE EDITORS

Duncan A. Campbell

Duncan A. Campbell is Assistant Professor of History at National University in La Jolla, California. Before that he was a lecturer in American Studies at the University of Wales Swansea. He is the author of *English Public Opinion and the American Civil War* (2003) and *Unlikely Allies: Britain, America and the Victorian Origins of the "Special Relationship"* (2007). He is, additionally, co-editor of *The 1980s: A Critical and Transitional Decade* (2011) and *The American Civil War* (2000) in the Helm Literary Sources and Documents series. His research interests lie in comparative history, especially that of the nineteenth-century Atlantic World.

David Levinson

David Levinson spent twenty years as lead researcher and vice-president of the Human Relations Area Files, Yale University. He is the editor or senior editor of major anthropological works including the *Encyclopedia of World Cultures*, the *Encyclopedia of Cultural Anthropology*, and *American Immigrant Cultures: Builders of a Nation*. His research focuses on forgotten or invisible peoples, ethnic relations, and local history and culture.

Michael Aaron Rockland

Michael Aaron Rockland is Professor of American Studies at Rutgers University and the author of fourteen books, including *An American Diplomat in Franco Spain* and *Navy Crazy*. Early in his career he served as a cultural attaché with the United States embassies in Argentina and Spain.

215

INDEX

automotive industry in, 179–180

Greening of Detroit (nonprofit organization), 183

immigrants in, 179–180

suburbanization, 180–182

vacancy of houses and real estate in, 182

diseases from the Old World, effects of on native populations, 6–8, 26–27

domestication of animals, 6

Douglass, Frederick (former slave, author, and orator), 28, 58

Du Bois, William Edward Burghardt (W. E. B.) (civil rights activist), 128–131, 194–195

political beliefs of, 130–131

Washington, Booker T. vs., 130

Dust Bowl, 170–172, 173

Dutch settlement. *See under* European settlement

See also "Pennsylvania Dutch"

E

Edison, Thomas Alva (inventor), 71–72

Eighteenth Amendment. *See under* amendments to the US Constitution

Eisenhower, Dwight D. (34th US president), 105, 112 (quote)

See also interstate highway system

election of 1912, importance of, 86, 87

See also Roosevelt, Theodore; Wilson, Woodrow

Emerson, Ralph Waldo (poet), 35, 79

English settlement. *See under* European settlement

Enlightenment, the, 41, 153

See also deism

environmentalism, 173–177, 187

See also Carson, Rachel; fracking; Santa Barbara oil spill

Erie Canal, 53, 178

European settlement of America

Dutch, 12–14

English, 14–16

French, 16–18

Spanish, 11–12

exceptionalism. *See* American exceptionalism

executive branch of government, 43

See also political system of the United States

F

Federal Deposit Insurance Corporation (FDIC), 109

federal system of government

in Latin America, 151

in the United States, 42, 43

See also political system of the United States

Federalist Papers (by James Madison, John Jay, and Alexander Hamilton), 43

feminism, 135–141

first wave international movement, 138–140

second wave international movement, 140–141

See also women's rights movement

Fifth Amendment. *See under* amendments to the US Constitution

Fifteenth Amendment. *See under* amendments to the US Constitution

firearms and gun control, 158–160

See also Second Amendment *under* amendments to the US Constitution

"fireside chats" (F. D. Roosevelt radio addresses), 109

First Amendment. *See under* amendments to the US Constitution

flappers, 94, 95

football. *See* sports

foreign policies of the United States, 81, 94, 150, 152

"forgotten war." *See* Korean War

founding fathers, 27

See also Adams, John; Franklin, Benjamin; Hamilton, Alexander; Jay, John; Jefferson, Thomas; Madison, James; Monroe, James; Washington, George

founding principles of the United States, 41–42

equality, 47–50

Know Nothings (anti-immigration political
party), 68
Korean War, 114
Ku Klux Klan (KKK), 65, 97

L

labor movements, 74–77
Haymarket Massacre, 76
strikes, 74, 75, 77, 89
unions, 75, 76, 77, 89, 98–99
See also Debs, Eugene V.
Lafayette, Marquis de (French general,
American Revolutionary War hero), 36
League of Nations, 93, 99
legislative branch of government, 42
See also political system of the United States
Lend-Lease Act, 100–101
Leopold, Aldo (environmentalist, forester),
166–167
A Sand County Almanac, 162, 166–167
Lewis and Clark expedition, 53
libertarians, 192
Lincoln, Abraham (16th US president, 1861–
1865), 59–63
assassination of, 60, 63
Emancipation Proclamation, 61
Gettysburg Address, 62
Republican Party and, 59, 61
suspension of *habeas corpus* during Civil
War, 66
Locke, John (English philosopher),
41–42, 125
Second Treatise of Civil Government, 41
See also founding principles of the United
States; individual rights
Louisiana Purchase, 52
Love Canal (site of toxic waste dump), 176
loyalists, 31, 80
Lusitania, RMS (British passenger ship), sinking
of, 91, 92
See also submarine warfare *under*
World War I

M

Madison, James (founding father, 4th US
President, 1809–1817), 27, 42, 43, 44, 45
See also Bill of Rights, *Federalist Papers*
Maine, ix
split from Massachusetts after War of 1812,
78, 79
maize (corn). *See* agriculture
malls. *See* sprawl
Marley, Bob (Jamaican reggae star), 30
Maryland, founding of as Roman Catholic
colony, 22
Massachusetts
Lexington and Concord, battle of, 35
refusal to fight Britain in War of
1812, 78
settlement of, 14
See also American Revolution; New England
McCarthyism, 112
Mesa Verde National Park. *See under* national
parks
Metacomet (Wampanoag leader, also known as
King Philip). *See* King Philip's War
Mexico
civil wars in, 82
Mexican-American War, ix, 55
revolution in, 81, 82
See also Zimmermann Telegram
See also under international relations with the
United States
military-industrial complex, 111–112
military power of the United States, 91,
106–107, 118–119
Milk, Harvey (first openly gay elected official in
United States), 144
See also gay rights movement
missions (religious), 19
See also Alamo *under* Texas, history of
Missouri Compromise of 1820. *See under*
slavery
Monroe, James (founding father, 5th US
president, 1817–1825), 81

PRAISE FOR BERKSHIRE'S "THIS WORLD OF OURS" SERIES

This Is America: A Short History of the United States is the latest in Berkshire's "This World Of Ours" series, acclaimed by some of the world's leading scholars. *This Fleeting World: A Short History of Humanity*, the first in the series, was praised by Bill Gates, founder of Microsoft and author of *The Road Ahead*. The books tackle big subjects such as China, America, Islam, sports, environmental history, and Africa—even the universe—in about a hundred pages. Each book is designed to be read in one or two sittings.

This Is China

"It is hard to imagine that such a short book can cover such a vast span of time and space. *This Is China: The First 5,000 Years* will help teachers, students, and general readers alike, as they seek for a preliminary guide to the contexts and complexities of Chinese culture."

> Jonathan Spence, professor of history,
> Yale University; author of
> *The Search for Modern China*

This Fleeting World

"I first became an avid student of David Christian by watching his course on DVD, and so I am very happy to see his enlightening presentation of the world's history captured in *This Fleeting World*. I hope it will introduce a wider audience to this gifted scientist and teacher."

> Bill Gates, founder of Microsoft

This Is Islam

"*This Is Islam* provides interested general readers and students with a concise but remarkably comprehensive introduction to Islam. It is a clearly presented guide that provides both a broad overview and important specifics in a way that is easy for both experts and non-specialists to use."

> John Voll, professor of Islamic history,
> Georgetown University

Forthcoming titles in the series include *This Good Earth: A Short History of Human Impact on the Natural World*, *This Sporting World*, and *This Is Africa*.

CPSIA information can be obtained at www.ICGtesting.com
Printed in the USA
LVOW01s0309220215

427852LV00002B/4/P